Teaching Psychology

TEACHING PSYCHOLOGY
CONCEPTS AND PEDAGOGIC STRATEGIES

A Resource Book for Teachers in Schools and Colleges

Namita Ranganathan
Vishakha Kumar
Vikas Baniwal
Rashmi Malhotra
Anshu Chaudhary

SHIPRA

Rs. 1250

ISBN: 978-81-7541-887-5

First Published in India in 2017

Teaching Psychology: Concepts and Pedagogic Strategies

Published by:

SHIPRA PUBLICATIONS
LG 18-19, Pankaj Central Market,
I.P. Ext., Patparganj, Delhi 110092, India
Ph.: 011- 2223 5152, 2223 6152
Email: info@shiprapublication.com
www.shiprapublication.com

Preface

This book is a result of collaboration and dialogue between teacher educators, teachers, university professors, and scholars in the field of Psychology. It started as a quest to reach out to those teachers who believe in classrooms as open spaces, where learners have voice and agency. Such teachers have faith in the ability of their learners and in the democratic process of learning. After much deliberation, discussion and heated debates it was felt that teachers need something more than basic books in psychology that can be used as a reference point, to inform their pedagogic practices. This Resource Book is intended to fill that void by addressing the pedagogic and perspective based queries of teachers, particularly in the context of students studying Psychology for the first time. Like most other disciplines, Psychology too has witnessed some major changes in last few decades in the way research is carried out and its body of knowledge is built. Recognising this, an attempt has been made in this book to deal with some of the fundamental questions of the discipline and various paradigms of research that it supports.

The inception of the idea for this book came from a workshop of Psychology teachers, teaching in Delhi schools, organised in 2012. It was during this workshop that the teachers expressed the need to have a platform which can facilitate ideation and sharing of pedagogic inputs. I would like to thank all those teachers of Psychology who were present in that workshop with special mention to Mrs. Vithika Rahul, the then Head of the Department, Delhi Public School, RK Puram, New Delhi for her support to the workshop. After the workshop, I met two of my scholars, Ms. Vishakha Kumar, who was then teaching Psychology at DPS, R.K. Puram and Ms. Rashmi Malhotra, who was also a Psychology teacher at Vasant Valley School, New Delhi, to deliberate on the possibility of bringing out a book that can act as source of inspiration, ideas and suggestions for teachers of Psychology. Dr.

Vikas Baniwal and Ms. Anshu Chaudhary also joined the project to expand the scope of the book so that it could address the needs of teachers teaching beginning learners, both at the school and college level, respectively. Their insight and commitment towards this project is immense.

In the course of writing this book, several people helped us in bringing it to fruition. I would like to thank my friend and colleague of several years, Dr. Geeta Sahni, Associate Professor, Faculty of Education, University of Delhi, for giving her valuable time to proof read the draft of the book. I would also like to thank Dr. Toolika Wadhwa, Assistant Professor, Shyama Prasad Mukherji College, University of Delhi, for constantly motivating us in the course of writing this book. She also painstakingly read the final draft of the book and gave her noteworthy suggestions. I would also like to thank Mr. D. Kumar, the publisher of the book, for his patience and guidance in completing the book. I hope that this book, which in the Indian Educational context, is the first of its kind will help to weave together a strong community of Psychology Teachers, where dialogue, discussion and further enrichment become the cherished goals.

This book has been written keeping in mind the diverse situations of Psychology Teachers and students across the country.

Prof. Namita Ranganathan

Contents

Psychological Disorders / 210

Therapeutic Approaches / 219

Developing Psychological Skills / 227

Introduction

This book is a result of collaboration and dialogue between teacher educators, teachers, university professors, and scholars in the field of Psychology. It started as a quest to reach out to those teachers who believe in classrooms as open spaces, where learners have voice and agency. Such teachers have faith in the ability of their learners and in the democratic process of learning. After much deliberation, discussion and heated debates it was felt that teachers need something more than basic books in Psychology that can be used as a reference point, to inform their pedagogic practices. This Resource Book is intended to fill that void by addressing the pedagogic and perspective based queries of teachers, particularly in the context of students studying Psychology for the first time. Like most other disciplines, Psychology too has witnessed some major changes in last few decades in the way research is carried out and its body of knowledge is built. Recognising this, an attempt has been made in this book to deal with some of the fundamental questions of the discipline and various paradigms of research that it supports.

The dominant methodology followed in teaching Psychology in contemporary times, is the constructivist approach. The present book recognises and addresses this aspect. It also takes into cognizance, the movement within Psychology from universalism to pluralism, and contextualism, emanating from the growth of cross-cultural and indigenous psychology. This movement makes it imperative to bring about a change in the pedagogic practices, basically, by creating space for experiential and inquiry based learning. The learner is no longer seen as a passive recipient of knowledge. Instead she/he has to be located in the context of where she/he belongs and perceived as having experiences and agency of her/his own. In this backdrop, one of the basic aims of the book is to encourage teachers to rethink their understanding about the nature of the learner, the discipline of Psychology and their own role as teachers.

School education is guided by the principles laid out in the National Curriculum Framework (2005). NCF 2005 makes a strong plea for learning to become an experiential engagement for the learner. It also promotes the idea that learners bring with them a fund of knowledge and experiences, drawn from their everyday lives, or what they have picked up from being part of a specific community or group. These must find space and expression in the classroom. In the absence of a corresponding curriculum framework document, in higher education, it may be useful to apply the same principles and objectives that NCF recommends. Most Psychology teachers have expressed the need for a resource book that can guide them towards building a constructivist classroom and promoting experiential learning. They have shared that they often find themselves in challenging situations, as they strive to balance the expectations of policy documents with the demand of high performance by the school, college and parents.

In response to this, this resource book tries to address the question: 'How to make the learning of Psychology experiential and constructive for learners?' It is important to point out here, that answers to 'how to' questions, should always be read with caution, since they require adaptation to cultural contexts and local concerns. Every Unit in this resource book, presents some activities and pedagogic suggestions that can be incorporated by any Psychology teacher, as long as he/she keeps in mind the cultural context of the learners, they are expected to teach.

The present resource book also attempts to dispel two common myths. The first myth is that an activity based approach is a time-consuming and less efficient way of teaching. The second myth is that only activity based classes can be constructivist. It does this by asserting that activity is a means of decentralising power in a classroom. Instead of a class where the teacher makes all decisions about learning and evaluation, activity enables learners to become active participants of that process. Once the learners feel involved and take responsibility for their own learning, the process will be far more rewarding. This will reduce the emphasis on rote learning and memorisation.

In addition, the resource book provides some strategies to introduce the discipline of Psychology to beginning learners of the subject. Teachers at both the school and college level, face the challenge of teaching in a way that is interesting, inspiring, and also does justice to its emergence as a discipline. This resource book provides examples, suggestions, and guidelines to enable teachers to realise this goal as well. It attempts to complement the present basic textbooks and readers that exist in Psychology with pedagogical inputs and information links that provide value addition to the theoretical understanding of concepts and ideas, discussed in each Unit.

Needless to say, the book places the concerns of a Psychology teacher first and foremost: that is how to teach psychology through innovative pedagogic strategies so that learners not only engage with the curriculum but also become reflective about the critical issues that have shaped the discipline. Some of the questions aligned with this objective, towards which a teacher may want to sensitize her/his learners, are as follows:

- What are the contributions of psychology to the society at large?
- What are the values and beliefs that have influenced research in Psychology?
- What are the epistemological questions that engage psychologists?
- Can the theories of Psychology be universally applied?
- What is the place of indigenous knowledge and cultural beliefs in the so called 'scientific' discipline of Psychology?
- What are the significant developments that have taken place in the Indian context?
- How is Psychology influenced by the socio-political-historical contexts in which it has evolved?
- What criticisms does the discipline face in academia?

Organisational Structure of the Resource book

The book is organised in two sections—

Section I is written exclusively for teachers. Its purpose is to encourage teachers to rethink and reflect upon some fundamental questions about the discipline that they teach. Particularly, it seeks to address critical issues that emerge from the paradigmatic understanding of research. It also presents a critique of how basic school and college texts deal with the content of Psychology, the idea being that teachers should also read them critically. Significant portions of the content of Section 1 can be used to build perspective among learners about the nature of Psychology, its basic concepts, ideas, research paradigms, its history and evolution and where it stands today.

Section II deals with specific topics and concepts that constitute the subject matter of Psychology. They are presented in the following format:

'Key Concept(s)'—In each unit some concepts have been identified and listed and then, activities have been designed for them. The concepts were chosen on the basis of their salience in that unit. Only key concepts have been covered in each Unit.

'Introduction' to each Unit is basically an overview of its contents. It also provides the backdrop in which the concepts and ideas of the Unit may be taught.

'Route' explains how each concept is to be transacted through a detailed description of an activity.

'Synthesis' basically connects the learning experiences of the activities with the concept or idea being studied. It establishes the link between the concept and the route. Based on this, teachers will be able to summarise all that has been learnt. To make this task easier for teachers, either the use of readings or a worksheet has been suggested. A list of core readings has been provided at the end of each Unit, along with a list of supplementary readings for both teacher educators, as well as students.

Finally, each Unit ends with a section titled 'Recent Trends'. This section was added to contemporise each unit. Very often books of general psychology only present the major researches and theories that have widespread acceptability. This section presents some recent developments in the discipline, in the hope that teachers will take them up and also add to their own knowledge base. Some references have been listed for teachers who want to read further.

The resource book also endeavours to introduce teachers to the new technologies of learning and progression in the discipline. It proposes some activities which will require teachers to access material from the internet and other more advanced Psychology books. The topics covered in Section II have been drawn from the Psychology syllabi of schools and colleges and pertains to General and Applied Psychology.

Prof. Namita Ranganathan

SECTION-I

Development of Psychology*

An Overview

Some Reflections on Psychology Textbooks

An introductory book in the form of a textbook is both an important part of the curriculum and a significant teaching-learning resource. It is very difficult to define an ideal format for a textbook. What is important to emphasise is that a textbook, like any other resource, ought to be used as only one of the many resources that are available and must be combined with other resources. However, the reality is that many teachers and students treat them as the only source of knowledge. The reliance on textbooks further increases when the entire system focuses on 'teaching to test'. Ideally, all teachers should reflect on the nature of textbooks by reading additional books to understand and critically examine the assumptions and orientation that underlies them, rather than treating them as sacrosanct. In other words, every teacher of Psychology must have an informed view about textbooks.

All popular textbooks of Psychology, irrespective of whether they are brought out by the National Council of Educational Resources and Training (NCERT) or come from the ilk of all time classics like *Introduction to Psychology* (Morgan, King, Weisz Schopler 1993) and *Psychology* (Baron, 2001). Baron and Morgan and King, highlight some key issues about the nature and teaching of Psychology as a discipline. These centre on exploring whether Psychology is a Science or a Social Science; whether it is interdisciplinary or not; whether newer trends of research in Psychology are incorporated in the textbooks or not; and whether these textbooks adequately prepare and motivate learners to pursue psychology at the level of higher education.

Likewise, all the popular textbooks, especially the NCERT textbooks, through their preface, encourage readers, particularly teachers and students to use multiple sources of information,

* Namita Ranganathan, Vishakha Kumar, and Vikas Baniwal

instead of focusing on information provided in the textbook alone, as the basis of knowledge. They project Psychology as one of the latest and fastest growing disciplines, highlight the biological, neurological and environmental basis of behaviour and affirm the applied aspects of the discipline. They present many examples to establish the different ways in which knowledge of Psychology can serve in dealing with personal, inter-personal, and professional challenges. They also either directly or indirectly, enlist the career prospects for students of Psychology.

The basic difference between the introductory texts written by foreign authors, like Morgan and King (1993) and Baron (2001) and the NCERT texts is that the former mostly represent the western perspective and draws examples from the western world. In contrast, the textbooks developed by NCERT try to introduce indigenous ideas, local examples and Indian perspectives, wherever possible. The elaboration on these ideas, however, is rather limited. The emergence of psychology as a discipline, especially in the Indian context, however, has been touched upon in the NCERT textbooks. Yet what seems to be missing in all the introductory texts are the alternate movements, perspectives, frameworks and voices that mark psychology as a discipline, such as Critical Psychology, Positive Psychology or Feminist Psychology.

It is important however to acknowledge that the effort that has been put into developing the NCERT texts, post NCF 2005, in a language and style that is simple, comprehensible and experiential. It is commendable, especially, in comparison to the textbooks used prior to the year 2000. In fact, the present NCERT books have helped in giving more rigour to psychology as an academic discipline. It is now placed and taught at par with other established subjects like History, Political Science, Economics and Geography. Its combinability with subjects of the Commerce and Science streams has also gained momentum. All these developments necessitate that psychology teachers discuss the nature of psychology, its historical evolution, its interdisciplinary nature and new emergences in the discipline in detail. A framework for the same has been presented in the subsequent sections.

Psychology: Science or Social Science?

Since, the textbook may be the first encounter of learners with the discipline, it becomes imperative that the identity of the discipline be discussed in detail and be adequately established through citing suitable examples. This unfortunately, as it has already been mentioned, has not received the kind of attention that it requires, in the books at the introductory level. One of the reasons for this could be the belief that this issue should be addressed in its full complexity only when a learner pursues Psychology at an advanced level, and studies specialised papers on 'History of Psychology' and 'Research Methodology'. Even so, there is no denying that lack of clarity about Psychology being a Science or Social Science, or the method it adopts, creates confusion in the minds of beginning learners.

Very often, since Psychology as a subject is an option for learners in the Humanities stream in schools, both the learners and their parents start subscribing to the belief that it is essentially a Social Science. The textbooks, however, discuss the interlinkages of Psychology with Neuroscience and Computer Science, and highlight that experimentation is the primary method, indicating to students that psychology has more to do with sciences. The confusion persists in higher education as well since Psychology is offered both as a Science and Arts degree in Undergraduate and Postgraduate courses. Whether the Science or Arts degree is better, is a frequent query in students' minds. In such a situation, the introductory texts at both the school and college levels must clearly discuss the identity of Psychology as both a Science and Social Science in order to dispel the confusion in the minds of learners. For the Psychology teacher this becomes the first debate to focus on.

Another issue, related to the identity of Psychology as a discipline, is that the criteria for categorising a discipline as a Science or Social Science, does not find adequate discussion. For instance, the introductory textbooks state that Psychology is both a Science and a Social Science, yet they give much more emphasis to the primary goals of research in Psychology being 'prediction and control'. The NCERT text gives greater emphasis to experimentation and the positivist paradigm of research. Discussion about the interpretive approach to research is limited to just one paragraph and the coverage is very cryptic. Considering how important it is for discourse building in the discipline, it needs elaboration and illustrations, in order to enable learners to understand it better. In order to dispel this confusion, the Method of Science and Social Science respectively, needs more elaboration, supported by examples for clarity and emphasis. The understanding that the different steps of research such as hypothesis formulation, data collection, analysis, and theorization, are essentially the same for both Sciences and Social Sciences, also needs to be emphasised. General differences between Natural Science and Social Science must also find articulation.

It is the teacher's responsibility to also point out that just because Psychology involves studying the behaviour of humans, locating it in a context, it alone does not make it a Social Science. Most teachers report that the difference between Psychology as a Science and Social Science becomes more complex with the introduction of terms like 'subjective', 'objective', and 'empirical'. The textbooks do little to ease out the confusion in this regard, leaving it to the teacher to take up the initiative to clarify the nature of the discipline. What is also true is that most of the introductory texts project the experimental method as being very high on reliability and validity, giving the impression to students that there is no possibility of arriving at alternate findings through other methods. This often leads to students' forming the notion that Psychology is monolithic. In order to change this perception, through different activities and class discussions, learners have to be encouraged by teachers to express the ideas and opinions, drawing from their lived experiences. Often, these may be contrary to the findings of the classical experiments described in the textbooks. This would help learners to appreciate that the findings emerging from experimental research in Psychology are not sacrosanct, universal laws. They would also begin to understand that Psychology is not only about scientific research, it is also about understanding human experience.

The Interdisciplinary Nature of Psychology

The discipline of Psychology has not developed in a vacuum. Over the years, it has engaged with other important disciplines like Philosophy, Sociology, Anthropology, Physics, Biology, Neuroscience, Law, and Management, drawing from their body of knowledge and frameworks. Thus, there are several inter-linkages between Psychology and these disciplines. The National Curriculum Framework (2005) acknowledges the interdisciplinary nature of Psychology. It emphasises the need for more porous borders across disciplines. Textbooks too have to carry these reflections. The Psychology textbooks in school do acknowledge the interdisciplinary nature of the discipline, but much more justice has to be done to the spectrum of discussion. For instance, the introductory textbook should give a number of illustrative examples to help students see the interface and interlinkages of Psychology with each of the disciplines that it draws upon, separately. What the textbooks are unable to do, then becomes the responsibility of the teacher.

What needs to be highlighted about the interdisciplinary nature of Psychology, both in the texts and teaching of teachers, is pertaining to ways in which certain methods, research findings, and constructs in psychology, are borrowed and adapted from other disciplines. Similarly, the ways in which theories, findings, and insights from Psychology apply to other disciplines also needs to be emphasised. For example, there are several studies done in Sociology and Anthropology that lend themselves to some of the debates in Developmental Psychology. The application of theories of motivation in 'Management Studies' can also be highlighted. A discussion on how various methods in psychology such as case study, ethnography, and narratives, have been borrowed from the frameworks of the Medical Sciences, Anthropology and Sociology, can also find expression. Since some of these explicit linkages are not there in the introductory texts, perspectives about them can be built through additional sources, or specially designed classroom activities.

Nature of Knowledge in the Texts: Selection and Representation

The most pressing concern with reference to the selection and representation of knowledge in Psychology texts is the predominance of Euro-American Psychology and its portrayal as mainstream psychology. Most of the textbooks draw upon research work done in these regions of the world. There is hardly any mention of psychological ideas from other parts of the world. This problem of representation creates an impression that Psychology as a discipline has developed and been advanced only in Europe and America and that India has nothing significant to contribute. This impression further alienates learners from the theories and researches in the introductory books and even the Indian textbooks, since they do not adequately reflect their cultural context. The learners are also not encouraged to examine the various theories critically. As a result, they start absorbing the content in the textbook passively to a point where their faculty for critical questioning ceases to get aroused. What is further seen is the less emphasis given to the dynamic nature of Psychology as a discipline. In effect, the way the introductory books and textbooks present information, gives the impression that knowledge in Psychology is timeless and universal. In order to address these concerns, all the basic texts should make it a point to include illustrative examples of researches and knowledge generation from different cultural contexts. For example, in textbooks in India, the contributions of Indian researchers to the discipline must find representation. This will give learners a sense of the relevance of the discipline to their own set up, apart from a sense of pride and achievement. They should also be encouraged by the teacher to link psychological concepts that they are studying to ideas, insights and experiences from their own culture, wherever possible.

Adequacy of School Textbooks as Preparation for Higher Education in Psychology

One of the aims of education at the senior secondary level is to help students to prepare for higher education, by making them more self-reliant. In order to ensure that the transition from school education to higher education is smooth, both the texts and how the teachers transact them, should work towards making students independent, curious, and critical. They should be encouraged to identify the sources of information, study them independently, critically analyse the content, and develop a well-informed opinion in the matter. An activity based approach to teaching promotes this transition, and hence, should form the basis of the teaching - learning process. However, the way the present textbooks have been designed, it does not promote activity based teaching. Teachers thus have to use their agency to obtain alternative resources for this.

Pedagogical Directions in Textbooks

The focus in this section is on analysing the NCERT texts, which are widely used at the Senior Secondary level, both in order to know the main topics of emphasis to be studied by learners and to know how much to teach and how to teach it. The NCERT books also become the source of guidance for other publishers and authors. It may be mentioned that the college textbooks do not provide pedagogical directions, but, carry the same content in a more elaborate form than the NCERT books. Thus, the directions spelt out for the NCERT textbooks may be equally relevant for beginning learners in higher education as well.

The pedagogic directions given in the NCERT textbooks emphasize the need for class participation, discussion, reflection, critical thinking, experiential and hands-on learning. The text mentions that while teaching the course it is imperative that teachers must strive to maintain a balance between scientific and experiential learning.

The preface, foreword, note for teachers, and note for students of the NCERT textbooks, set the tone for a teaching-learning process derived from the constructivist paradigm. In other words, the locus for learning is on students while the teacher acts as a facilitator with the responsibility of making the teaching-learning experience a rewarding one. The textbook also suggests that teachers should use techniques like brainstorming, role-play, interviews, and learning-diaries to ensure interaction and participation in the class. Keeping in mind these pedagogic directions, the NCERT textbooks have activities interwoven in each unit to help learners move beyond rote-memorization and likewise for teachers to move beyond lectures and didactic teaching. The activities and examples given in the texts also help to bring the everyday experiences and observations of learners to the classroom, thereby making them feel both comfortable and motivated. At the end of each unit, there are some project ideas, pedagogical hints, and web links given to facilitate the teachers and the students.

Although the pedagogic directions given through activities and projects in the texts are meaningful, given the width and dynamic nature of Psychology as a discipline, they appear to be somewhat limited. If teachers wish to do a meaningful transaction of the curriculum through an activity-based approach, they need to have access to more teaching resources, web-links, videos, activities, games etc.

Revisiting the History of Psychology

To understand the contemporary thrusts and concerns in Psychology, and locate their emergence, it is imperative to delve into the history of the discipline. The trajectory that marks the growth of the discipline of Psychology, can assist teachers in taking important decisions about how to teach specific units, with the aim to understand psychology in a larger framework.

Carr (1961, p.3) believes that "when we attempt to answer the question 'What is History?' our answer, consciously or unconsciously, reflects our own position in time, and forms part of our answer to the broader question of 'what view we take about the society in which we live". Most historians would select those events from the past that they consider significant according to their present context. One way of understanding history, is through reconstruction of the past, based on the present. Harris (1997) suggests three ways of writing the Histories of Psychology: Celebratory Histories of Psychology, Revisionist Histories of Psychology, and Critical Histories of Psychology.

In the Celebratory Histories of Psychology, there are two visible biases: first is the *presentist bias,* which is "the tendency to write a history to justify the current status quo. It is also known as Whig history- after the tendency to believe that history was inevitably progressive and so the current state of affairs must be the most advanced" (Jones & Elcock, 2001, p. 9). The second bias is to view Psychology as an independent discipline. This is the *internalist bias,* which ignores the inter-disciplinary and contextualized nuances of the development of a discipline. It focuses on "the history of theoretical change within the discipline, as if it was only driven by empirical and theoretical change" (Jones & Elcock, 2001, p. 10).

Writing revisionist and critical histories is the prevalent trend. Highlighting the differences between the old way of writing history and the new ways of looking at history, Jones & Elcock (2001, p. 3) highlight that "old style histories tended to have a narrow, intellectual focus, tracing the chronological development of the discipline. In such histories, the progressive development of the discipline occurs in intellectual and cultural isolation, and so are immune to contamination by outside forces". Harris (1997) argues that the traditional histories of psychology aim to strengthen its nature as fixed. They tend to ignore the role of political and ideological factors in the evolution of Psychology and instead, depict the progress of Psychology in a linear fashion.

Although the revisionist and critical histories save themselves from the progressivist or *internalist* bias "the *presentist* approach is harder to avoid - it is clearly impossible to write history from anything other than the present. Even so, it is important to avoid the trap of discussing contemporary theories as largely true" (Jones & Elcock, 2001, p. 3). Two examples of the new ways of writing histories are: first, Danziger's (1990) 'Constructing the Subject', which "focuses on the way in which Psychology has created its own subject matter, and particularly on the way in which much of what is now accepted as a necessary component of psychological research is a social construction" (Jones & Elcock, 2001, p. 5). It questions the understanding that the current methodologies are the best possible methods that have evolved historically. Second is Herman's (1995) 'The romance of American Psychology', which focuses on "the role of psychologists in the pursuit of political and cultural authority, and the impact of this pursuit on the nature of theories produced" (Jones & Elcock, 2001, p. 5). Such recent histories depict how political interests and social contexts influence research and evolution of a discipline. They attempt to internationalize the history of psychology rather than limiting it to the American-European context. For example, Brock (2006) asserts that only those European psychologists are included in traditional histories whose work had an influence in the United States. Thus, even "Wundt is included because he had American students, and some of the Gestalt psychologists are included because they migrated to the United States" (p. 2).

The old histories of Psychology justify their linear accounts, on the basis of the apparent progress that the discipline has made because of its methods that have evolved along the years. The understanding of Psychology as a discipline, with its own methods has grown over the last century, which is referred to as 'the century for psychology' (Fuller, Walsh, & McGinley, 2013). The eminent Dutch psychologist, Gerard Heymans had predicted as early as 1909 that Psychology will bring wisdom and it will enter the lives of people to bring happiness that technological innovation could not bring. This optimism about Psychology could not sustain itself. Mehryar (1984) was of the view that in the third world countries, Psychology served to remind people about the need for political struggle, to relieve them from their position of poverty.

However, the twentieth century turned out to be the century of measurement and experiments. Almost a century ago, in 1920's Simon and Binet constructed the first intelligence test and this development led to an unprecedented growth of tools of psychological measurement, for prediction of future performance in schools and for employment purposes. Several issues have been raised about the over generalization that psychologists made on obtained test results (Poortinga, 1997). Subsequently, Psychology diversified into several specialized areas of work: Developmental Psychology, Clinical Psychology, Community Psychology,

Educational Psychology to name a few, which have expanded exponentially and continue to contribute to the development of the discipline. The development of clinical diagnosis and clinical practice have provided evidences about the lack of success of experimental paradigms. Even within the area of Clinical Psychology, several theories and methods of treatment have emerged, which appeared to be mutually inconsistent if not incompatible, because, the nature of experimentation had very limited applicability to everyday behaviour.

The shift from quantitative methods to qualitative methods kindled the debate concerning Psychology being a Science or a Social Science. The fact that most scholars consider the setting of a laboratory in Leipzig, Germany, by Wilhelm Wundt, as the beginning of Psychology as a distinct discipline, itself hints at the quest of psychology to establish itself as a science - for which a laboratory is imperative. It also points towards the dominance of positivism in the methods of research, not just in Science but also in other disciplines that were competing to become a science - Psychology being one of them.

However, the seminal work of Morawski (1988) and Danziger (1990) indicates that the History of Psychology cannot be considered at par with the history of experimental laboratory research that is said to have started in 1870 when Wundt founded the first psychological laboratory. They brought out the fact that Wundt, the founder of modern Psychology, was interested in private individual consciousness, not in behaviour. Wundt "warned that experimental method should apply to basic psychological phenomena only while the higher, more complex psychological phenomena must be studied from cultural perspectives, on which he wrote the ten volumes of Folk Psychology" (Teo, 2014, p. 1177). He did not see the experimental method as the only possible method for gaining knowledge. Instead, he proposed that Psychology ought also to engage in ethnographic studies of human nature. However, to attain the status of being scientific, the experimental method became the method of choice for mainstream American Psychology.

Post Wundt, the attention shifted from introspection to 'observable behaviour' and from the individual to groups of subjects. There are two probable reasons cited for this. First, a growing body of psychologists believed that only the natural sciences could be the role model for Psychology if it wanted itself to be a 'real' science. Secondly, Psychology as an established discipline needed to apply its results to the outside world and only those practices that were marketable, were likely to find promotion (Danziger, 1990).

In the wake of the Industrial Revolution, Behaviourist Psychology and Cognitive Psychology dominated the discipline. It was their claim to prescriptiveness and homogeneity that made them popular for employee management in an organizational setup. Another school of Psychology that became quite popular in America was Psychoanalysis, which gained prominence with its use for propaganda and advertisement by Freud's nephew, Edward Bernays. The main intent of the use of these different schools of Psychology was to control and manipulate human behaviour at both the individual and collective level.

> *"Evidences can be garnered to substantiate that mainstream psychological theorizing is still elitist and skewed against the non-Caucasian modes of thought and social relations. For instance, Galtonian axioms are still sought to justify the prevailing social distribution of cognitive and personality traits across class, gender, and ethnic groups" (Arvind, 2006, p. 42).*

Against this understanding of Psychology as a tool for domination and propaganda, many thinkers in Psychology, like Parker (2007), emphasise the ways in which revolutions in society and other disciplines have revolutionised Psychology as well. They also ask whether Psychology as a discipline would ever have the potential to bring about any kind of revolution. This issue will find discussion in the next section, where contemporary developments in the discipline of Psychology, are covered.

However, another, more open way of understanding the various shifts in the history of Psychology is by referring to changes in the conception of the method of psychological research or paradigms of research. A paradigm is a framework or a way of answering three important questions: first, ontological questions or what is the nature of reality; second, epistemological questions or what is the nature of relationship between the knower and known; and third, axiological questions which include the questions of ethics and aesthetics.

The model of the natural sciences that is defined by the method that it adopts, is the first paradigm of psychological research, namely positivism, which assumes that there exists an objective reality outside of human subjectivity. Positivism attempts to "either exclude agency, experience, and meaning or reduce them to biological, chemical, and physical processes so that technical manipulation can be carried out and objective evidence can be found" (Teo, 2014, p. 1177). The quantitative approach gives precedence to the verification of a priori hypotheses giving little significance to the insights of creative and divergent thinking. Besides the intra-paradigmatic critique, questions pertaining to positivism, not recognizing that 'theory and facts' as well as 'value and facts' are not distinct entities. In fact, even theories in themselves can be value statements. Further, the inquirer is not someone distant from the phenomena; rather his presence interacts with the phenomena.

The second paradigm, which is a meek critique of the positivist one, is the post-positivist paradigm. It rests on critical realism, which asserts that reality is constructed only imperfectly and probabilistically.

The third paradigm is that of Critical Theory. This is an umbrella term for several alternative paradigms like Marxism, Feminism, Materialism, and Participatory Inquiry. Ontologically, critical theorists believe that reality is a function of the social, political, cultural, economic, ethnic, and gender values that crystallize over time. This may have increased their theoretical rigour on one hand, but it has reduced their applicability and generalizability, on the other. These paradigms have no allegiance to any pre-defined meaning and purpose of human life. Critical theorists use a dialectical model for research. The transactional nature of inquiry requires a dialogue between the investigator and the subject of inquiry. These dialogues must be dialectical in nature, to transform ignorance and misapprehensions into a more informed consciousness. It links historical understanding to elements of critique and hope.

The fourth paradigm, Constructivism, relies on the model of hermeneutics for understanding of meaning, in a context. The nature of social constructions suggests that an individual construction is possible only through interaction between the investigator and respondent. Those constructions are interpreted using hermeneutical techniques (Guba & Lincoln, 1994). This has emerged with acceptance of the fact that qualitative data can provide a rich insight into human behaviour. It was a response to the growing criticism against mainstream psychology for failing to provide adequate accounts of non-mainstream lives. Further, most of the grand theories seem very far removed from realities.

Notwithstanding this, both the Scientific models: Positivism and Post-positivism- and the Hermeneutic models: Critical theory and Constructivism, have been critiqued by the Phenomenological thinkers on the grounds that they do not take into account the intentionality of human behaviour. They claim that the study of human reality is as opaque as the study of the nature of human beings themselves. They question the possibility of a knowing subject's knowledge of itself. They question the positivist framework because it leaves out human phenomena like freedom and creativity outside the purview of its inquiry. Phenomenologists would disagree with positivists by asserting that one must look for intentions and meaning instead of real existence of things in the world. They argue that it is the consciousness to which meaning is related.

Further, Psychoanalysis, to some extent, and Existentialism, which agree with Phenomenological thought to some extent, explicitly question even the relevance of a 'method' of knowing, since they believe that reality is essentially personal. They focus on the lived experiences of human beings, as they experience reality, instead of how the researcher perceives reality.

These paradigms and models of understanding human nature form a continuum with positivistic determinism on the one hand and existential freedom on the other. One can place psychological researches and theories at different places in this continuum. However, as discussed above, most textbooks in Psychology tend to present a naïve picture of its history as the linear development towards these two approaches. They are shown to be essentially a refinement of the experimental and psychometric approaches. Even the paradigmatic way of understanding progression in psychological inquiry, appears to fall into the progressivist or *presentist* bias as it somewhere connotes that these transitions have been linear and the present way of doing research is the most advanced one. Here, one needs to challenge the simplistic and linear fashion in which the History of Psychology is presented in the texts.

In order to develop a perspectival understanding of the varied ways in which Psychology has developed, teachers may like to refer to the references, listed at the end of Section 1 of this book, to understand the alternative histories of the development of Psychology in detail.

The section that follows presents a brief overview of the recent developments in Psychology that have made the Historians of Psychology rethink and retrace its developmental path.

Contemporary Developments in Psychology

As discussed in the previous section, the shift in the history of Psychology has been from a linear perspective toward a non-linear and non-additive development model. This movement has taken place in the wake of the critique of the mainstream methods as over-generalizing with a neglect of several contextual factors that influence human behaviour. Understood in a broader context, Psychology is not only about what is out there, which can be studied objectively by experiments and testing. It is also about the meanings that unfold and get discovered by engaging in dialogue. An attempt has been made in the text that follows, to outline some of those voices that have had a strong impact in the development of Psychology as a discipline in the present century. The attempt is to draw attention of the various stakeholders towards these emerging trends in Psychology and better contextualize the subject matter of Psychology, at both the school and undergraduate level. Even at the beginning level, students can be motivated to observe, analyse, think, and discuss realities that they see around them. We believe that in order to develop a critical understanding of any discipline one ought to engage in a classroom with a pedagogy that develops the capability of learners to be critical. A critical perspective is not about knowing certain issues or critique but about developing a critical attitude.

Various perspectives and forms of psychologies have emerged as a response to Euro-American Psychology with their own underlying moral and ethical concerns. These psychologies had not only moral questions as part of their concern, but also political questions at the helm of their focus. The last two decades show mainstream Psychology to be in a state of flux. There appears to be an unprecedented degree of questioning about the subject matter, the boundaries of the discipline, and the method of enquiry. Much of the discussion revolves around what constitutes the theoretical foundations of mainstream Psychology. The post-modernist and constructivist perspectives have rejected the assumptions of the positivist paradigms and thus have denied the possibility of universal laws governing human behaviour. These perspectives emphasize understanding of the unique behaviour event in its contextuality (Shweder, 1991), its intentionality (Eckensberger & Meacham, 1984), and its historicity (Gergen, 1973). These alternative voices are strongest in the area of Social Psychology.

In recent years, a deliberate attempt to move away from the behaviourist methods is apparent in contemporary mainstream Psychology. What has emerged as an alternative is the cognitivist perspective? The main concern is thus no longer with the measurement of behaviour but with the understanding and mapping of cognitive functions and mental processing. Despite this shift, some issues of concern continue to persist. For instance, there is still a dominant need for prediction, control and prescription. There is still search for universality and homogeneity. In the recent years, although there has been a shift from cognitivism to constructivism, yet, mainstream Psychology continues to subscribe to positivistic notions and empiricist impulses, which were at the heart of outdated behaviourist experimentation. "Against the view that methods are free from theory and value, critical theorists argue that any method necessarily makes a particular assumption about the subject matter (ontology), the nature of knowledge (epistemology), and practical orientation" (Teo, 2014, p. 1177). Typically, mainstream cognitivist and behaviourist psychology, understand psychological phenomena as atomistic, reducible, mechanical, individualistic, decontextualized, and ahistorical. With this ontological assumption, "in order to apply experimental and statistical methods, mainstream psychologists break holistic psychological event into atomistic parts, which are then converted into variables and numbers" (Teo, 2014, p. 1177).

Critical perspectives in Psychology challenge many of the assumptions of mainstream Psychology. One is the significance given to the individual vis-a-vis the society and group, of which the individual is an important part. Secondly, by focusing on individualism and competitiveness, mainstream Psychology neglects and marginalises the powerless. Teo (2009, p.49) argues that Psychology's embeddedness in capitalism, conflicts with its potential as an emancipatory science. Capitalism rests on the individualistic worldview where economic class is seen as a given and not as a social construction. Psychology, by focusing on the individual neglects the social explanation of several phenomena like work stress. For example, the mainstream therapist would work at the level of the individual but the problem experienced by several people can also be analysed from the societal perspective.

Psychology has made its way to several other fields like Sports, Education for Persons with Disabilities, Public policy, Public health, Education etc. Terminologies with their origin in Psychology, like 'IQ', 'introvert- extrovert', 'repression', and 'unconscious mind' etc., are also seen to be in popular usage. What Stanley Hall wrote in 1923 (p. 437), "All the great problems of our age are becoming more and more psychological; the better we understand them", holds true in the present context also. In sharp contrast however, psychologists like Lasch (1978) and Gross & Lasch (1978) hold Psychology responsible for many of the present day problems. Gross has stated that the 'psychological society' has created a culture of vulnerability where everyone seeks guidance (1978). The roots of this kind of Psychology lie in Western society with its focus on individualism.

Another significant movement in Psychology is the change within Social Psychology where there has been movement towards symbolic interactions. This focuses on showing how selves, attitudes, motives, gender and emotions are products of conversations instead of being mental entities. Social interactions also focus on meanings that emerge in due course of social interaction. The interpretive interactionists do not believe in grand theories. In contrast, they see society as an emergent phenomenon having diverse forms of social actions. They are more interested in local narratives about how people do things together. They look at the actual experiences of people instead of focusing on the objective things in the world. Within the social interaction perspective, there was a movement toward taking up problems related to gendered selves, identities, desire, sexuality etc. These problems have found attention within the framework of Critical Psychology from the 1970s. Critical Psychology looks at the already existing work of psychology as a cover-up to hide gross inequalities of gender, class, ethnic groups and race. It reviews the present approach of Psychology with a quest to incorporate local factors that influence human phenomena. However, most of these voices still remain peripheral and are not yet part of mainstream Psychology.

There has also been a significant increase in the interest of psychologists in the domain of indigenous and cultural psychology (Kim, Yang, & Hwang, 2006; Berry *et al.*, 2011), which attempts to understand phenomena in cultural and local contexts. This movement in Psychology has brought into light the cultural and indigenous theories as opposed to universal theories. In recent years, increasingly greater involvement is visible with regard to historical sensibility, appreciation of the reciprocal relationship between culture and psychology, development of alternative paradigms for constructing realities, the consolidation of indigenization, cultural-psychological exploration, and the use of qualitative methods. These efforts are making Psychology a multi-voiced organism (Misra, 2011).

For example, Sudhir Kakar and Ashish Nandy are two such voices in the field of psychoanalysis, which itself is struggling to find its proper place in India. These two Indian psychologists, are often seen to be at the edge of what constitutes mainstream discourse in Psychology. Reviewing the status of psychoanalysis in India, Vahali (2011) analysed the work of Kakar and Nandy. He found that a strong cultural perspective was emerging in India, South Asia and other non-European countries, which was revisiting and questioning some of the core psychoanalytic assumptions, like cultural variations in the unfolding of the Oedipal complex, divergent ways in which the human psyche could develop and the influence of karmic notions and beliefs in the world of spirits. In 'Inner World: Psychoanalytic Study of Childhood and Society in India' (1978), Kakar examined socio-cultural phenomena methodologically, as is done in social sciences. While analysing the myths, fantasies and unconscious processes, Kakar also analyses social institutions like family, caste, the guru and the deep religiosity of our society. He uses ethnography extensively as a methodological framework for his work 'Shamans, Mystics and Doctors: Journeying through the domains of traditional healers' (1982). The work makes an important point that psychological healing can take place when there is some convergence between the world of the client and the healer, or the psychotherapist. Secondly, his writings also indicate that practices of psychotherapy are embodied in local worldviews and draw credibility from the linkage that they can make with the unconscious of the seeker. Kakar has used the vast store of cultural stories, mythologies, and religious practices to analyse the cultural influence on the human psyche. Thus, through his work, he makes a strong case for cultural psychology by appreciating the role of cultural systems and their ritualised practices (Vahali, 2011).

Politically inclined psychologists, like Nandy and Kakar (see Nandy & Kakar, 1980; Kakar, 1995) have made a clear attempt to use the psychoanalytical tradition to remember the forgotten, to discover the subaltern, and to reconnoitre the often neglected voice of the ahistorical common population of India. Nandy uses the enterprise of history, as a state-sponsored exercise providing a certain structure to the past by prioritizing some memories over others. He argues that the process of writing history is not an innocent exercise. Rather, the prioritizing of some memories and feeling states over others, serves the interest of the powerful, more articulate and dominant social classes, political parties or cultural groups. He connects the historical factors to the deeper intra-psychic space in his methodology. He uses the psychoanalytical method and psycho-biographical orientation to study the lives of the common people whom he calls 'ahistorical'. A few writings, like Hartnack's (2001), acquire a language of protest and argue against the tendency of creating universal psychoanalytical conceptualizations that explain experiences of selfhood, or view them as essentially inferior, less worthy, deficient or else simply pathological (Vahali, 2011).

There has also been a significant increase in the interest of psychologists rooted in particular cultures, like Indian psychology, which "represents an approach to psychological issues that developed in the long and rich intellectual and cultural traditions of India" (Paranjpe A., 2014, p. 942). Indian Psychology has emerged as another strong force in psychology that has been able to make a place for itself worldwide (Rao, Paranjpe, & Dalal, 2008). This revival is seen by many as a resistance to the baggage imposed by the British during the colonial period. It is an attempt to return to the roots by resisting the continued denigration of the various Indian knowledge systems (Paranjpe A. C., 2002; Rao & Paranjpe, 2016). With the acknowledgement of Indian psychology as a viable alternative, various Departments of Psychology and Neuroscience are researching and exploring the spiritual aspect of human personality.

This journey of psychology needs to be communicated to the learners appropriately, based on their previous knowledge, level of discussion, and as a response to their queries. Thus, a psychology teacher must also be aware of some essential pedagogical methods, tools, and strategies to be able to communicate and engage effectively with the learners.

Pedagogy in the Psychology Classroom

As important as knowing one's content for teaching is the way one teaches it. Thus, pedagogical understanding of a teacher becomes significant in the teacher-student relationship and the teaching-learning process. Pedagogy has the potential to make learners appreciate the importance of an idea in their lives. It can make the discourse come alive for students, making it an experience of their everyday life. It can ignite their passion for the discipline. The teacher, through the pedagogy that she/he adopts, can motivate students to think, ideate, reflect and analyse so that their interest in the subject remains sustained. Appropriate subject pedagogy can make any class an experience in itself, something that learners look forward to. In a non-engaging classroom, learners start disliking a subject or underestimate its importance for life. Thus, appropriate choice of pedagogy has the potential to raise the level of engagement of any class, be it about brain functions or holistic development.

Pedagogical knowledge can thus play a major enabling role in the teaching of Psychology, more so where it is the first exposure of the student to the discipline. The discipline should not come across as only an assemblage of theories and practicum to learners, but should appear as a way of life. For students, Psychology can become a discipline that can help them to live a healthy and productive life and become a more meaningful and cognitively enriching experience.

In order to select the most appropriate method of teaching, it is important for a psychology teacher to know her/his learners, their concerns, interests, and their outlook. A psychology teacher also needs to know about the ways in which the students spend their time and the activities they engage in so that she/he can guide them towards becoming mentally healthy persons.

A well-established fact, which applies to Psychology as well, is that teaching ought to be facilitative rather than an external imposition. This will strengthen the relationship between the teacher, learner, and the content. A classroom has to be a space that allows learners' views to emerge in relation to the prescribed syllabus. Their voice has to be heard and so they ought to get primacy in the learning process. There is potential to go beyond textbook knowledge once the learners become engrossed in the process. It is very important to know where to step in and where to step back and let learners emerge as forerunners.

Understanding the Nature of Learner

Beginning Psychology learners are typically in their late teen years. At this developmental life stage, most of them experience strong emotions, think critically and idealistically, are curious, engage intensely with the world and with people around them. These days they are quite digitally active and their online engagement is usually with their peers, with whom they explore friendships and relationships. Idealism, utopian ideas and self-exploration are characteristic features of this life stage. Alongside is the pull of learning to accommodate societal expectations in their behaviour and attitudes. In fulfilling the latter, at times they may experience overwhelming contradictions and disillusionment.

There is thus a need to prepare all learners to reconcile the personal and societal ways of being. To begin with, they have to first understand the larger societal world and then carve out niches and spaces for themselves. As articulated in NCF, 2005, (p.16) during adolescence, the "process of acquiring a sense of self is linked to physiological changes, and also learning to negotiate the social and psychological demands of being young adults". The emphasis on Life Skills Education and Adolescence Education as preparation for this, flow from this realisation. There is also no denying that at this life stage, the learners live and experience career choice pressures, peer-pressure, vulnerability to substance misuse and strong emotional outbursts, relationship conflicts, sexuality drives and strong ideological pulls and conflicts. For a psychology teacher, it is thus important to have understanding and perspective on all these.

Intellectually, psychology learners at the senior secondary level are at a higher level of cognitive functioning with a prominent capacity to reason, analyse, argue, and conceptualize. Their language abilities, both in terms of vocabulary and verbalisation are highly developed. Many of them are fluent in three languages: English, Hindi and their Mother tongue. Developmentally speaking, they are able to do complex problem-solving and analytical tasks rather than relying on only trial-and-error approaches to problem solving. They are capable of hypothetico-deductive reasoning and other logical operations like induction, deduction, reflection, analysis and judgement. Their cognitive capabilities and abilities can also be channelized to develop understanding of themselves, their ability to introspect, along with various other life-skills, like judgement making, evaluative thinking and problem solving, reflection, critical analysis.

The vision of a psychology student that we intend to share here is that of a person who has developed an understanding of human nature, oneself and others, and the understanding that development of one's self takes place in a context. A student of psychology would develop sensitivity towards others, greater tolerance and appreciation for differences, respect for phenomenological reality, and healthy adaptive attitude. These qualities, we believe, will not only enable learners to live a healthy life but also to commit themselves to a social cause. Any student gets inspired when she/he believes that his/ her teacher lives by these values. The personality of the teacher plays a major role in inspiring students to become a better human being.

The Psychology Teacher: Important Considerations

Teaching psychology to adolescents and young adults is a challenging task in many ways, because of the heterogeneous mix of students that teachers have to engage with, in the Indian schools or because of the very diverse nature of topics in the course of Psychology. Just as a teacher has to be sensitive towards his/ her learners, she/he also has to be self-reflective and sensitive to the social context, that is the background and ethos in which classroom engagements have to be located. A teacher should also care for her own growth. When the entire emphasis is on performing well in a job, invariably at the cost of one's personal wishes or desires, there are chances of stress and burn out. However, if the emphasis is on the growth of both the teacher and the learner, then there is always a quest to do more. Thus, it is imperative for a psychology teacher to be a reflective teacher so that he/she also grows.

A reflective teacher, simply defined, does not teach different things but teaches differently. For a reflective teacher, every new teaching situation is a new challenge in itself rather than a repetition of the same lesson plan taught previously. She/he is always in a sort of dialogue with the learners, their needs, their developmental course, their ways of thinking, and the impetus that is required for their holistic growth and development. Every class, for a reflective teacher, is a new avenue to explore; a space where learners' minds and hearts may unravel their beauty. To facilitate expression of learners and to take up the challenge to guide them is a constant risk that a reflective teacher is happy to take. She/he is not only aware of how learners feel and think about the discipline, the class, and herself, but also about the kind of emotions that are aroused within oneself, while interacting with various learners. A reflective teacher is aware of the issues of equality, justice, liberty, freedom, gender, and the like, and she/he knows that teaching and learning occur in a context. A reflective teacher is also capable of raising the level of engagement to a level where the questions of being, becoming, spirituality, and self-actualization take the centre stage. The quest of a reflective teacher is to create learning opportunities for oneself and for the students. Every question, pun, incident, observation, and concern has the potential of becoming a moment of learning and a reflective teacher is acutely aware of such moments. These are the moments in which the subject matter and its implications become alive and relevant to the learners; when they realise that their textbooks and their existential reality has a connection, which needs to be explored further. A reflective teacher is not one who only transfers the knowledge of various theories and propositions to the learners, but is the one who enables the learners to develop wisdom and the power to discriminate between a contextually appropriate theory, or one that is not relevant in the context.

Thus, a psychology teacher need not only be one who shares knowledge that she/he has, but, also become a researcher who generates new knowledge of the discipline and of ways of teaching as well. She/he would reflect on the classroom discourse and the context of learning to identify challenges and questions that need further exploration. She/he might also carry out some small class-based researches- action research- improve the pedagogic engagement in the classroom, and she might also take up some small group projects in order to understand the lived realities of the students better. Such researches and reflections also help the teacher to mould and develop curriculum for the class. A Psychology teacher also needs to understand the importance of personal and professional development. Since, there are limited spaces, like training workshops, meetings, or in-service seminars, where psychology teachers can find avenues for self-growth, professional development or peer sharing and discussion, they have to enhance their knowledge through their personal efforts.

The expectations of a teacher from the learners should be in tandem with her/ his expectations from her/himself. As a teacher, one might feel surprised at first, but often students rise to the level of the teacher's expectations. It is important that the standards set by the teacher about the expectations from students, be realistic. They should factor in the developmental stage of the learner, preoccupation with other work, the pedagogical inputs that are required for learning, their interests, and the different aspects of the topic that need to be covered.

In light of the framework provided by the National Curriculum

Framework (2005) viewing the learner as a constructor of knowledge is imminent. This requires that the psychology teacher also follow this approach in her engagement with students. The implications are many for his/her pedagogic stance, creation of an appropriate learning environment and methods of evaluation.

A very important mandate for psychology teachers is dispelling the myths and misconceptions that prevail about Psychology as a discipline and the sense of awe and bewilderment that accompany them. Apart from taking a proactive stance in society to address this matter, a yearly event in the institution by the Psychology club, could be discussion and critique of these popular myths in varied forms of representation. This would enable other students and teachers to understand the real nature of Psychology and dispel their incorrect beliefs. Such an engagement might also help in removing the stigma attached to the profession of a Psychologist and to those who consult Psychologists. As part of his/her social responsibility, the teacher must also find ways in which basic psychological education can be disseminated in society through community awareness drives, street plays, surveys, panel discussions with significant persons on the panel, awareness campaigns, and screening of movies and documentaries.

Methods and Strategies for Teaching Psychology

The spirit of any discipline is realised through personal engagements with texts, symbols and relics, and through interaction with the practitioners of the discipline. The same is true for Psychology as well. First-time learners of Psychology need an engagement with the discipline that makes it come alive for them. The use of appropriate teaching methods can help teachers in this regard.

Usually teaching methods in Psychology are referred to as Experiential or Experimental; Objective or Subjective, depending on the content of the lesson. One can infer from such a division that there is a clear distinction between teaching through practical experiments as part of classroom engagement and teaching through enabling the sharing of experiences and feelings by all. The latter characterises the experiential learning approach. As the authors of this Resource book, we believe that for an effective teaching-learning engagement, one needs to involve the whole being of every student in every class. If we broadly conceive of human nature as an assimilation of the thinking, feeling, and affective aspects of a person, then one needs to integrate all of them into the pedagogic interaction. Every engagement has the potential of becoming an experience. It is in this background, that some methods and strategies of teaching Psychology are discussed below. The choice of method and specific strategy will depend on the nature of the topic to be covered and the interaction and bond that exist between the teacher and the learners.

Lecture Method

Of all the teaching methods, lecture is the one that is most widely used. It places most of the responsibility on the teacher since he/she has to select the topic, plan the lecture, prepare for it, and present it to the learners. Here, the onus for fulfilling the intent and objectives of the lesson is on the teacher, but the teacher also has the freedom to engage students in the preparatory stages and to involve them in various activities after the lecture. "The prototype of the outstanding lecture may be of a powerful speaker mesmerizing the audience across the entire class period" (Hobbs, 2006, p. 50). Some other strategies for making lectures effective, include: "speaking softly when beginning, such that complete classroom silence is required" (Hobbs, 2006, p. 50); beginning the lecture with a problem situation or a case study; using anecdotes, a computer presentation or demonstration; asking provocative or unconventional questions; giving voice to students' feelings and views as the initial activity; making appropriate eye-contact and modification of the content of the lecture as per the students' responses, expressed in their body-language and facial expressions. One important aspect of a lecture is enthusiasm, or passion (Benjamin, 2002), and fascination with the discipline that is reflected in the style of narration of the teacher. To ensure that there is significant impact stemming from the lecture, variations in the volume and tone of voice and through the gestures and movement of the teacher can be done.

A teacher can also motivate learners to develop interest in topics by the use of humour, wit, and creativity. Intelligent and witty psychological jokes, language games, puzzles, one-liners or statements of famous personalities in Psychology, reference to anecdotes, and real-life situations can add moments worth remembering in the classroom. Reference to popular cinema, poems, stories, characters, cartoons, movies, and documentaries can be of real help in developing a lecture as well as in driving the point home.

Group-work

Group work in a classroom, can be organized in many ways. For instance, as a starting point, instructions need to be given to learners to work collaboratively on a problem- solving task, project work, mini research, analysis of a case-vignette or engage in a theme based group discussion with a follow up summarization. As a general method of collaborative group-work, a problem or a task is assigned to the learners, to be solved or completed. Finding the tools for solving the problem constitutes the learning of the students. The duration of the task could range from a single class to many classes or it could also be an after-class task.

The basic assumption of any group work is that the students will learn better if they are able to interact with each other in small groups. Well-structured and effectively managed group-work enables learners to become sensitive about each-others' strengths and weaknesses, to appreciate the value of cooperation and collaboration, to have a sense of responsibility towards others, learn negotiation skills, appreciate diversity, plurality, and alternative interpretations. Group work is also useful for generating ideas for further research projects through processes like brainstorming or idea pooling.

Experiments

Experimentation holds special significance in Psychology. Historically, it is through experimentation that Psychology claimed the status of being a Science. Many theories of learning, memory, perception, emotions, social cognition, attitudes and inter-personal attraction have emerged from the experimental method. Thus, familiarizing the learners with these experiments and making them replicate these experiments in the lab or in the classroom are crucial for teaching of these concepts. Some experiments can be part of the practicums, as prescribed in the curriculum; others can be illustrated or discussed in the classroom as simple field experiments or simulation exercises. While teaching using the experimental method, teachers may examine the earlier hypotheses or help learners create new hypotheses with reference to the problems that they wish to study.

Generally, when students engage in doing experiments, they seek perfect replication of previous experiments and look for validation of hypotheses, as predicted by the existing theory. However, the teacher should caution students against this tendency and emphasize that the replication of results is not necessary for successful experimentation. Often, there are factors in the form of intervening variables that are beyond control. Such factors influence the relationship between the independent and dependent variable in an experiment. What the teacher should help learners to understand is that even when hypotheses fail to get validated, the research does not become futile. It may lead to modification of the existing theory and the emergence of new theories. The teacher should also emphasize on the significance of adhering to the scientific method and the values that it encompasses. Students have to be made fully conversant with all the steps of the experiment and their underlying rationales.

Project-Based Learning or Problem Solving

One of the interesting ways of designing the teaching-learning process is through initiating a project. A project involves teaching learners to choose different problems or issues for exploration based on some assumptions and conceptual understanding. For a teacher, it is important to understand that a project or a problem entails learning to understand the world holistically, which often requires a multi-disciplinary approach. Concepts, ideas, and methods from various subjects, like History, Sciences, Social Sciences, Mathematics, and Languages can thus be drawn upon and used wherever necessary. The projects might even include the study of the arts and culture of a society. This pedagogical engagement would help to build the research potential of the learner. Aspects related to choice of a project, method of study, responsibilities of the researcher, dealing with the challenges and problems faced during the project, and optimal ways of sharing the knowledge or findings that have emerged, should be discussed both at the inception stage and through the duration of the task.

T-Groups, Encounter Groups, and Sharing Groups

A method widely used in Psychology is that of encounter groups, sharing groups, or transactional groups. Such groups help to build perspective and understanding of those topics in which sharing of real-life experiences are of importance for students' learning. For example, experiences of different forms of addiction, trauma, job-experience, reflective exercises, personality or learning challenges when shared, help considerably. However, such a learning method is more suited for advanced learners. For beginning students, it can be used for ice breaking or establishing the importance of personal experiences in learning Psychology.

Role Play

Role play is another method where students learn about the cognitive aspect of a situation, and also get a glimpse into their own self and that of others. Unlike a context of learning in which students may have to engage with other people directly, through role- play, learners are encouraged to step into those lived realities that are different from their own context. It could also be a safe way for students to act out their own fears and complex emotions, and to learn vicariously, since one of the important competencies of a psychologist is to be able to understand one's emotions and to respond to others thoughtfully rather than react indiscriminately. Qualities like empathy, active listening, questioning, clarifying, suggesting, providing support and trust, usually develop among learners through role-play.

Questioning as a Pedagogical Technique

To motivate any learner in the process of knowing, curiosity plays a role that is fundamental as well as so close to oneself; something that one usually does not even reflect upon. Human curiosity to know about other human beings more and to understand why they do what they do, makes Psychology a relevant subject. The constant interaction that one has with other human beings is even greater than the internal reflection or contemplation that one engages in for oneself. This curiosity finds expression in the questions one asks of oneself, others, or the world one lives in. In these questions, a teacher can gauge the readiness of learners and the depth and extent to which they can engage with the content, and maybe even the sequencing of topics. Questioning can play a significant role for a teacher to introduce a topic or even to develop a lesson with the help of learner interaction. Questions that probe the curiosity and native and experiential knowledge of learners can help the teacher to enhance their sense of self-worth and the confidence to share their own ideas and insights.

Use of ICT in the Classroom

The role of the teacher cannot be limited to being a transmitter of information but as one where he/she enables the learners to make sense of the world, both by presenting the world in different ways and by helping them to interpret it with reference to their own contexts. In this backdrop that ICT has been introduced only as a resource that a teacher can use as part of her/his pedagogical effort. It is not a replacement for the teacher. The biggest argument in favour of ICT is that it enables a teacher to bring the world to the learners within the bounds of the classroom, in contexts where taking the learners out is not feasible. A teacher needs to understand that ICT is suitable for various purposes in the classroom, like, introduction of a topic, to enable reflection and discussion, to depict social and existential reality, to assess and evaluate learning, to promote discussions, to depict a historical context or progression for a clear understanding of the learners.

Assessment and Evaluation

Assessment is one crucial aspect of learning and schooling with which teachers struggle. This is because on the one hand, teachers are expected to maintain high levels of performance and so they 'teach to test'; on the other hand, as they attempt to promote creativity and originality among learners, assessment takes a backstage. Here, one must understand that there is a close association between the method of assessment and the larger goal of enhancing learning. The purpose of assessment is not to judge and categorise learners; rather it serves as a feedback and the crucial point to initiate a new discussion, dialogue and enhance learning. When a teacher asks a question in class, the objective must be to engage the learner and to ignite his/her curiosity. He/she can use various strategies for assessment, like varieties of worksheets, in which some items are objective type like fill in the blanks, true and false, or match the following, while others may be subjective, like writing a detailed account of one's observations or other reflective exercises. They may also be in the form of crosswords and puzzles. Assessment tools and other evaluation strategies aim to keep the learners, parents, and the teachers informed about the progress of a learner's learning. Thus, assessment and evaluation mechanisms not only help the teachers in identifying learning gaps, they also help in pedagogical planning which in turn aims to foster the development of critical thinking and reasoning among learners.

The Framework for this Resource Book

Considering the discussion in the foregoing sections and the nature of Psychology textbooks at the school and college level, the present resource book aims to give some additional value inputs and knowledge that Psychology teachers can use to do better justice to the discipline.

The dominant ideology in Psychology in contemporary times, endorsed by the National Curriculum Framework for School Education (2005) is constructivism and so the aims of teaching and the pedagogic strategies to realise the aims have to follow constructivism. In this approach, the learner is located in the context in which he/she lives and grows. So theoretically, he/she is seen as having agency. As Bruner (1996) puts it, the teacher's method of teaching depends on what he/she thinks about his/her learners and how he/she thinks the mind works. It also depends on how he/she construes the basic nature of the subject and what identity he/she wants to communicate to the students. Therefore, the purpose of this Resource Book is to encourage teachers to rethink the nature of the learner, nature of the discipline and re-define their own role as a Psychology teacher. All these it is hoped, will help teachers to create more engaging classrooms where the learners construct knowledge more meaningfully.

The Resource Book covers the core concepts, ideas and theories that form the courses for all beginning learners of Psychology. They relate to important areas of General Psychology and Applied Psychology. Some activities have been suggested in each of the identified content areas. They are presented in the format given below: –

- Key Concept(s): This focuses on the concept(s) that is/ are discussed in the activity.
- Introduction to each Unit
- Route: It explains the procedure for conducting the activity.
- Synthesis: It explains the objectives to be achieved through the activity. We have either suggested the use of readings or a worksheet to synthesise the activities. A list of suggested core readings is provided at the end of each unit, along with a list of supplementary readings for both teacher educators, as well as student teachers.

- Further readings and web links: To facilitate further reading and innovative teaching methods, further readings and web links have been provided at the end of each Unit.

Note

The activities suggested in this handbook are only indicative and one of the many teaching-learning resources. Teachers must use their discretion and knowledge of their contexts in selecting which activities would be relevant and useful for the topics and classes that they have to teach. Each class undoubtedly throws different opportunities for a teacher. This handbook is like a resource to help teachers brainstorm and come up with innovative ideas. It tries to overcome the isolation that teachers have steadily been experiencing over the years. We grow when we have someone to share our ideas with and this Resource Book may act as a sounding board. Teachers must use these activities and share their feedback so that others can benefit from their experience. There are chances that some activities work well in a given context and may not yield the same results in another context.

References for Section- I

Arvind, G. R. (2006). Culture, cognition, and pedagogy: Evolving a discourse of possibility. *Kul'turno-istoricheskaya psikhologiya = Cultural-Historical Psychology, 4*, 42–51. doi:http://dx.doi.org/10.17759/chp

Baron, R.A. (2001). *Psychology* (5th ed.) New Delhi: Pearson.

Benjamin, L. T. (2002). Lecturing. In S. F. Davis, & W. Buskist (Eds.), *The teaching of psychology: Essays in honor of Wilbert J. McKeachie and Charles L. Brewer* (pp. 57-68). New Jersey: Lawrence Erlbaum Associates.

Berry, J. W., Poortinga, Y. H., Breugelmans, S. M., Chasiotis, A., & Sam, D. L. (2011). *Cross-cultural Psychology: Research and Applications.* Cambridge: Cambridge University Press.

Boring, E. (1950). *A History of Experimental Psychology* (2 ed.). Englewood Cliffs, NJ: Prentice-Hall.

Brock, A. C. (Ed.). (2006). *Internationalizing the History of Psychology.* New York: New York University Press.

Bruner, J. S. (1996). *The Culture of Education*. London: Harvard University Press.

Carr, E. H. (1961). *What is History*? London: Penguin.

Danziger, K. (1990). *Constructing the Subject: Historical Origins of Psychological Research.* Cambridge: Cambridge University Press.

Eckensberger, L. H., & Meacham, J. A. (Eds.). (1984). Action theory, control and motivation: A symposium. *Human Development, 27*, 163-210.

Fuller, R., Walsh, P. N., & McGinley, P. (Eds.). (2013). *A Century of Psychology: Progress, Paradigms and Prospects for the new Millennium.* London: Routledge.

Gergen, K. J. (1973). Social psychology as history. *Journal of Personality and Social Psychology, 26*, 309-320.

Gross, M., & Lasch, C. (1978). *The Psychological Society.* New York: Random House.

Guba, E. G., & Lincoln, Y. S. (1994). Competing paradigms in qualitative research. In N. K. Denzin, & Y. S. Lincoln (Eds.), *Handbook of Qualitative Research* (pp. 105-117). London: Sage.

Hall, G. S. (1923). *Life and Confessions of a Psychologist*. New York: Ayer Company Pub.

Harris, B. (1997). Repoliticising: The history of psychology. In D. Fox, & I. Prilleltensky, *Critical Psychology: An Introduction.* London: Sage.

Hartnack, C. (2001). *Psychoanalysis in Colonial India.* New Delhi: Oxford University Press.

Herman, E. (1995). *The Romance of American Psychology.* Berkeley: University of California Press.

Hobbs, S. H. (2006). The classroom lecture. In W. Buskist, & S. F. Davis (Eds.), *Handbook of the teaching of psychology* (pp. 49-53). London: Blackwell Publishing Ltd.

Jones, D., & Elcock, J. (2001). *History and Theories of Psychology: A Critical Perspective.* London: Arnold.

Kakar, S. (1978). *The Inner World: A Psychoanalytic Study of Childhood and Society in India.* New Delhi: Oxford University Press.

Kakar, S. (1982). *Shamans, Mystics, and Doctors: A Psychological Inquiry into India and Its Healing Traditions.* New York: Knopf Doubleday Publishing Group.

Kakar, S. (1995). *The Colors of Violence.* New Delhi: Oxford University Press.

Kim, U., Yang, K.-S., & Hwang, K. K. (Eds.). (2006). *Indigenous and Cultural Psychology: Understanding People in Context.* New York: Springer.

Lasch, C. (1978). *The Culture of Narcissism: American Life in an age of Diminishing Expectations.* New York: W.W. Norton.

Mehryar, A. (1984). The role of psychology in nation development: Wishful thinking and reality. *International journal of psychology, 19*, 159-167.

Misra, G. (Ed.). (2011). *Handbook of Psychology in India.* New Delhi: Oxford University Press.

Morawski, J. (1988). *The Rise of Experimentation in American Psychology.* New Haven: Yale university press.

Morgan, C.T.; King, R.A.; Weisz, J.R. & Schopler, J. (1993). *Introduction to Psychology*. New Delhi: Tata McGrawHill.

Nandy, A., & Kakar, S. (1980). Culture and personality. In U. Pareek (Ed.), *A Survey of Research in Psychology, 1971–76*, 1, 141–158. Bombay: Popular Prakashan.

National Curriculum Framework. (2005). *NCF Position paper of national focus group on teacher education for curriculum renewal.* New Delhi: NCERT.

Paranjpe, A. (2014). Indian psychology. In T. Teo (Ed.), *Encyclopedia of Critical psychology* (pp. 941-947). New York: Springer.

Paranjpe, A. C. (2002). Indigenous psychology in the post-colonial context: A historical perspective. *Psychology and Developing Societies, 14,* 27-43.

Parker, I. (2007). *Revolution in Psychology: Alienation to Emancipation.* London: Pluto Press.

Poortinga, Y. H. (1997). Brown, Heisenberg and Lorenz predecessors of twenty first century psychology? In R. Fuller, P. N. Walsh, & P. McGinley (Eds.), *A Century of Psychology: Progress, Paradigms and Prospects of the new Millennium* (pp. 1-15). London: Routledge.

Rao, K. R., & Paranjpe, A. C. (2016). *Psychology in the Indian Tradition.* New Delhi: Springer.

Rao, K. R., Paranjpe, A. C., & Dalal, A. K. (Eds.). (2008). *Handbook of Indian psychology.* New Delhi: Cambridge University Press.

Shweder, R. A. (1991). *Thinking through Cultures: Expeditions in Cultural Psychology.* Cambridge: Harvard University Press.

Teo, T. (2005). *The Critique of Psychology: From Kant to Postcolonial Theory.* New York: Springer.

Teo, T. (2009). Philosophical concerns in critical psychology. In *Critical Psychology: An Introduction* (2nd ed.) and, pp. 36-54, London: SAGE.

Teo, T. (Ed.). (2014). *Encyclopaedia of Critical Psychology.* London: Springer.

Vahali, H. O. (2011). Landscaping a perspective: India and the psychoanalytic vista. In G. Misra (Ed.), *Psychology in India: Theoretical and Methodological Developments* 4, 1–91. New Delhi: Pearson Education.

Vazin, T., & Reile, P. (2006). Collaborative learning: Maximizing S\students' Potential for success. In W. Buskist, & S. F. Davis (Eds.), *Handbook of the Teaching of Psychology* (pp. 65-69). London: Blackwell Publishing Ltd.

SECTION-II

Activities

The Nature of Psychology*

Introduction

There are a number of misconceptions associated with Psychology as a discipline. Some of them include: the study of Psychology can help one to read others' minds; with the use of Psychology one can manipulate others; or one can make predictions about an individual's future life. Many myths and fallacies are also seen to exist about the roles that psychologists perform. There is also a sense of wonder about what constitutes the subject matter of Psychology. In order to demystify the real nature of Psychology and enable students to appreciate its relevance, both in everyday life and in specific contexts and settings, various activities can be planned and conducted in the classroom. The activities introduced in this section aim at presenting an overview of Psychology as a discipline. They also build up an understanding of how the definition of Psychology has evolved over a period of time. This unit also initiates discussion on the distinction between science and social science and tries to locate Psychology on the continuum of the two disciplines. In the first section, the epistemological basis of the debate of whether Psychology is a science or a social science, or both, is elaborated. The teachers can simplify and share some of the basic tenets related to this with their learners.

Activities in this section have been designed to enable learners to understand the uniqueness of Psychology as a discipline and recognise its cross-linkages and kinship with other disciplines. The dual status of Psychology both as a science and social science can be made more explicit through discussion and deliberation on the

---

* Rashmi Malhotra

different methods that make science distinct from social science. Psychology, as an area of study, has a two-way relationship with the human world. It attempts to study human behaviour, as well as influence it. This unit will enable students to deliberate on how knowledge generated by research in Psychology is applied to different aspects of life. It will also be an exercise to inquire about various branches of Psychology.

ACTIVITY 1: NATURE OF PSYCHOLOGY: SUBJECT MATTER AND DEFINITION

Route: The teacher can ask a few students to come to the board and write any three things, which they think are a part of Psychology. Repetition of responses by students should not be allowed so that they are forced to think beyond the usual responses. From the obtained responses which are likely to include ideas like mind, thoughts, behaviour, soul, feelings, etc., the teacher can club together similar ones and evolve categories. For instance, responses such as,' thoughts, decisions', etc. can be clubbed together under the category 'cognitive processes'. Similarly, responses like, 'feelings, sentiments, likes and dislikes' can be clubbed under 'emotions'. Through this process, what constitutes the definition and subject matter of Psychology can be arrived at and then discussed elaborately.

Synthesis: To facilitate greater clarity of some issues, such as what constitutes the subject matter of Psychology, the teacher can raise some questions to enable the learners to understand with more clarity, as to what the subject matter and definition of Psychology consist of. Some suggested questions are:

1. If you are a psychologist who is interested in studying the students of class XI, what all do you think you would need to know about them?
2. What are the different ways through which a psychologist can get to know the students of class XI in the best possible way? (The obtained responses may be further used to differentiate between Psychology as a science and a social science)

(The teacher may evolve more questions on her/his own).

ACTIVITY 2: DISPELLING MYTHS AND MISCONCEPTIONS ABOUT PSYCHOLOGY

Route: The teacher can list out all the myths and facts related to Psychology on different slips of paper. Alternatively, he/she can ask students about what they think the subject matter of Psychology consists of. Students may state some of the myths that they hold about Psychology. They may then be asked the source of their information. The class can then be divided into groups of 4-5 students each. Each group can be given around 4 slips to discuss and find out which one is a reality and which one is a myth about Psychology. Each group should be asked to support their answer with a reason. Some of the myths that can be used to conduct this task are:

- Psychologists can predict the future.
- Psychologists can do face reading.
- Psychology is all about telling you what is going on in your mind.
- In Psychology, there are different perspectives to study the same thing.
- Any psychologist can work in any field.
- The only job of a psychologist is to counsel people.

(The teacher may add many more.)

Synthesis: The discussion can be used by the teacher to dispel myths that are associated with psychology and arrive at an appropriate understanding of the discipline. The discussion on the sources of information can be used later to distinguish between common sense knowledge and knowledge generated through research (linkage with Unit II). Some of the myths about Psychology also exist due to popular notions being presented in magazines and movies that are accepted as facts about the subject. The notion of pop psychology can also be introduced.

ACTIVITY 3: IDENTITY OF PSYCHOLOGY AS A DISCIPLINE

Route: The teacher can draw two columns on the board, as given below and ask the students to find common factors and differences between the subjects listed on the board and Psychology.

Physics, Biology, Chemistry	*History, Political Science*
Similarities	
Differences	

As the students come out with similarities and differences, the teacher can help them to understand how to place Psychology as a science or as a social science or both. The teacher can highlight that any science is a systematic study of any area. She/he can further discuss the difference between terms such as 'objectivity' and 'subjectivity'. She/he can also discuss the steps of conducting research in science and social science. While differentiating between science and social science, the teacher may also bring in the historical dimension pertaining to the period of enlightenment when scientific temper began to get emphasised. This may also help to situate the evolution of Psychology as a discipline.

Synthesis: The discussion will help the students to understand the different nuances of the subject and how different subjects are placed in the category of science and social science - their characteristics such as systematic study, ability to test and retest the data, etc.

ACTIVITY 4: PSYCHOLOGY AS AN APPLIED DISCIPLINE AND ITS KEY BRANCHES

Route: The students can be divided into groups. Each group can be allotted a field of study, such as Philosophy, Medicine, Economics, Computer Science, Political Science, Music, Law and Criminology, and asked to think about and work around the following points:

- How a psychologist can work with professionals to improve the work in that field?
- How Psychology benefits from that field and what Psychology can use from it to develop itself?

The discussions should be presented in a whole class mode where the class can add further to the group's learning and the teacher can use this to build up the required understanding.

Synthesis: The teacher can use the discussion to elaborate on the scope of Psychology and how various fields interact with each other to help in understanding human dynamics.

ACTIVITY 5: EVOLUTION OF PSYCHOLOGY

Route: The teacher can discuss the evolution of Psychology through narrating it as a story, where some select key foci are discussed. The storyline given below may be used. Based on the history of Psychology, teachers are also free to put together their own stories and use elements of detail as per the need.

"Once upon a time a group of people wanted to understand human beings very closely. They were interested in finding out who humans are and how and why every human being is different. They did not know where to go to find answers, nor where to begin their study. An inference that they made was drawn from religion, wherein they speculated that probably the whole essence of the human being lay in his/her soul. Issues related to mind, soul and body and the relationship between them dominated their strain of thought. At this stage, Psychology was seen as a part of Philosophy where the focus was on knowing the soul, the mind, the body and their complex inter-relationship. With the need for Psychology to extricate itself from Philosophy, in the late nineteenth century, a group of thinkers decided to use the method of science in the study of Psychology. As a consequence, the view that emerged was that just as science was studied in a laboratory, processes of human behaviour ought also to be studied in a laboratory setting. The underlying idea was that Psychology must study human behaviour that can be observed, predicted and understood through laboratory experimentation. The problem that arose however was that it was not always possible to do experiments of varied kinds on human beings. The solution to this problem was found in replacing human beings with animals. The argument was that humans share some commonalities with animals. So if animals were studied experimentally, the findings that emerged could be applied to human beings as well. This approach dominated the study of Psychology in the first half of the twentieth century. However, in the middle of the twentieth century, another group of thinkers felt that the laboratory

experiments did not adequately explain everything about human beings. Their argument was that human beings think, solve problems, remember things and reason and so they asserted that Psychology should not focus on behaviour alone. It should take into its fold the study of mental processes as well. Yet another group of thinkers raised the argument that every human being is different because he/she experiences life differently, so why not study the experiences which make him/her distinct? Finally, it was thought that all three arguments have some merit. Therefore, Psychology decided to include all three groups and today, Psychology is defined as the study of behaviour, human experience and mental processes..."

(Teachers may add some other twists and turns to make the story interesting and outline the evolution of psychology broadly. The purpose is not to give details of the history of psychology but to intrigue students in a way that they want to read further.)

Synthesis: The teacher can introduce students to different schools of thought in Psychology which have contributed to the growth of the discipline and have led to its present definition. The terms 'behaviourism', 'psychodynamics' 'existentialism', and 'humanism', as the important schools of Psychology, can be briefly introduced here.

ACTIVITY 6: PSYCHOLOGY AND EVERYDAY LIFE

Route: Students are asked to draw pictures or list out on a sheet of paper, where all they think they can use Psychology in their immediate life or in the future. They are encouraged to think in terms of where they will be working in future, about their relationships ten years from now, about what they would like to do for society, or any other cause they would like to work on like environment, media, etc. This will help in developing their critical thinking. Students can be asked to draw stick figures, if they are not comfortable with drawing.

Synthesis: This activity can enable learners to think about the practical applications of Psychology. It also helps in linking everyday life with the systematic study of a discipline.

ACTIVITY 7: HUMAN WHOLENESS IN PSYCHOLOGY

Route: Students may be asked to enlist the aspects of human nature that they would like to study and know more about in their

Psychology classroom. Their responses may then be written on the board under three categories: thinking, feeling, and behaviour. The responses may be used to highlight the holistic integrative nature of human beings and the attempt that Psychology makes to study them through different methods. The discussion may also be related to the debate of whether Psychology is a science or a social science.

Synthesis: The teacher may ask the learners about their assumptions of the nature of human beings and what they would like to study,

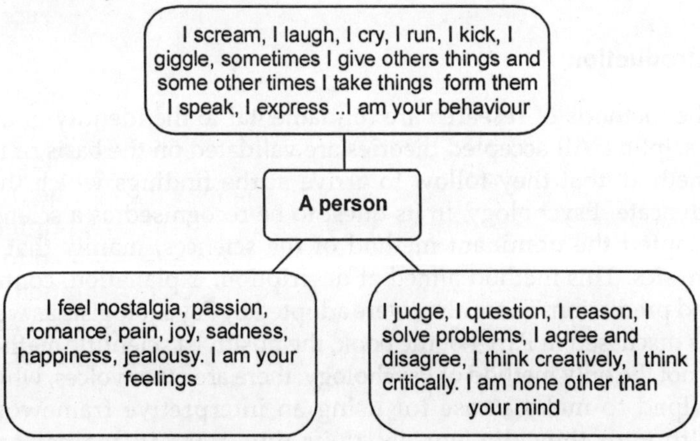

Figure 1: Aspects of Human Nature

Web-links and Readings

Ambridge, B. (2015, February). 10 myths about psychology, debunked. TED Talks. Retrieved October 22, 2015, from https://www.ted.com/talks/ben_ambridge_10_myths_about_psychology_ debunked/transcript?language=en

APA (n.d.). *Psychotherapy: Myths versus Reality*. Retrieved October 22, 2015, from American Psychological Association: http://www.apa.org/helpcenter/psychotherapy-myths.aspx

Butler, G., & McManus, F. (2014). *Psychology: A Very Short Introduction*. Oxford: Oxford University Press.

Schacter, D. L., Gilbert, D. T., & Wegner, D. M. (2014). *Introducing Psychology* (2 ed.). London: Worth Publishers.

Whitbourne, S. K. (2011, December 17). *The Top 10 Psychology Myths*. Retrieved October 22, 2015, from www.psychologytoday.com/: https://www.psychologytoday.com/blog/fulfillment-any-age/201112/the-top-10-psychology-myths

Methods of Enquiry in Psychology*

Introduction

The methods of research are fundamental to the identity of any discipline. All accepted theories are validated on the basis of the 'method' that they follow to arrive at the findings which they advocate. Psychology, in its quest to be recognised as a science, adopted the dominant method of the sciences, mainly that of Physics. This method aimed at description, explanation, control and prediction. These aims were adopted by Psychologists as well. As discussed in Part-I of the book, the positivist scientific method is not the only method of Psychology: there are other voices, which helped to make a case for using an interpretive framework. Although they did not get their due place in mainstream psychology at the time of their emergence, yet their voice made an impact and today, some of them find space and expression.

In most textbooks and basic readers of Psychology that constitute core reading, near total emphasis has been given to describing the experimental method. Other methods that take into cognisance the interpretive and critical perspectives that inform how Psychology is understood in present times find very little space or discussion. This needs to be recognised by teachers as a major limitation and taken up through more elaborate discussions in class.

One way to initiate a discussion about methods is to locate them in the debate on whether Psychology is a science or a social science. Subsequently the different methods of research that are followed by the sciences and social sciences, can be discussed. Another strategy found to be effective for teaching methods of

---

* Vikas Baniwal

research, is to make learners plan and replicate some of the classical experiments in Psychology. Through this replication, they will be able to understand how experiments are conceived, designed, conducted and analysed by researchers in different parts of the world. The teacher can also encourage learners to conceive of their own simple psychological experiments and carry them out as mini-projects, in the class. These projects can also be assessed. In addition, teachers may access and utilise material from internet and other more advanced Psychology books. Most books of General Psychology do not elaborate upon the reasons why a particular method was used in a certain kind of research. Teachers need to bridge this gap.

Another practice that a teacher can adopt to make this topic more engaging is to position it after the learners have read some other units of study like Perception, Emotions and Motivation. The benefit of reorganising the sequence is that learners will begin to have some idea of what Psychology studies and the kind of inferences that are drawn from research studies within it.

The intent to discuss Research Methods is also to break the various myths associated with Psychology and emphasize that research is a systematic process, distinct from the way we form opinions in our everyday life. Learners need to understand the ways in which any opinion or belief can become accepted knowledge, i.e. by problematizing different opinions, formulating research questions, attempting to find solutions to these questions, and arrive at answers to them as researchers.

In this backdrop, this Unit will introduce learners to the various ways in which research is conducted in Psychology. The suggested activities that follow introduce the beginning learner to the different steps that a researcher typically follows to create knowledge in Psychology. Most teachers report that learners find this Unit terse, boring, and difficult to grasp. The challenge lies in teachers devising ways of encouraging learners to engage with these methods in different ways that provide a sense of wonder and excitement on the one hand and deeper conceptual and experiential understanding, on the other.

ACTIVITY 1: UNDERSTANDING PSYCHOLOGICAL RESEARCH

Route: To sensitize learners to the difference between a common-sense understanding of human behaviour and that of knowledge derived from scientific theories of human behaviour, the teacher can present them with a hypothetical scenario involving different possible outcomes/ behavioural explanations and ask them to reflect on them. These responses can be further examined to see if the basis of the explanation is rooted in common sense or scientific research. The examples should be such that the common sense explanation is different from the explanation derived from psychological theory. One such illustration of a hypothetical example is presented below:

> *"A person named Hamid is walking on the road in the morning. It is a busy street. He is suddenly hit by a scooter and falls on the road. He seems to be hurt. What are the chances that Hamid will get help and will be given adequate medical help on time?"*

Most of the learners may reply that chances are very high that Hamid will get help because it is a busy street and it is daylight. Some of the learners may also say that sometimes people get scared to help someone who has met with an accident because it may wrongly implicate them. The teacher must probe further to explore the reasons behind the learners' responses. After a brief discussion, the teacher can share that research shows that if there are many people around, then the chances of a person getting help are less, as compared to a situation in which there are only a few people around. The teacher can also share how this research was conducted and how the researchers arrived at the conclusion. He/ she can refer to the famous study done by John Darley and Bib Latane (1968). A brief description of the study is as follows:

Participants were invited into the laboratory under the pretext they were taking part in a discussion about 'personal problems' (Darley & Latane, 1968). They were made to talk to a number of unknown others, varying from one to four, in each of the experimental trials. Because of the sensitive nature of the discussion, they were told that the actual discussion would take place over an intercom. In fact, this was just a ruse to ensure that the participants couldn't physically see the other people they were talking to. During the discussion, one member of the group would suddenly appear to be having an epileptic seizure. The experimenters then measured how long it took for participants to go the person's aid. They clearly found that when the number of people involved in the group discussion was more, the response to the apparent emergency was slower. It seemed that the presence of others inhibited people's helping behaviours.

This is explained as the bystander effect and diffusion of responsibility. The term 'bystander effect' refers to the phenomenon, in which, the greater the number of people present; the less likely it is that people will help a person in distress.

The teacher can share other experiments in Psychology which indicate research findings different from common-sense understanding. One such experiment is the Robbers Cave experiment. The Robbers Cave experiment is a classic experiment in Social Psychology, conducted with two groups of 11-year old boys at a state park in Oklahoma. It shows how easily an exclusive group identity is adopted and how quickly the group can degenerate into prejudice and antagonism towards outsiders.

Narrating different experiments conducted in Social Psychology may serve two purposes. First, they may give some idea to the learners about what kinds of experiments are conducted in Psychology. Secondly, it may also motivate them to read further.

Certain questions which the teacher can pose to learners, to help them understand the concept better, may include:

- Have they ever experienced that what they thought to be true, has been contradicted by research?

If learners do not come up with an answer the teacher can ask them some questions, such as:

- Have you experienced or observed teasing and stalking happening to you or around you? If yes, can you give a description of the people who may be involved in these acts?
- What is your view about rape and terrorism? Can you describe the type of people who participate in such crimes?
- Is there a difference between views that you hear from your friends, others around you and the news that appears in newspapers?
- Do you think news in newspapers is based on research?

Synthesis: From the responses that come up, the teacher can cite some researches which contradict the common perceptions. For instance, most learners may say that rapists and those who engage in teasing or stalking belong to a particular social class or age group, but research contradicts these views. The teacher must direct learners' attention towards the day to day process of thinking and point out how scientific research is different from this process.

ACTIVITY 2: GOALS OF PSYCHOLOGICAL INQUIRY

Route: The teacher takes a few newspaper cuttings with different kinds of research results published in them to the class. The aim is to discuss the process that the writer is likely to have followed to reach those results. The teacher can then ask learners to compare them with actual research articles. Some examples are given below:

Mental Stress Can Raise Physical Fatigue

WASHINGTON: Worried about something at work? You may find yourself more exhausted at the end of the day, according to a new study by Indian-origin researchers who have found that mental stress can increase physical fatigue.

This phenomenon is a result of the activation of a specific area of the brain when we attempt to participate in both physical and mental tasks simultaneously, researchers said.

http://timesofindia.indiatimes.com/home/science/Mental-stress-can-raise-physical-fatigue-study/articleshow/48298006.cms

What does it mean to be Middle class in India today?

Let us first look at what it meant 20 years back, meaning one generation ago. It was the last period without mobile phones and when there was no internet. Life was really, palpably different. Middle class then meant 'not poor'. Its membership comprised those urban families whose men were occupied in small business or white-collar jobs. How different is it today, one generation on? Here are 10 of my casual observations:

(Aakar Patel, August 8, 2015 *Times of India*)
http://blogs.timesofindia.indiatimes.com/aakarvani/what-does-it-mean-to-be-middle-class-in-india-today/

97 per cent Engineering graduates cannot speak English fluently: Survey

As many as 97 per cent Engineering graduates in the country cannot speak English, which is required for jobs in corporate sales or business consulting, revealed a new survey. Engineering remains one of the most popular choices among aspirants for under-graduate courses.

The survey also found that 51 per cent of them are not employable based on their spoken English scores and of the 6 lakh engineers that graduate annually, only 2.9 per cent candidates are fluent while speaking English. Pronunciation and fluency were found to be major barriers in effective spoken English.

(Apoorva Puranik, *Hindustan Times*, Mumbai August 8,2015)
http://blogs.timesofindia.indiatimes.com/aakarvani/what-does-it-mean-to-be-middle-class-in-india-today/

After showing these news reports the teacher can ask learners:

1. How do you think reporters of these news clippings arrived at these conclusions?
2. What procedure would they have followed?
3. Do you think that the findings are reliable?
4. What are the chances that these findings can be contradicted?

Learners may say that some of these studies are based on measuring fatigue levels in different conditions or by studying people who report greater fatigue etc. Since the size of the sample is not known, it is difficult to comment on the reliability of the findings. The teacher can direct learners' attention to the scientific procedure followed in some study, such as the first one.

Synthesis: This activity can be used to discuss the goals of psychological inquiry by elaborating on the significance of research studies in our daily lives. The learners may be able to understand that research is used for understanding, explaining, or predicting some phenomena.

ACTIVITY 3: STEPS FOR CONDUCING PSYCHOLOGICAL RESEARCH

Route: The teacher should encourage the learners to discuss a topic related to Psychology that they wish to explore and research.

Step 1: The learners could be divided into small groups. Each group should be instructed to formulate a problem they would like to research and list out the steps that they would like to follow.

Step 2: Each group can then be asked to discuss the research problem and its objectives, which they formulated with the rest of the class. Everyone can comment on the feasibility of the research and the suitability of the research objectives. The discussion on these should be facilitated by the teacher, so that it leads to consolidation of the research study.

Step 3: Following this, the group may be asked to reconvene and think about the steps they would like to undertake for the study.

Step 4: Now, each group may present to the rest of the class, the steps involved in undertaking their research study for final feedback. At this stage, the teacher can moderate the discussion and help learners to think through each step of their research study, so that they come up with a workable research proposal as a group.

The teacher can facilitate discussion in the class, raising the following questions:

- What is the importance of proceeding step by step in research?
- Is research a linear process?
- What will happen if the outcomes of the research are contrary to what was expected?
- What if the findings of the research are not significant?

Synthesis: The teacher will help learners formulate a research problem and outline the steps to conduct the study. This process of formulating the research problem and steps and discussing them in their peer group, is likely to help learners to get initiated into the world of psychological research on firmer ground. At this stage, the teacher can introduce to the learners, the predominant ways of conducting psychological research: both quantitative and qualitative techniques. In light of the discussion, learners may be encouraged to reflect on their own inclinations based on their choice of research questions.

ACTIVITY 4: SIMULATED EXPERIMENT

Route: The teacher can identify 8-9 learners and carry out a simulation experiment in class without revealing the nature and the purpose of what is being done. He/she may instruct the learners as follows:

"Today, we would be playing a small game in the class. We would be replicating the prison scenario in the class for a brief while. Some of you would be made prisoners while others would be acting as prison guards. We would be enacting the daily routine at the prison. The role of the prisoners is to follow the rules laid out by the prison authorities and the task for the prison guards is to ensure that the prisoners follow the rules."

For this exercise, a small area of the class can be converted into a prison. The learners can just imagine bars as demarcating prisoners from the guards. To make the scenario look more real, the learners may use certain props. Certain rules should be set for the prison in advance which should be enforced by the prison guards on prisoners. The teacher can then ask them to enact the daily routine of a prison. This can go on for approximately twenty minutes, during which the teacher and the remaining learners can carefully observe the role-play. The teacher should be ready for some noise and confusion during the exercise. The learners may get excited as they assume the assigned role of prison guards and prisoners. They may also start playing the role with utmost seriousness as if they are actually in a prison.

After the role-play ends, the teacher may facilitate a class discussion on the experience of the learners playing the role and the observations made by the learner observers. A discussion can ensue around the following questions:

- How did you feel while playing as the prison guard/ prisoner? (The learners involved in role play should respond to this question.)
- How were the prison guards and prisoners behaving? (The learners involved in role play should respond to this question.)
- Did playing the role of prison guards or prisoners lead to any change in the general personality of the learner assuming the role?
- How do you think labelling in real life such as being a 'bully' or 'bookworm' influences an individual's behaviour?
- What do you think this exercise was meant for?

After the discussion and the exercise, the teacher can narrate to learners the Stanford Prison Experiment by Zimbardo (1973). Alternatively, the teacher may also ask learners to find out about the study from the library or web sources. They can also be encouraged to watch the movie/ documentary made on the Stanford Prison study. The teacher may also introduce ethics of research here (which are discussed in detail later). The learners may also be asked to critique the study on some ethical grounds as an extension of the discussion.

ACTIVITY 5: EXPERIMENTAL METHOD

Route: The teacher must bring to the attention of her learners, the steps that are followed in an experiment. The following terms and their significance in experiments must be discussed:

- Problem
- Hypothesis
- Independent variable

- Dependent variable
- Controls

Synthesis: Since most of the topics that learners identify are difficult to investigate through experimentation, the teacher can clarify on the importance of experimentation for some dimensions by giving concrete examples and also introduce alternative methods to experimentation that can be used for researching the topics of interest, selected by students. She/he can further highlight, how experiments in Psychology are very different from the experiments that learners may have come across in Science. Learners must be given a chance to read different experiments conducted in Psychology. She/he can also give them an opportunity to design their own experiments within the school setting and conduct them as well.

ACTIVITY 6: OBSERVATION

Route: The teacher can divide the class into groups and ask the groups to go to different places in the school like the library, playing field, art room, wash room, yoga room etc., to observe the behaviour of students that they see, in these places. On the basis of what they have observed, they can be asked to prepare an observation checklist. This will help them to understand that observation is a scientific process and not something that is mere recording of impressions and pre-determined expectations. It requires certain tools.

Synthesis: The teacher can use this task to differentiate between impressions and scientific observation. She/he can also take it ahead to build understanding on types of observation: participant and non-participant observation, and the ways of using them.

ACTIVITY 7: CORRELATIONAL RESEARCH

Route: The teacher must collect some clippings of correlational researches published in newspapers, magazines or journals which relate to human behaviour. She/he must then read these out in the class and ask learners to identify the different variables which have been found to be correlated. These clippings may be used to discuss different aspects of correlational research. The difference between positive and negative correlation can also be discussed. Some examples of the kind of clippings that can be used are:

- Biometric machines lead to better punctuality in offices.
- Girls perform better than boys yet again, in the CBSE Class 12 Board Examination.
- Heavy smokers gain more weight after quitting.
- Children who stay at home and watch TV all the time, become obese during adolescence.

Synthesis: The difference between correlation and a cause and effect relation should be highlighted by the teacher. The teacher can also draw learners' attention to the fact that correlational research is used for prediction of one variable when another variable is known. Many instances such as correlation between marks in pre-boards and the board result, between practice and performance in sports are used in everyday life.

ACTIVITY 8: SURVEY METHOD: DESIGN, STANDARDIZATION AND UTILITY

Route: The teacher can ask learners to bring a cutting of a survey that relates to some aspect/s of human behaviour from internet sources, magazines or newspapers. Some of the surveys brought by learners can then be discussed with reference to how they were designed, the sample of participants, contents of the survey tool and the issues of standardization, suitability and rigour. For this, the teacher may involve the learners in discussing the following questions:

- What was the objective of the survey?
- Were there any questions in the tool that you found to be irrelevant or repetitive?
- Do you think the questions capture all the areas and aspects of the topic chosen? Would you like to add any more questions?
- Will there be any difference if the questions are posed as a questionnaire, or carried out in the form of a personal interview or a group interview or a telephone survey?
- Have you ever participated in any survey? If yes, share your experience.
- What are the benefits and limitations of conducting surveys?

Synthesis: This exercise can be used by the teacher to build understanding about survey as a method of research. It can also be used to sensitize learners to the differences between scientifically designed surveys and pop-surveys. Apart from describing the different ways in which surveys can be employed in Psychology, the teacher should be able to highlight the specific contexts in which survey researches are useful and significant.

ACTIVITY 9: CASE STUDY

Route: The teacher can divide the class into groups for this activity. Each group can be instructed to work together to find a famous documented case study. The teacher can give examples of case studies from different fields in Psychology such as Human Development, Organizational Behaviour, Clinical Psychology etc. Some of the case examples are as follows:

- The Krishnamurti Foundation Schools
- John Nash's case of Schizophrenia
- Piaget's Study on his children
- Freud's clinical cases

These cases can be circulated in the class in a way that all learners have access to them. The teacher may ask them to read the cases in advance. Discussion can then be taken up in the class around the following points:

- What are the similarities and differences between the case studies?
- Can you try to list out the different tools that the psychologists may have used to gather information about the different cases discussed in the case studies?
- Do the case studies give complete information? Is there any more information that could have been added to the case studies?
- List out other areas where the case study method can be used.

Synthesis: The teacher should highlight how the method of case study in Psychology has been adapted from the field of Medicine. The Psychoanalytic heritage of the use of case study as method of research along with the contributions of Sigmund Freud should also be discussed. The learners should be able to appreciate the uniqueness of case study as a method of enquiry and its relevance in contemporary qualitative research. They should also be able to understand that case studies are used for individuals and institutions and for diagnosis and success stories.

Ethics of Research

The teacher should sensitize learners to the issue of ethics in research, particularly because Psychology is the study of human behaviour. Why ethics are important, issues of victimisation, labelling, confidentiality, privacy, seeking consent etc. should all be discussed across methods of research. The discussion may be also be related to the larger question of human and animal rights.

Recent Trends

Section-I of this book explicates the different paradigms of research in psychology. Though the emphasis in introductory psychology books is primarily on positivist paradigm of research it is worthy to note here that critical theory and interpretivism are alternate paradigms of research in social science. They are elaborated in section one of this book and the teacher can refer to them while teaching this unit. We feel that there is a need to elaborate on the general characteristics of qualitative research and on some methods that are used in this approach. The methods of research discussed above are the ones that are referred to establish the discipline of psychology as science, however, there are many other methods that establish psychology as a rigorous social science as well. For example, methods like case-study, in-depth interview, ethnography, and content analysis are quite often used by psychologists to understand human actions.

Qualitative Research: It is difficult to provide strict criterion to define qualitative research, however some points can be mentioned here to differentiate this approach from other approaches. As discussed earlier, positivism concerns itself with the search for valid truths that can be generalised. But the goal of interpretivist qualitative research is to understand a particular context. This is possible by immersing oneself in the context that we want to understand. In sharp contrast to positivism's goal of prediction and control, interpretive framework seeks to understand. In this approach the boundary between the researcher and subject or participant is blurred. Qualitative research may also want to generalize, draw hypothesis and theories to explain patterns of behaviour. But the difference in these theories is that they do not offer a law like generalisation that can be universally applicable. Rather they offer a perspective which may or may not be applicable in another context. It presents a situated understanding and lays emphasis on the local truths.

Qualitative research is also free from the boundaries of knowledge. It cuts across all disciplines and borrows from any source that it deems relevant. It is open to a variety of methods with its commitment to study and thought. It also emphasises the need for multiple perspectives. This approach holds that human beings have agency and act on their own initiative. It disagrees with the realist notion that reality is out there. Instead they contend that reality is socially constructed through interaction and communication. This implies that reality is dynamic and changes according to changes in human interaction. The idea of multiple realities comes from their belief that external reality can never be known directly. Different cultures have different views about the world. Acceptance of multiple realities enables us to understand why people living in different parts of the world or different cultural groups have different behaviour patterns.

Ethnography: Ethnography is an umbrella term which encompasses fieldwork, interviewing and other methods of gathering data. It is sometimes treated as a synonym to fieldwork. The research is conducted in a natural environment instead of a contrived environment. In this method the researcher is expected to spend time in the field and build relationship with the participants. With the passage of time the participants get used to the presence of the researcher and start acting naturally. They may start sharing their thoughts more explicitly with the researcher. The researcher has to maintain notes which help in presenting thick description of the field. The researcher may also use still photography and video recording to gather data. They can then analyse data. Ethnography is not a particular well defined method. Rather, it is a broad conceptual framework (Willis,2007).

Case Studies: Case study, like ethnography, is a broad framework, a methodology and not a specific method. A case study is an examination of specific phenomenon such as a programme, event, institution or a social group. The focus of case studies is on a particular context. The context could be a person, family or a classroom. The researcher explores a case over a period of time, through detailed, in-depth data collection using multiple sources of information and reports a case description. Case study approach was popularised in Psychology by the work of Sigmund Freud.

This approach is widely prevalent in medicine, law and political science. Case study can be done using both quantitative and qualitative methods (Yin,2003).

The biggest challenge in case study is the identification of a case. The case itself must be an issue and worthy of study. The researcher may study more than one case also. There is no set number of cases that a researcher can study but the more the number of cases the more diluted the case study may become (Creswell, 2007). To explain a case, the researcher must establish a rationale for its selection. They must also develop a matrix that specifies the amount of information they are likely to collect about the case.

Narrative Research: Narrative is a term used for a variety of analytical practices in social science. It can refer to text or discourse. It can also refer to stories told by individuals within a certain context that gives an account of an event or a series of events that are connected. As a method, narrative begins with lived experiences that are told by individuals in the form of stories. This study consists of focusing on one or two individuals, gathering data by collecting their stories, reporting their individual experiences and chronologically ordering those experiences. The researcher must also locate those stories in historical context and their culture (Creswell, 2007). Finally the researcher analyses them and then re-states them in a framework that makes sense. At this stage the researcher can analyse the key elements of the stories for time, place, plot and scene. The researcher may also provide causal links among different ideas in the story. The participant in narrative analysis is an active part of the research process. This research originated from literature, history, anthropology, sociology, socio-linguistics and education. Different fields have adapted it to meet their requirements.

Phenomenological Research: Phenomenological research emphasises the importance of personal meaning and lived experiences of any phenomenon. It is somewhat similar to narrative research but narrative inquiry restricts itself to reporting life stories of one or two individuals. Phenomenological research describes what participants have in common when they experience a phenomenon. The purpose of this research is to take individual experiences to express a universal essence of what and how they experienced a particular phenomenon. This research draws heavily from philosophy, especially from the work of Edmund Husserl (1859-1938).

Grounded Theory: Grounded theory goes beyond phenomenology to generate and discover a theory, an abstract analytical schema of a process. It begins with description of an event or phenomenon and on the basis of that it develops a theory that might explain the practice or provide framework for further research. This study is grounded in the data that is collected from the participants. This design was developed by two researchers Barney Glaser and Anselm Strauss in Sociology in 1967. They felt that theories in research are often inappropriate for participants under study. They hold that theories should be grounded in the data from the field. They should capture the interaction and social processes of the people (Cerswell, 2007).

The above mentioned approaches indicate an interpretive flow. It is difficult to step aside and be objective about what you see and write. Qualitative research engages in personal experiences, cultures, histories and backgrounds. It demands reflexivity in what a researcher sees, hears and writes. Research writing is more of a researcher's interpretation of an event, people and their activities. There can be other interpretations of the same study. Thus, a piece of writing in qualitative research can only be a discourse with a tentative conclusion. It is a part of dynamic process which is open to changes (Creswell, 2007).

Web-links and Readings

Cohen, L., Manion, L., & Morrison, K. (1997). *Research Methods in Education* (6 ed.). New York: Routledge.

Creswell, J. W. (2007). *Qualitative Inquiry and Research Design Choosing among five approaches.* New Delhi: Sage Publications.

Frankfort-Nachmias, C., & Nachmias, D. (1996). *Research Methods in the Social Sciences* (5 ed.). New York: St Martin's Press.

Indo-Asian News Service. (2015, August 14). *Heavy smokers gain more weight after quitting.* Retrieved from India Today: http://indiatoday.intoday.in/story/heavy-smokers-gain-more-weight-after-quitting-cigarettes-obesity/1/458646.html

Darley, J. M., & Latane, B. (1968). Bystander intervention in emergencies: diffusion of responsibility. *Journal of Personality and Social Psychology, 8*(4), 377-383.

Kelly, D. (2015, August 26). *10 Fascinating case studies from Sigmund Freud's career.* Retrieved from Listverse: http://listverse.com/2015/08/26/10-fascinating-case-studies-from-sigmund-freuds-career/

Kitchener, K. S. (2000). *Foundations of Ethical Practice, Research, and Teaching in Psychology.* New Jersey: Lawrence Erlbaum Associates, Inc.

Lillie, W. (2003). *An Introduction to Ethics.* New Delhi: Allied Publishers Pvt Ltd.

Mayan, M. J. (2001). *An Introduction to Qualitative Methods: A Training Module for Students and Professionals.* Edmonton: International Institute for Methodology, University of Alberta.

Norton, B. G. (1982, Spring). Environmental Ethics and Nonhuman Rights. *Environmental Ethics,* 4(1), 17-36.

Nutt, A. E. (2015, May 26). *Did John Nash's schizophrenia boost his 'beautiful mind'?* Retrieved from The Washington Post: https://www.washingtonpost.com/news/to-your-health/wp/2015/05/26/did-john-nashs-schizophrenia-boost-his-beautiful-mind/

Oliver, P. (2003). *The Student's Guide to Research Ethics.* Berkshire: Open University Press.

Singer, P. (2011). *Practical Ethics* (3 ed.). Cambridge: Cambridge University Press.

The Editors of Encyclopaedia Britannica. (2016). *Jean Piaget.* Retrieved from Encyclopaedia Britannica: http://www.britannica.com/biography/Jean-Piaget

Willis, J. W. (2007). *Foundations of Qualitative Research.* New Delhi: Sage Publication.

Yin, R. K. (2003). *Case Study Research: Design and Methods.* (3 ed.) California: Sage Publications.

Zimbardo, P.G. (1971). The Power and Pathology of Imprisonment. Congressional Record, 15, 10-25.

Sensation and Perception*

Introduction

When Psychology established itself as a formal discipline in the University of Leipzig, Germany in 1879, a major part of research in the discipline was devoted to the study of sensation and perception. However, with the advent of Behaviourism in America, the focus shifted to prediction and control of all forms of behaviour. This remained the pattern in the 1940s and 50s. Contiguous with this, the work of Gestalt psychologists once again revived interest in the study of perception. Subsequently, Cognitive Psychology introduced the concept of top down and bottom up processes. This opened up an altogether new area of research in perception. The Cognitivists, Gestalt studies and Gibson's research, all emphasised the top down processes. The advent of the Information Processing Approach in the 1960s gave a new impetus to the study of sensation and perception. It emphasised unravelling and understanding of underlying mental processes. Concomitant with this, the Cognitive Science Approach coupled with Artificial Intelligence, began to emphasise the nature of mental representations. A major part of research work in perception today revolves around visual perception and relies heavily on a mathematical framework.

Through this unit, learners will get an overview of some of the earliest experiments that took place in various Psychology laboratories to measure sensation. To understand sensation, it becomes important to understand how the various sense organs function, and how their respective structures limit the range of sensations that a human mind can perceive. Learners will also be acquainted with a branch of Psychology called Psychophysics. Closely linked to the study of sensation are two more processes,

---

* Rashmi Malhotra

namely, perception and attention. The teacher can use a lot of visual imagery to discuss principles of organization, monocular, and binocular cues. Overall, there is a lot of scope for creativity and activity based teaching in this Unit. One of the best ways to teach the Unit is with the help of simple experiments and demonstrations, conducted in the classroom, to facilitate better understanding of various concepts. The teacher should not be too concerned about exact measurements, because the purpose of these activities is to make learners conversant with the method and to have an engaging teaching-learning interaction.

ACTIVITY 1: DRAWING THE RELATION BETWEEN SENSATION, ATTENTION AND PERCEPTION

Route: The teacher can take learners for a 5-minute nature-walk to their school/college garden. The learners' task during this walk is to notice their surroundings. Later, when they are back in the class, they will have to describe the things they saw, sounds they heard, any strange smells they encountered and anything peculiar that they touched while they walked. The teacher's role is to discuss how they experienced these things and make linkages to establish the relationship between the three processes.

Alternatively, the teacher can ask learners to recount what all they saw or heard in the morning, on their way to class. He/she can then discuss the experiences of some of the learners and lead the discussion towards the importance of sensation and perception. The uniqueness and subjectivity of these processes and yet how they intersect, can be emphasised.

Synthesis: The teacher can then discuss the difference between sensation, attention and perception. There may be several stimuli in the surroundings that stimulate the sensory receptors, but attend to only some of them. When the sensory information to which we attend is recognised, interpreted or given meaning, then we can say that we have perceived something. On the way to school, learners are likely to have come across several things, but while asking them about all that they saw, they are only able to recollect a few things. The reason for this is that not every sensation translates into perception.

ACTIVITY 2: VISUAL AND AUDITORY SENSATIONS

Route: The teacher will divide the class into four groups. Each group is required to go for a nature walk, but under different conditions. The idea is that after the walk, all of them will converge in class and share their experiences.

Group 1: Learners in this group have to support the other three groups and make sure that no one falls or gets hurt in any of the groups.

Group 2: Learners in this group will at first, be blindfolded. Then they will proceed for a nature walk, with the first group.

Group 3: Learners in this group have to stuff cotton bobs in their ears so that any sound is blocked. They can even tie a cloth or wear headphones. They have to go for the walk in this condition.

Group 4: Learners in this group will be both blindfolded and have cotton in their ears so that both vision and sound senses are blocked. They too have to go for a nature walk with the first group.

After the nature walk, the teacher would encourage the groups to discuss their experiences. The main point of discussion has to be the nature of experiences that everyone had. Learners will be encouraged to reflect on the different experiences and analyse what the reasons could be for these differences. The teacher can then relate the discussion to the processes of sensation, perception and attention. The teacher may also use this activity to introduce visual and auditory sensation to them.

Synthesis: The teacher must discuss that sensation is the experience that results from stimulation of the sensory organs. It is the most elementary experience. When a person attends to a particular sensation then it goes for higher processing. Finally, perception is the process by which we recognize, interpret and give meaning to the information provided by the sense organs.

ACTIVITY 3: 'ABSOLUTE THRESHOLD' AND 'DIFFERENTIAL THRESHOLD'

Route: A simple classroom experiment can be conducted by the teacher to demonstrate the concept of threshold.

The teacher can play a song on her mobile phone at very low volume and ask the learners whether they can hear it or not. Slowly she can increase the sound level and take it to a point where the learners can hear it. The volume, at which the learners can hear the song, is the critical point. The teacher can then explain that this point is the absolute threshold. The point at which they can understand the difference in volume is the differential threshold.

The teacher can ask the following questions to take the

discussion further:

1. Why do we feel the touch of the wind but not air, even though it is present all the time?
2. Do you think we can hear all the sounds present around us?

Synthesis: The above experiment is aimed to demonstrate that the human sense organs have some limitations. None of the learners could hear the music when the volume was very low. As humans, we function within a limited range of stimulation. Absolute threshold is the minimum value required to activate a sensory system. The point at which a person can detect the difference between two stimuli, is the differential threshold. A branch of Psychology known as the Psychophysics tried to study this by conducting such experiments in laboratory settings.

ACTIVITY 4: ATTENTIONAL PROCESSES

Route: The teacher asks any two learners to close their eyes and recall all the things that they think are present in their classroom. During this time, the remaining class listens carefully and checks whether the things, recalled by their two classmates, are actually present or not. One of the learners from the class can note down the list of things and then compare it with the actual situation in the class. The class can then discuss the activity with the help of the following questions:

1. Why did she/he miss some things?
2. Why is it that we recall some things faster as compared to others?

Synthesis: In most conditions, learners themselves will say that they recalled only people or objects to which they paid attention. There may be several objects and people in our environment; however, it is not possible to register all the stimuli at one point in time. Only those things which we attend to, or which draw our attention, are perceived.

ACTIVITY 5: SPAN OF ATTENTION

Route: The teacher puts a few things like sharpener, eraser, pencil, toffee, piece of coloured paper, scissor, nail cutter, etc. in a box and covers it. Two learners volunteer as participants. They are told that the box will be opened for 15 seconds, during which they have to view and subsequently remember, what is present in the box. After this, they make a list of all the things they saw on a sheet of paper. The box is then brought out to check how many items have been correctly remembered and listed by them.

Synthesis: This activity is useful in explaining the concept of span of attention. Our attention also has limited capacity to hold information unless and until we organize it. The number of objects we can remember for a brief time is our 'span of attention'. Miller (1956), in his study found that the number of objects we can remember at one go, is 7 ± 2.

ACTIVITY 6: ALERTNESS AND CONCENTRATION

Route: The teacher will show the learners some picture puzzles to spot the difference as quickly as they can. After the learners have completed the task, the teacher will ask them what was involved in the completion of the task. Learners may respond with terms like, attention, focus, concentration, etc. The teacher will then introduce the ideas- concentration and attention.

Synthesis: The teacher can discuss how alertness and concentration are part of the process called attention. Concentration refers to focusing attention on a particular object while excluding others.

ACTIVITY 7: FOCUS AND FRINGE

Route: The learners are asked to describe a chart put up on the display board, or the teacher can carry any painting to the class, which she can ask the learners to describe. The teacher may then ask them to focus on any one part of the drawing and talk about it. Whatever the learners describe in detail is the focus. There may be other things near the border of the painting or picture, which the learners may have noticed but not described, because they were not paying as much attention to it. That is the fringe. The teacher can then discuss how this activity elucidates the concept of focus and fringe.

Synthesis: The teacher must discuss that focus is the object on which the field of awareness is centred, whereas fringe, as the name suggests, is away from the field of awareness and the individual is only vaguely aware of them.

ACTIVITY 8: SELECTIVE ATTENTION AND INTERNAL AND EXTERNAL FACTORS AFFECTING ATTENTION

Route: The teacher can carry some old newspapers to the class and divide the class into groups of 4-5 learners. Each group gets one or two newspapers. They are asked to cut out advertisements of different sizes, which they think are attractive. They then share with the class as to why they found those advertisements attractive. The learners may say that the colour, design or the tag line of the advertisement was attractive, or that the product displayed was of interest to them. They may also say that they have not seen such an advertisement before. The teacher can then discuss these factors and introduce them as factors affecting selective attention. They can be then be asked to categorize their responses as internal and external factors as well.

Synthesis: The teacher can facilitate the categorization of learners' responses into external and internal factors that affect selective attention. When learners attribute the reason for their selection to the qualities of the advertisement, then they become external factors of selective attention. Whereas, when the learners identify factors that lie within them, then those become internal factors of selective attention.

Alternatively

Route: The teacher may ask the learners to discuss in detail any one advertisement that they had seen and really liked. Learners may describe an audio-visual advertisement or a print advertisement. The teacher then asks them to deliberate on why they remember audio-visual advertisements more than print ones.

Synthesis: This activity serves to bring out various factors affecting selective attention. Research indicates that certain qualities of the stimuli such as those objects, which are large, colourful and move easily, catch attention. Similarly, rhythmic auditory stimuli are more easily attended to, than verbal narration.

ACTIVITY 9: FILTERING BY SELECTIVE ATTENTION

Route: The teacher can organise a small experiment in class with the help of three learners.

Step 1: One learner is made to sit in the centre while two other learners will be asked to sit on two sides of the learner. They will read aloud from two different textbooks of different subjects simultaneously. This would continue for about 5 minutes. The teacher would then ask the learner sitting in the middle, about what he/she heard and whether he/she is able to recall anything from the readings.

Step 2: In the next stage, the teacher will call one of the readers quietly and tell him/ her to say the name of the child sitting in the centre after every line. Then the learner sitting in the centre will recall whatever s/he has heard. The results of step 1 and step 2, will be compared. If the learner attends to the one who is taking his name after every two lines, then the teacher can discuss the reasons for increased receptivity in step 2. The rest of the class thinks of how we attend to a stimulus and how some stimuli escape the filter to enter higher processing.

Synthesis: The teacher will discuss the results of the experiment to explain filter attenuation theory. According to this theory, whenever there are competing stimuli, the selective filter allows only one stimulus to pass through for higher processing. However, some stimuli escape this filter and enter higher level of processing. Research indicates that some personally relevant stimuli enter the filter, even at a very low sound.

ACTIVITY 10: PROCESSING APPROACHES IN PERCEPTION

Route: The teacher will prepare slips with the names of various objects such as a musical band, a guitar or a harmonium, a place, a book, etc. He/she will divide the class into two teams. Each team member will send a person to pick up a chit and explain the object to his team, without using the name of the object. Every time the team guesses it correctly, the team gets 10 points. Each team will get 2-3 chances depending on the time at hand. Now the teacher will ask learners to reflect on their mental processes during this game. She can ask the following questions:

1. How did you identify the object?
2. Do you think the team member who saw the chit and the others followed the same type of processing?

The teacher can explain top-down and bottom-up processing with the help of this game and responses to the question. The members, who have seen the chit, perceive the object as a whole. The perceiver identifies the object and then tries to explain to others with the help of some of its characteristics. This is top down processing. However, the other team members first observe the characteristics of the object and then identify it. They are using the bottom up approach, since the stimulus characteristics are driving their perception.

Synthesis: The learners should discuss that we employ both bottom-up and top down processing in our everyday life. Both these processes facilitate identification of objects around us.

ACTIVITY 11: PERCEIVER'S SIGNIFICANCE

Route: The teacher will display one or two logos of different organizations or movements such as Doordarshan, or the prevention of AIDS logo (shown below). Learners would then be asked to think why they said Doordarshan or AIDS and not a red-ribbon or circle? The responses of learners may indicate their previous repeated exposure to the shape, alphabet, colours etc. arranged in a particular manner, as the reason for such a response. The teacher can steer the discussion towards the concept of perceptual set and build on how cultural background affects the process of assigning meaning to different symbols.

Synthesis: The discussion should enable learners to understand that the perceiver's knowledge and expectations also influence the process of perception. Sometimes perceptual set acts as a hindrance too, because we are unable to see other uses of the same object.

ACTIVITY 12: PERCEPTION OF SPACE, DEPTH AND DISTANCE

Route: The teacher will display printouts of different paintings or can project them in the class, or can even take learners to the art room to show various forms of artwork. The teacher will ask learners to find out the different strategies to paint a dimensional perspective.

The teacher would then compile and categorise the responses of the learners, for example, relative size, leading line, and angles.

Similarly, the artist may have used overlapping objects, linear perspective, aerial perspective, effect of light and shade, relative height and texture gradient, to create various effects.

Synthesis: The cues used by the artist in paintings with a two-dimensional space, are called monocular cues. As the name suggests, there is no difference in the perception with one eye, or both eyes. These cues enable the artist to create varied effects on the canvas.

Alternatively

Route: The teacher can invite the art teacher to talk about various strategies they use while painting. If possible, she can demonstrate some of the tricks that they use to create perception of depth and distance. The session is followed by a detailed discussion between the psychology teacher and the art teacher. All the monocular cues such as relative size, overlapping objects, linear perspective, aerial perspective, effect of light and shade, relative height, and texture gradient would be part of the discussion.

Synthesis: The cues used by the artist in paintings, which is a two dimensional space, are called monocular cues. As the name suggests, they are perceived with one eye only. These cues enable the artist to create varied effects on the canvas.

ACTIVITY 13: ILLUSIONS

Route: The teacher can share various pictures (given below) to show different kinds of illusions and have a discussion around them. The teacher can also show a video demonstrating the various illusions.

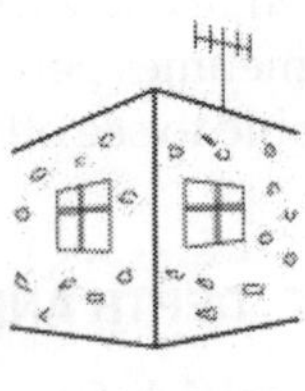

In the first drawing the learners have to guess which wall has greater height. The second picture shows that the road is converging. Even though we know that it is not possible, yet most of us experience this. Learners have to develop various illusory devices to be displayed, in the annual fair or in the psychology club.

Synthesis: Illusion is a misperception resulting from misinterpretation of information received by our sensory organs. Some illusions are commonly experienced. There are scientific explanations for every illusion.

Recent Trends

Visual Perception: The study of perception became an important area of research for neuroscientists and researchers who are working on disabilities along with psychologists. Among several works published during the 1970s and 80s, a book by David Marr (1982), a neuroscientist, titled 'Vision: A Computational Investigation into the Human Representation and Processing of Visual Information' became a landmark. He discussed both mental processes and mental representations in his book. He also elaborated about how raw sensory data goes through several layers of representation before it reaches a three dimensional representation of the world outside as subjective experience of our perception. He also discussed the role of various computational processes to reach a particular level of representation. Marr's work continues to hold sway in the recent developments in perception.

The work of Kubovy (1994) on grouping by proximity in dot lattices draws from Marr's computational framework. The dot lattice or the dot pattern was, for the first time, used by Gestalt psychologists to demonstrate grouping by proximity. The study of periodic dot patterns has advanced manifold now. Bravais (1949) had demonstrated five types of periodic dot patterns consisting of oblique, rectangular, centred rectangular, square and hexagonal. Gestalt psychologists had studied grouping by proximity in rectangle and square patterns. Kobovy (1994) took the work of Bravais (1949) further and divided the centred rectangular lattice into two parts; centred rectangular and rhombic. He also introduced the concept of degree of instability of lattices and demonstrated how to order lattices from least stable to most stable.

David Marr (1982) had put forth another important question about how the visual system integrates several sources of information in order to achieve object perception. The retinal image is continuously changing every fraction of a second and the viewer makes saccadic eye movements to bring new information in high-resolution central vision. A saccade is a quick movement of both eyes in same direction in between two fixations. There are several studies to understand how the visual information is integrated across saccades.

Inter Sensory Integration: Our brain receives information from all sensory organs. The key to effective perception is the integration of all this information. When we are talking to someone, we see the talking person and not the voice and face separately. Researchers see this ability to see the world in a multimodal, integrated fashion, in an evolutionary perspective because such integration reduces the processing time. But the question that surrounded the researchers was that when does this ability develop? Do infants have this ability at birth? One explanation that Piaget (1971) offered was that each system develops independently and when it reaches a certain level of competence, the integration of separate sources takes place. Later studies present quite a different picture. The work of J. Gibson (1969), Werner (1973), Bower (1974), Thelen and Smith (1994) indicates that senses are integrated right from birth. The present studies in perception draw from E. Gibson's (1982, 1984) general theory of perceptual development. His theory is an extension of the work of J.J. Gibson (1969) who postulated a relationship of mutuality in the child and the structure. An infant is an active seeker of perceptual structure and the structure actively influences the way the infants see it.

Recent consensual data indicates that inter-sensory perceptual abilities are present from a very early stage in human development. However, the next question is: what are the underlying processes that make multi-modal integration possible? David Lewkowicz (2000), in his paper attempts to explain these processes. He states that that responsiveness to four inter sensory temporal relations forms the basis of inter sensory integration. These relations are temporal synchrony, duration, temporal rate and rhythm. Their development proceeds in a sequential and hierarchical manner. Of these, inter sensory synchrony is the most fundamental basis for development of integration of intersensory temporal relations. That is why inter sensory synchrony is the most researched area among researchers working on inter sensory perception in infants. Findings indicate that infants are responsive to inter sensory temporal synchrony. The development of the remaining more complex processes, takes place in a sequential and hierarchical manner.

Web-links and Readings

Bach, M. (n.d.). *Optical Illusions & Visual Phenomena: 123 of them.* Retrieved February 4, 2016, from Optical Illusions & Visual Phenomena: http://www.michaelbach.de/ot/

Bravais, A. (1949). *On the Systems formed by points regularly distributed on a plane or in space* (A. L. Shaler, Trans.). Crystallographic Society of America. (Original work published 1850)

Bower, T. G. R. (1974). *Development in Infancy*. San Francisco: Freeman.

d'Ydewalle, G. (1997). Visual Perception at the Edge of the Century. In R. Fuller, P. N. Walsh, & P. Mc Ginley (Eds.), *A Century of Psychology Progress, Paradigms and Prospects for the new Millennium*. London: Routledge.

Gibson, E. J. (1969). *Principles of Perceptual Learning and Development*. New York: Appleton.

Gibson, E. J. (1982). The concept of affordances in development: the renascence of functionalism. In W. A. Collins (Ed.), *The Concept of Development: The Minnesota Symposia on Child Psychology* (pp. 55-81). Hillsdale, N.J.: Lawrence Erlbaum.

Gibson, E. J. (1984). Perceptual development from the ecological approach. In M. E. Lamb, A. L. Brown, & B. Rogoff (Eds.), *Advances in Developmental Psychology* (pp. 243-286). Hillsdale, N.J.: Lawrence Erlbaum Associates.

Gibson, J. J. (1966). *The Senses Considered as Perceptual Systems*. Boston: Houghton-Mifflin.

Gibson, J. J. (1979). *An Ecological Approach to Perception*. Boston: Houghton Mifflin.

Henriques, G. (2013, May 01). *Perception and Perceptual Illusions*. Retrieved March 10, 2016, from Psychology Today: https://www.psychology today.com/blog/theory-knowledge/201305/perception-and-perceptual-illusions.

Kubovy, M. (1994). The perceptual organisation of dot lattices. *Psychonomic Bulletin & Review*, 1(2), 182-190, Springer.

Lewkowicz, D. (2000). The development of intersensory temporal perception: An epigenetic systems view. *Psychological Bulletin*. 126(2), 281-308.

Marr, D. (1982). *Vision: A Computational Investigation into the Human Representation and Processing of Visual Information*. San Fransisco, CA: Henry Holt & Company.

MashupZone. (2014, August 12). *Cool Optical Illusions Compilation 2014 [NEW]*. Retrieved March 10, 2016, from YouTube: https://www.youtube.com/watch?v=hrhGTR54E5k.

Miller, G. A. (1956). The magical number seven, plus or minus two: Some limits on our capacity for processing information. *Psychological Review*. 63(2): 81–97. doi:10.1037/h0043158.

Rookes, P., & Willson, J. (2000). *Perception: Theory, Development and Organisation*. London: Routledge.

Thelen, E., & Smith, L. B. (1994). *A dynamic systems approach to the development of cognition and action*. Cambridge, MA: MIT Press.

Werner, H. (1973). *Comparative psychology of mental development*. New York: International Universities Press.

Human Memory*

Introduction

Human memory is a fascinating area of study. Several movies and television shows have used the various possibilities and limits of human memory as the primary theme, around which the story is built. Yet there are many questions related to human memory that continue to engage researchers, like, can eye witness testimony be trusted? Can the capacity to remember information be enhanced? Is it possible that human memory is influenced by suggestion? Do we remember exactly what we have experienced or do we remember something altogether different? Finding answers to these questions can be both exciting and intimidating. Exciting, because they open up new vistas of how we can enhance and work better in our day to day life; and intimidating, because they point out that many times, we falter in recollecting our experiences.

In this Unit, learners need to get acquainted with the different models that explain how human memory functions. They will read about the working of the memory systems, which include the sensory memory, short term memory, and long term memory. They will also be enabled to connect the models of memory with their experiences. For instance, if they are asked to think about how they ensure that whatever they have read will be retained for a longer time, most of them will be able to describe some strategies. This Unit gives ample opportunity for relating learners' experiences with the subject matter. Another useful approach to teaching this unit can be through classroom experiments. The teacher can repeat some classic experiments and promote learner participation in both, designing material for these experiments and conducting them.

---

* Vishakha Kumar

ACTIVITY 1: NATURE OF MEMORY

Route: The teacher can show a small movie or a documentary clip for about ten minutes to the class. If the classroom does not have a projector, the teacher can take a collage with a number of images and some newspaper headlines. Before showing the movie or collage the teacher can give instructions that the learners must view the movie or observe the collage carefully, as they will be asked to describe all that they have seen. The responses of learners about what they saw will help the teacher to initiate discussion on the nature of memory. The discussion can start from reflecting upon the following questions:

1. Why did you remember only a few things?
2. Why did these things catch your attention?
3. Why didn't you recall everything that you had noticed?

What is likely to emerge though this activity is that encoded information that caught their attention, or which they deliberately paid attention to was what learners had processed and stored. When the teacher asks them to recall the information, they are able to retrieve it. However, if the teacher shows them the collage or clip again, they are likely to be able to recollect much more information, which they may have inadvertently skipped or had failed to store appropriately.

Synthesis: Memory is generally conceptualised as a process that consists of three sub- processes namely, encoding, storage, and retrieval. All the three processes are closely inter-related. The first of these processes is encoding. Here the information received for the first time is registered. This process is akin to perception. The second stage is storage, where the information encoded is saved for later usage. Finally, the third process is retrieval, in which the encoded and stored information is recalled at a time when it is required.

This activity can also be used to discuss short term memory.

ACTIVITY 2: LONG TERM MEMORY

Route: In this activity, the intent is to demonstrate the role of long-term memory. So, the teacher can ask the learners some questions related to the concepts that they learnt in class 6-8, or about landmarks in their personal lives, or about specific things that they had learnt at school or at home. The learners will be asked to answer questions, as exemplified below, or perform some activities, as described below:

1. Where were you born?
2. What is the difference between a compound and a mixture?
3. What are latitudes?
4. What is the capital of Punjab?
5. Name any three Mughal emperors.
6. Recall any happy moment from your life.
7. Learners will be provided with a square piece of paper and would be asked to make something out of it. (origami)
8. Demonstrate any 5 exercises they have learnt in school.

The teacher will then discuss their responses and categorize them as 'semantic' or 'procedural'. The teacher can then draw upon this categorisation to explain the concept and types of LTM.

Synthesis: The information that passes through the short term memory enters the long term memory where it is permanently stored. Long term memory consists of declarative and procedural memory.

ACTIVITY 3: MAINTENANCE REHEARSAL AND ELABORATIVE REHEARSAL

Route: The teacher can divide the class into two groups. The first group will be given a list of words to remember. The second group will first be given a passage to read and then given the same list to remember. Both the groups would then be asked to recall the words. The teacher will note the number of words that each group could recall.

Control: Both groups should be given equal time to learn the list

Group I: The following list can be given to this group for 2 minutes to read and remember. Then the teacher would close the list and ask the learners to write the words that they remember.

1. Summer
2. Ocean
3. Parasailing
4. Exhilarated
5. Cauldron

6. Drummer
7. Skydiving
8. Vacation
9. Humdrum
10. Occasionally
11. Percussion
12. Current
13. Contribute
14. Zorbing
15. Quaint

Group II: This group would be given a passage to read. After 2 minutes they will be given the same list of words, as given to Group1, to remember.

> *This summer, after several failed attempts, I finally planned a vacation to Andaman and Nicobar Islands. The ocean was deep blue and I desperately wanted to go for parasailing. There were other sports as well, like skydiving and zorbing, but I always had a penchant for parasailing. The experience was exhilarating and I wish I could do it again and again. I felt like a free bird and wanted to fly high. We were staying in a resort close to the ocean and they played live music in the resort. I particularly developed a liking for drum. The percussion of drum seemed to have a magical effect on me. No matter what I was thinking or doing I would just sit and listen to the drummer play till it was late in the evening. As I was sitting and listening to the drum, my thoughts drifted to my life back in Delhi. Occasionally, I had thought of leaving the humdrum of the city life and settling in a quaint place, but the cauldron of life pulled me back. But now sitting here I was happy and satisfied with life. I could inhale the clean air and feel the freshness around me. My state of mind was peaceful and calm. I was now ready to go back to work and contribute in some meaningful way. But, before leaving, I made a promise to myself that in every six months I will gift myself a vacation, away from the city life.*

(Kumar, 2015)

Both the groups would then be asked to recall words they had learnt. Each person should be asked to write down the words he/ she can recall. The teacher will then collect the list of words from each person and collate the results.

	Number of Words Recalled by Different Learners	Average
Group 1	5,6,7....	
Group 2	7,8,9....	

After discussing the data, learners will then be asked to share their experiences on the following:

1. Which words did you remember more easily? *(During the discussion the teacher can gauge if learners thought that they remembered those words with which they were familiar, or there was primacy, recency effect, etc.)*
2. What process did you use to memorise the list? (Learners may say that they used images or made a story)
3. Which group recalled more words? Why?

Synthesis: The teacher can initiate a discussion on the implicit processes that we follow to remember information. For instance, if one looks at the list above, it has words that can be linked to images and can be also memorised in the form of a story. The teacher can also discuss the difference in the performance between the two groups. It is usually seen that the second group remembers more words. The reason for it is that words become more meaningful and contextual in a passage and thus can be learnt and remembered better. The first group gets only a discrete recall list. So in the first group, what the learners do is merely maintenance rehearsal whereas in the second group, they engage in elaborative rehearsal. The learners can then be made to reflect on the memory processes they use at present and how memory can actually be enhanced using elaborative rehearsal.

ACTIVITY 4: MEMORY SYSTEM

Route

Step 1: The teacher should put together, ten to fifteen objects in a box. Some of the objects can be familiar, others unfamiliar. Some examples of objects that can be used are DVDs, postcards, pictures of some sportspersons who are not very popular, paintings, books, small art work, stationery, etc. The teacher can also use some words from some other language such as French or German in place of objects. He/she can show each object for 5 seconds and after showing all the objects, ask learners to recall and describe all the objects that were presented. The following questions may be asked to know how much information the learners are actually able to recall. The important point of emphasis is that it may be difficult to remember all features of the objects that are presented because the duration of viewing is limited to a few seconds and sensory memory lasts only for a few seconds. Some questions that may be asked are along the following pattern.

1. What all did I present in front of you now?
2. What was the colour of the pencil that I had shown you or what was the colour of the shirt that the actor was wearing?

Step 2: The teacher can show the same objects again and this time ask the learners to pay attention to the information. They will be asked to recall it. When the teacher asks the learners to remember the information, learners are more alert to receiving information.

Step 3: The teacher can again show the same or different objects. Each time he/she shows an object, he/she narrates a story around that object. For example, after showing a postcard of Kerala, he/she can tell them that this is a postcard showing Munnar, a hill station in Kerala. This place is famous for spices like cardamom, cinnamon as well as jasmine. There are also tea plantations in this region. Likewise, after showing the DVD of the film, 'Dead Poets Society', the teacher can tell them that this film is about a teacher and how he wants to change the conservative and rigid system of the school. The teacher can also elaborate on why the film was named 'Dead Poets Society'. Basically, each object should be pegged with some elaboration and story. Then teacher can then ask learners to recall the names of the objects and even write a story, using all the information that she had presented to them.

Synthesis: The teacher can discuss how the information moves from sensory memory to short term memory and finally reaches the long term memory. In this activity both elaborative and maintenance rehearsal are used. The teacher can discuss the entire memory system while discussing the learners' responses at each step.

ACTIVITY 5: MEMORY AS A RECONSTRUCTIVE PROCESS

Route: The teacher can give any one of the tasks, mentioned below, to make learners reflect on how our memory is constantly undergoing changes.

Task 1: The teacher can ask the learners to write down three important events of their lives that they remember vividly. They can then cross check the facts that they have written with their friends, parents, or anyone else who was present there. They should try to identify the inconsistencies that they find between their own response and what was told to them by the person whom they consulted. They should be asked to reflect on why there could be a difference in the two versions.

Task 2: The teacher can ask learners to remember an instance from their life when they fought with someone in their class. They may be asked to write about it. What they write can be compared.

Task 3: The teacher can prepare two learners to enact something in front of the class. The rest of the class should not know about it and the enactment must appear spontaneous. The act can show that two very good friends get into an argument that turns sour. The teacher may then enter the classroom and try to sort out the fight. Both learners can put forth their arguments. The remaining class would then be asked to write an exact account of what happened in the class.

Task 4: The teacher can ask learners to write the story of a film that they viewed about five years back. She/he can ask them to write a vivid description that can include costumes and locations too. They can cross check the facts with each other or with the film.

Task 5: Narrating a story: The teacher can narrate the following story to the class and ask a few questions. The purpose of asking questions is to make learners think of those details which were not present in the story.

> *Surya, a teenager, lived in a coastal town. He stayed aloof most of the time and had few friends. The only time he ventured outside his classroom, was to play football and occasionally table tennis. While preparing for his exams he realised that he was in need of some guidance, so he called up a classmate for notes. His classmate refused to give him the notes. Next day Surya got confused in the exam and messed up his paper. However, he somehow finished it and rushed to the ground. That evening he played with the ball till sunset and then walked back to his house.*

On his way back he saw his classmate lying on the road. He had met with an accident and was bleeding profusely. Surya looked around and saw a number of people at the place of accident. Surya walked away from the spot towards his home.

(Kumar, 2015)

The teacher should ask a few questions which make leaners think about some details which were not there in the story. They can be as follows:

1. Why do you think Surya stayed aloof most of the time?
2. Why did his classmate refuse to give him notes?
3. Why did Surya decide to stay late in the school?
4. Do you think Surya deliberately did not want to help his classmate?

The purpose of these questions is only to make learners fill details without being aware that they were not part of the original story. Most learners will add or modify the story when they are asked to narrate it. If there is a time interval of one or two days between when they first read it and now, when they were being asked to recall it, the chances of modification are much higher. The teacher can then discuss how memory is reconstructed.

Alternative Story

Shanta practiced magic tricks on the bank of a river. Once a month she would conduct a show for children in her village. She travelled to distant villages to display her art. One day after she returned from her day's work she saw a haggard person at her entrance. She wondered what brought the person to her door steps. The person showed her a black box that had few sticks inside it. Shanta looked inside the box carefully and the sticks turned into gold leaves. Before Shanta could believe her eyes the person vanished into thin air. That night she could not sleep properly. When she woke up she had a severe headache. After sometime she vomited blood and in the evening she collapsed on the ground. When she regained consciousness, she found herself surrounded by other villagers who were staring at her. One of them asked her who she was and how she had entered the village.

(Kumar, 2015)

Some questions to be posed to learners:

1. What would Shanta have thought when she saw the haggard person at her entrance?

2. Do you think the box was responsible for Shanta's subsequent illness?
3. Do you find the villagers' question, peculiar? Why?
4. What could be the probable reasons for Shanta's illness?

(While narrating the story the teacher must be careful about his/her tone. He/she should try not to add intonations and expressions while narrating the story. After the narration is completed, the learners must be asked to read something from their textbook for 10-15 minutes. A day or two later, the teacher should ask learners to reproduce the story of Shanta, that she had narrated to them).

Synthesis: The purpose of this set of tasks, was to make learners reflect on how memory changes over a period of time. The first three tasks would require the person to check the details they have written with someone else. Task 4 is an adaptation of the original task used by Bartlett. The nature of questions raised and the discussion that follows, can be used to explain what happens in reconstructing memory. The teacher can also discuss the notion of false memory. The questions asked after the story presentation, for example, may create memories of events that may not be part of the story.

ACTIVITY 6: ICONIC AND ECHOIC MEMORY

Route: The teacher can show an image to the learners for about 20 seconds and ask them to focus on some aspect of the picture. For example, she/he can ask learners to identify a mango tree in the image or a house. The learners could then be asked to draw it. Following this, the teacher can ask learners to reflect on the process they used, in drawing the image.

Similarly, to illustrate and explain echoic memory, the teacher can play a song in the class for one minute and then ask learners to sing it. He/she can then steer the discussion towards how learners are able to remember the music, even after the song has been muted or paused.

Synthesis: Sensory memory lasts for a very short while, but it has a large capacity. It registers information from all sense organs with great accuracy. We tend to experience after images for few seconds after the visual field is stimulated and sound reverberations, after we hear a sound track. This is because of the sensory memory. Iconic and Echoic memory are kinds of sensory memory. There are more such memories corresponding to the various senses, for example, if a learner presses a coin on the forehead of another student for about 20 seconds, then even after removing the coin, the second learner may feel it to be there on his/ her forehead.

ACTIVITY 7: CHUNKING

The teacher can play the game of Chinese Whisper in the class. Starting from one end he/she can whisper any one sentence to one of the learners and ask him/ her to share it with the next student and so on. The sentences could be as follows:

1. Siya stepped out of the physics classroom to work in the lab and by mistake smashed her head against the glass pane that was placed as a divider between physics and chemistry lab.
2. Ronjoy was aghast when he discovered a grisly black creature on the top drawer of his rack; he screamed and ran towards the door to call for help.
3. Dr. Geeta teaches perception using projectors and film snippets in her psychology classes.

The teacher may also ask the learners to repeat the sentence immediately after she finishes reading it. Most of the learners may not remember the complete sentence till they break it in smaller parts. The sentence can be divided in three or four chunks to memorise. Learners may also be asked to reflect upon their way of memorising the sentence. They may also be asked to reflect on the difficulties that they face in remembering different sentences.

Synthesis: Chunking is one of the processes by which the capacity of short term memory can be enhanced. Researchers have found that short term memory can hold five to nine objects, at a time (7±2). If a large pool of information is divided into smaller chunks, then each chunk can be treated as a unit. This process enhances the ability to retain more information.

ACTIVITY 8: TYPES OF LONG TERM MEMORY

Route

Step 1: Learners can be asked to make a detailed list of their everyday activities staring from the time they wake up; until the time they sleep. They must include activities they do in school and after school. Then the teacher can discuss the concept of procedural, declarative memory, episodic and semantic memory.

Step 2: Learners will be asked to indicate the kind of memory that they think is involved in the following actions:

- Brushing teeth
- Dressing up
- Having breakfast
- Catching the bus
- Driving a motorcycle/ walking
- School assembly
- Climbing stairs
- Studying different subjects
- Having conversation with friends
- Preparing for debate
- Playing football
- Dance rehearsals
- Witnessing a fight on the street and reporting it to parents
- Playing badminton with friends with friends
- Having conversation with parents

Synthesis: Memory functions pertaining to names, facts, dates are part of declarative memory. Procedural memories are related to procedures that a person follows to accomplish some tasks. Things like using hands to express yourself while talking, shaking your leg while studying, using hand while singing, etc can be procedural. Many a times the person may not be aware of these and may not explain these behaviours.

Tulving (1972), a psychologist gave another classification in which declarative memory can be episodic and semantic. Episodic memory consists of biographical details of a person's life. Semantic memory on the other hand consists of ideas, rules, and concepts.

ACTIVITY 9: CONCEPT

Route: Learners will be asked to draw whatever comes to their mind, or describe in 30-40 words, the ideas that come to them, when the following words are read out.

(Any 4 words can be chosen to either draw an image, or write a description)

- School
- Book
- Trust
- Bird
- Jealousy
- Compassion

Drawing from the work of each learner, after consulting them, the teachers can analyse some of the images to indicate the concept/ideas, conveyed through them. For example a learner may draw a red brick building of a school with a playground, learners dressed in uniform studying in a classroom or a teacher dressed in formal attire. For concrete objects, learners may choose to draw an image and for abstract terms, they may write a description.

Synthesis: The teacher can then indicate that each of the features in these images forms a part of the framework that represents our knowledge about that word. This framework is called schema. The dual coding hypothesis by Paivio (1983) states that concrete nouns and concrete information are encoded and stored in the form of images, while information related to abstract ideas assume verbal and descriptive code.

ACTIVITY 10: THE HIERARCHICAL NETWORK MODEL

Route

Step 1: The learners will be given a list of words to classify. They would have to first identify a broad category and find a classification system which can subsume all the concepts that are given for classification. Then, they would have to categorise and sub categorise the list items. A format for classification has been pictorially presented below:

Broad Category			
Category 1		Category 2	
Sub category a	Sub category b	Sub category a	Sub category b
Further categories, if needed			

Examples

Classify the following:

1. Sparrow, eagle, lion, hyena, whale, star fish, dinosaur, salmon, snake, ostrich, deer, pomfret, tuna, wild boar, peacock, orangutan

Animal		
Birds	Reptiles	Mammals

2. Socks, nurse, kettle, hair band, lying, groundnuts, jogging, bitter gourd, pen-drive, Pomeranian, ironing, deep sea diving, lavender, homemaker, chocolate, parrot, fennel seeds, salmon, cry, pomegranate, aeroplane, scratch, chef

Probable Classification:

VERB	NOUN		
	Animate	Inanimate	
		Edible	Inedible

The classification may be more difficult if the categories are not conventional. In such examples, learners would have to think critically to place each concept under some category. They may come up with more innovative categories. This will be a deliberate process that will help them understand the Hierarchical Network Model. The teacher should encourage learners to find their own classification categories, since the ones given above are only suggestive.

Step 2: The teacher can ask the learners to describe the procedure or steps they followed for making this classification.

Synthesis: The teacher can then discuss Allan Collins and Rose Quillian's classification system. The learner in all probability will try to find common features among each of the words given. The category on top will subsume the category below it. And automatically, the lower category will be understood as having all the qualities of the category mentioned above. This model suggests that knowledge is arranged in a hierarchical manner. Nodes are the central elements of this network, wherein, the connection between nodes represents the point of relationship.

Recent Trends

The Role of Metacognition: Metacognition is people's awareness of their own cognition and how their cognition works (Meichenbaum, 1985). It refers to knowledge about knowing and learning. This can be used to monitor and regulate several cognitive processes such as problem solving, decision making, comprehension etc. (Woolfolk, 2016). People differ in their metacognitive skills and these differences manifest in their ability to learn new tasks. Metacognitions can be divided into three types of knowledge: one is the explicit knowledge which is also called as declarative knowledge, the second is the implicit knowledge also termed as procedural knowledge and the third is conditional. Explicit metacognitive knowledge includes such information about tasks, strategies and people that we use in our everyday life. It is basically knowledge about characteristics of our own learning. One simple instance can be of the fallibility of our own memory. Children as young as six years old, accept that they can forget information. However, a five-year-old may be unable to appreciate that some information that is learnt, can also be forgotten. With age, children begin to understand their memory capabilities better and are able to estimate the time and effort they require to master a task. Similarly, as one gets older we are able to draw better strategies and minimise hindrances.

Implicit knowledge about our cognition comes much earlier in comparison to explicit knowledge. There are evidences to show that even toddlers can monitor their use of language and correct their mistakes in pronunciation and grammar. This shows that even young children experience a feeling of knowing that helps them anticipate, how well they will remember later. It is also found that the ability to monitor one's own comprehension distinguishes a good reader from a poor one.

There are three skills which facilitate regulation of thinking and learning. They are planning, monitoring and evaluating. In the planning stage, one decides such things as the time to be allotted, how much time has to be allocated to it and resources to be used. Monitoring is an on-going process where we ask ourselves whether the plan is going in the right direction or not. Finally, evaluation entails making judgements about the outcomes.

Self-regulation: Self-regulation is defined as a process that is used to activate and sustain thoughts, behaviour and emotions in order to reach our goals. The basic objective of self-regulation is to enable learners to become independent and develop the ability to direct their learning. It is closely related to a person's ability to actively participate in his/her learning in terms of metacognition and motivation (Zimmerman, 1989). Self-regulation comprises of three phases: preparation or forethought phase, implementation or the performance phase and reflection phase. The first phase includes setting of goals and analysis of the task at hand. At this stage, a person's beliefs about his/her ability to accomplish the goals also becomes pertinent. Then at the implementation stage, a person lays down strategies to achieve the goal. The person must have self-observation and self-control to work towards the goal. Self-control is based on use of appropriate strategies to achieve the goal. Self-observation is based on monitoring the activity and the effects of learning. A person has to focus his/her attention on the goal and continuously monitor his/her actions, too. Finally, after the performance stage, a person has to look back and evaluate his/her performance. The last phase influences the first one and in this sense, self-regulation is a cyclical process and not linear one (Woolfolk, 2016). Researches have indicated that writing involves the use of self-regulation and meta-cognition because this is one activity that learners have to do, all alone. They have to plan, implement and monitor what they are writing continuously.

Web-links and Readings

Cera, R., Mancini, M., & Antonietti, A. (2013). Relationship between Metacognition, Self-efficacy and Self-regulation in Learning. *ECPS Journal,* 115-141. Vol. 7.

Graf, P. & Ohta, N. (2002). *Lifespan Development of Human Memory.* Cambridge: MIT Press. Retrieved from https://books.google.com/books?id= dUFtZfeDgEgC&pgis=1

Kraft Classroom. (2013). Learn How Human Memory Works. Retrieved February 3, 2016, from https://www.youtube.com/watch?v=VISKge TTWKA

Kumar, V. (2015). *Reflections*. New Delhi: Unpublished.

Meichenbaum, D., Burland, S., Gruson, L., & Cameron, R. (1985). Metacognitive assessment. *The growth of reflection in children*, 3-30.

Paivio, A. (1983). The empirical case for dual coding theory. In Yuille, J. C. (ed.) *Imagery, Memory and Cognition: Essays in Honor of Allan Paivio*, pp. 307–332, Hillsdale: Lawrence Erlbaum Associates, Inc.

Tulving, E. (1972). Episodic and Semantic Memory. *Organisation of Memory, 381*(4).

Woolfolk, A. (2016). *Educational Psychology*. Boston: MA: Allyn and Bacon.

Thinking*

Introduction

In its developmental years, pursuing the quest to be a science, Psychology defined mental processes like perception, learning, and human memory in ways that made them amenable to experimentation and testing. Thinking is one such mental process, allied to the development of Experimental Psychology and Cognitive Psychology. Teaching learners about thinking can be very challenging, because of the enormity of research that has gone into the area and the continuous fresh insights and theories that keep on emerging. At the same time, it can be very exciting, because of its familiarity and closeness to learners' everyday lived experiences. Through the pedagogic stance that a teacher adopts, he/she can demystify the content related to thinking and cognition. He/she can in addition, facilitate the development of meta-cognitive awareness and self-regulation among the learners.

To transact this unit more meaningfully, the teacher can use puzzles, construction and visualization games, case vignettes for analysis, news clips and research cuttings for discussion, and topics for debates. These will help to concretise understanding, raise unanswered questions and transact the course through experiential learning. Peer learning and sharing can be encouraged. Learners' cognitive abilities like reflection, reasoning, judgement and debating, must also find space in classroom tasks, so that they are able to build some understanding about how these processes relate to thinking. Teachers can also use classroom, school, and community related issues and concerns as problems to be solved and ask learners to search for some creative solutions. This will help to build basic understanding about problem solving and

---

* Vishakha Kumar and Rashmi Malhotra

creative thinking. A number of activities suggested in this unit are open to adaptation. The teacher is free to change them as per need.

As part of this unit, learners must be familiarised with the theory of mind and social cognition. It would be interesting to reflect on how human beings have an intuitive ability to make judgements about what others are thinking and attribute intentions to them. There is a lot of research that is trying to study the belief system and its influence on decision making of different cultural groups. The teacher can ask learners to do their own small study to find out the latest developments in this domain.

ACTIVITY 1: DEFINITION OF THINKING

Route: A collage, or a painting should be displayed in the class for learners to observe. Following this, learners should be encouraged to describe whatever comes to their mind as they view it. To do this, they are given the option of either verbally sharing their ideas, or writing them in their notebooks and subsequently sharing them.

Synthesis: The teacher can draw learners' attention to the processes of observation, reflection and writing in which they were involved. He/she can then move on to explaining how cognitive processes like describing, explaining, and analysing all fall under the larger umbrella of 'thinking'. Learners must then be encouraged to discuss their understanding of terms like thinking, images and concepts, which the unit deals with and try to define them on their own. Subsequently they should compare their own definitions, with the ones given in the book and analyse the commonalities and differences. This will help them to deconstruct the notion of thinking. They will also begin to understand that thinking is an integral part of their everyday world and basic to all human beings.

ACTIVITY 2: DEFINITION OF THINKING

Route: Some scenarios depicting different situations that require learners to use their thinking skills are shared with them. The idea is that each scenario would require them to analyse, reflect and make decisions in order to solve a problem.

Scenario 1: You have fifteen minutes left to complete your exam paper. There are two questions remaining, of which, one is a four marker, the answer of which you know really well and the other is an eight marker for which you might have to think hard before writing. You have to make a decision about which one should you attempt first?

Probable responses that learners may come up with include:

- I would weigh the time left and the time I may take to finish a four marker question.
- It would depend on how confident am I about the eight marker question.
- I can finish the four marker question and then focus on the eight marker one.
- I would write the main points in both questions, distributing the time.

Scenario 2: You have lost your diary and you are desperately trying to find it. What would you do?

Probable responses:

- Think of places in my home where I keep my things.
- Ask friends and family to help.
- Announce it on Facebook or send a message to close friends.

Scenario 3: You have the option of choosing any four items from among a paper, water, sand, gum, water-colours, thread, dry colours, colour pens, different coloured cloth swatches, coloured threads and a needle, to create your own product. Reflect on the various ways in which the items selected by you, will be used to make the product. Describe the process involved.

Scenario 1 relates primarily to problem solving, scenario 2 requires the use of imagery, and scenario 3 involves creative thinking. After learners have engaged in all the three processes, the teacher can pose the following questions:

- How did they arrive at their answers in the different scenarios?
- Can they identify the common processes involved in all these scenarios?

After they arrive at the understanding that all these scenarios involved 'thinking', then the teacher would ask them to think of characteristics of thinking and a tentative definition of thinking. The teacher can try to scaffold them to arrive at the following points:

- Thinking involves manipulation and analysis of information that one receives from the environment.
- It goes beyond what one receives as input from the environment.

- It is a mental process involving manipulation and analysis of the information.
- The sub-processes involved in thinking include reasoning, creative thinking, problem solving, judging, decision making, imagining and abstraction.
- Mental imagery is part of thinking such as the image of one's diary, image of the prospective product that one wishes to create from existing objects, etc.

Synthesis: Learners can then analyse and discuss about 'thinking' by referring to any book on Basic Psychology.

ACTIVITY 3: BUILDING BLOCKS OF THOUGHT

Route: Learners are directed to write and/ or draw anything that comes to their mind, when they hear the word 'India'. They have five minutes to complete the task. Using their responses, the teacher explains how the various ideas and symbols come together as building blocks of thinking to construct understanding about anything.

Synthesis: Thinking emerges from the knowledge that one has, which can be stored as images, words, and/or concepts. These constitute the building blocks of thinking.

ACTIVITY 4: UNDERSTANDING CONCEPTS

Route: A handout carrying a list of situations is prepared and distributed in the class. Learners are asked to reflect upon the probable answers to them. There are no right or wrong answers. Each response will relate to some concept that they know. The teacher's focus should be on the process of selection of information and inferences drawn by the learners and not on the correct answer.

Situation 1: While walking on a street you see a hoarding stating the following:

There is something super exciting coming up for teenagers and young adults in the coming week. There will be opportunities for learning as well as having fun. For further details:

Contact Ms. Amrita Sehgal at 9811456780

What all can you infer from the hoarding? Why did you draw these inferences?

(Probable responses: Some weekend dance classes, theatre classes, music competition, book fair etc.)

Situation 2: You go to the latest gadget shop. You see a sleek gadget that has a rectangular shape. It has a small screen and is black in colour. It has some digits printed on it with some symbols. What would be your guess about the nature of the gadget?

(Probable answers: iPod, small audio recorder, mp3 player, music shuffler, pen drive, mobile phone etc.)

Situation 3: You visit your local grocery shop. You find a boy arranging things outside the counter. There is no one at the shop. Who do you think the boy is?

(Probable answers: owner of the shop, assistant in the shop, person who comes to clean the shop, etc.)

Situation 4: You are walking down the road and you come across a woman dressed in a saree wearing a white coat. You start thinking about who she might be. Who do you think she is?

(Probable answers: doctor, nurse, chemist, etc.)

Situation 5: Your teacher informs you that she will take you to a place where you will get to know more about outer space, spaceships and earth. What do you think the place will be?

(Probable answers: planetarium, museum, movie hall, library, etc.)

Synthesis: The learners are asked to give probable answers and justify them. Even if the answers are far-fetched, the teacher must allow them to think freely. Every response could highlight a concept that the learners hold. The teacher will conclude by making a chart of the characteristics and knowledge that combines to form a concept.

ACTIVITY 5: PROBLEM SOLVING

Route: The teacher can engage learners in solving the problems described below for a fixed length of time. After this, he/she can discuss the steps that they went through in solving the problem.

Problem 1: The teacher can take along 4-5 sets of tangrams made of paper to the class. He/she divides the learners into groups of 4-5. They are instructed to make as many shapes as they can in 5 minutes from the tangrams, keep a record of them and share their achievements with the rest of the class.

Problem 2: Rearrange the anagrams to make words

- OONMATIVT
- SEROVIUP
- TCCAAIYP

Problem 3: An eighteen-year-old girl is facing issues in school/ college. She feels that she is not attractive and is overweight. She avoids going to school/college and going out with her peers. She tried hard to lose weight but since she is very fond of eating sweets, she is not very successful. How do you think she can cope with her present life situation?

After discussion on the above three problems the teacher can ask the students to reflect on the process involved in solving these problems. Through discussion the class can arrive at the steps of problem solving

Synthesis: Problem solving is always a goal directed process. The steps of problem solving include:

- Identification of a problem
- Representation of the problem
- Setting sub-goals
- Evaluating the solutions
- Selecting one solution
- Evaluating the outcome
- Rethinking and redefining the problem

ACTIVITY 6: CREATIVE THINKING

Route: The teacher can give a table with list of objects to the learners and ask them to complete it. What the table requires them to think about is the most obvious use of an object. They are also required to think of alternative uses of same objects. They are encouraged to think of as many alternative uses as they can. The list of objects is as follows:

Items	*Conventional Use(s)*	*Alternative Use(s)*
Cup and plate	Drink tea	Planter, pencil holder,
Bicycle	Riding a cycle	Flower pot and decoration item
Shoe box	Keeping shoes	Magazine holder
Dustbin	To throw waste	Foot rest
Ear bud	To clean ear wax	Paint brush
Paper	Writing	Origami, Paper Mache

After the learners have completed the table, the teacher can ask them to reflect on the difficulties that they faced in thinking of the alternative uses of the listed objects. Then they can discuss the hurdles to creative thinking.

Synthesis: Five broad categories of blocks emerge as interfering with the process of creative thinking. These are emotional, motivational, habitual, perceptual and cultural in nature. Learners may be encouraged to identify their own habits and perceptions that interfere with creative thinking.

ACTIVITY 7: CHARACTERISTICS OF CREATIVE THINKING

Route: The teacher can present the following cases to the learners and ask them to discuss who amongst them is a creative person and why?

Case 1: *Shailendra weaves the most beautiful Benaresi fabric. Most weavers in Benares are from traditional families of weavers. While Shailendra is no exception to this tradition, his workmanship is unique. He has gradually moved away from weaving traditional sarees to producing scarves, dupattas, and other dress material. He has also picked up colour schemes from fashion magazines and now weaves designs and colour combinations to match the demands of the fashion markets even outside India.*

Case 2: *Surekha loves to read and write. She started writing short stories and couplets when she was twelve years old. Irrespective of the topic, she can write a couplet on whatever she has read. She also adds humour to her lessons by writing a short commentary on each of them.*

Case 3: *Amit enjoys doodling on whatever he can lay his hands on. From the cover of his books to the walls of his house, everything has an imprint of his handiwork. He draws caricatures of people and things around him and gives it a theme. Although, his parents wonder where he picks up his ideas, they often feel fed up with his habit since there is not a single corner of the house that is without any artwork.*

Case 4: *A person in Rajasthan has invented a fridge that runs without electricity. It is completely an environment friendly fridge.*

Case 5: *Bheem is a farmer in a village. Every alternate year the village suffers from drought and there is crop failure leading to lot of problem. There are times when there is untimely rain. With the assistance of his friends, he started building a water reservoir in his village. He spoke to some experts and located the reservoir in the low lying area of the village. His group made several connecting channels to the reservoir so that the water, instead of flowing away, can flow towards the reservoir. The reservoir was a success and his group subsequently decided to start water harvesting in the region. This benefitted the villagers and solved their problem to some extent.*

The teacher can initiate the discussion on creativity through each of these cases. She can ask her learners to name someone in their class/school whom they find creative and give reasons for naming them. Learners can further be engaged in answering the following questions:

- What is common in all the case studies?
- How do you think they came up with new things?
- Why is everyone not able to come up with new ideas?
- How can we encourage our students to come up with more and more new ideas?

Synthesis: All five people mentioned in the case studies are creative in some way or the other. A creative person is one with divergent thinking, one who can come up with a number of solutions to a problem (fluency), he/she can think of multiple uses of same object (flexibility), is able to think of new ideas that are rare and unusual, and finally is able to work out the details of these ideas. There are certain attitudes, dispositions and skills that can facilitate creative thinking. Thus, creative thinking can be cultivated to some extent by using strategies like brainstorming, building an eye for detail, identifying problems and finding solutions to them, listing the attributes of an object and giving vent to one's imagination.

ACTIVITY 8: LANGUAGE AND THOUGHT

Route: The teacher can divide the class in two groups. The task of the two teams is to debate on the relationship between language and thought. The first group can argue that language comes first and it influences the development of thinking. The second group can argue that thought precedes language development. The teacher should encourage learners to think on their own of various possibilities without looking at any research findings. This is more of a reflective exercise that should make them think about the most fundamental thing that they engage in, in their everyday life. This discussion paves the way for taking up the great debate on the nature of relationship between thought and language. The teacher can raise more questions for discussion, such as:

- Do people throughout the world think in similar way?
- Do people who speak different languages experience the world in a different manner?

Synthesis: The teacher can culminate the discussion by

presenting the three possible relations:

1. *Language shapes thought:* This is the Sapir-Whorf hypothesis (see Hoijer, 1954). According to this hypothesis, language has a profound impact on the way the world around is experienced by the people. Language provides the basis for the interpretation of the world and this leads to variations in the manner in which a particular event tends to be interpreted by different cultures.
2. *Thought shapes Language:* Jean Piaget, laid greater emphasis on the development of representational thought. According to him, representational thought, such as mental imagery, forms the basis of language development. He saw language development as dependent on cognitive development rather than causing it.
3. *Language and thought influence each other:* Lev Vygotsky advocated this position. According to him, thought and language originate independently of each other. They intertwine by the time a child attains two years of age and thereafter start influencing one another. Language becomes a means to express the cognitive understanding. It also starts directing children's thoughts and action. (Seigler, 1991)

The teacher should further discuss the great debate between B.F. Skinner and Chomsky on the mechanism that enables children to acquire language. Skinner argued that children learnt grammar in the same way as they learnt everything else; using reinforcement. They start by imitation of what people around them are saying and parents reinforce the child for statements they feel are correct. According to him, parents shape children's language by constantly correcting them. Noam Chomsky on the other hand said that even a three-year-old could create statements that he has never heard. He suggested that children do not learn specific language, rather they learn grammatical rules. He went further and theorised that people are born with innate knowledge of universal grammar, which is a system of basic properties that are common to all languages in the world.

Recent Trends

Theory of Mind and Intention: The phrase theory of mind refers to the ability to attribute mental states to self and others. In other words, it is used to convey an understanding that other people are people too, with their own minds, thoughts, feelings, beliefs and desires (Flavell, Miller and Miller; 2002). Folk Psychology, Common Sense Psychology and Naïve Psychology focus on this. Some important questions that they focus on are as follows: How do people attain this ability? How do they make judgements about others states when they are not observable? How people self-ascribe mental states? Do they follow the same process as they use for inferring about others or is it a different process?

Studies indicate that by two years of age, most children learn to convey their own intentions such as 'I want to sleep' or 'I want to go out and play'. Slowly, children understand that others also have feelings and experiences that can be different from theirs (Woolfolk, Misra, & Jha 2010). The word theory conveys that mental states are not observable, so they have to be inferred from observable behaviour. Secondly, the inferences help to predict behaviour. For instance, if someone is a bully in school then why he/she is a bully, or if someone is shy and recluse then why is he/she like that?

Folk Psychology: Jerome Bruner in his work 'The Culture of Education' (1996) has dedicated an entire chapter to Folk Psychology. According to him, "our interactions with others are deeply affected by our everyday intuitive theories about how others' minds work". These theories are very rarely discussed explicitly, yet they are present everywhere. These theories reveal the deep-seated cultural beliefs of a group about how mind works, how children learn and what helps them grow. Bruner argues that without knowing folk psychology it is difficult to introduce major changes in the education system because new theories have to compete with these existing theories that guide the behaviour of teachers and learners (Bruner, 1996). For example, his book urges teachers to allow learners to arrive at the concepts with the help of activities. This view can go against the belief of a teacher who feels that teachers are authority figures, who should use the lecture method to teach learners because they are supposed to memorise information to get good grades.

The Origins of Cultural Cognition: Michael Tomasello, an American cultural and developmental psychologist is currently working in Max Planck institute for Evolutionary Anthropology in Germany. He has proposed that the major difference between human cognition and that of other species is their ability to participate with each other in collaborative activities. He coined the term, 'shared intentionality' to convey that for any collaborative activity it is important to have shared goals and intentions. This ability distinguishes human beings from other species. The second distinguishing feature of human beings is their unique motivation to share emotions, experiences and activities with other people. These two aspects enable people to participate in cultural activities and acquire words, phrases and concepts of their language. This results in cultural cognition and evolution, specific to human beings (Tomasello, 2010).

Web-links and Readings

Bruner, J. (1996). *The Culture of Education*. Massachusetts: Harvard University Press.

Eysenck, M. W., & Keane, M. T. (2005). *Cognitive Psychology: A Student's Handbook* (5 ed.). NY, USA: Taylor & Francis.

Flavell, J. H., Miller, P. H., & Miller, S. A. (1993). *Cognitive Development*. Engelwoods Cliff, NJ: Prentice-Hall.

Hoijer, H. (1954). The Sapir-Whorf Hypothesis. *Language in Culture*, 92-105. Conference on the interrelations of language and other aspects of culture. Chicago: University of Chicago Press.

Siegler, R. (1991). *Children's Thinking*. New Jersey: Prentice Hall.

TEDx Talks. (2014, March 11). *Creative thinking - how to get out of the box and generate ideas*: Giovanni Corazza at TEDxRoma. (Università Telematica Internazionale, Editor) Retrieved March 2, 2016, from YouTube: https://www.youtube.com/watch?v=bEusrD8g-dM

The Silent Observers. (2013, June 26). Psychology Chapter 7: *Thinking and Intelligence*. Retrieved March 2, 2016, from YouTube: https://www.youtube.com/watch?v=HFbq6XZNmP4

Tomasello, M., Carpenter, M., Call, J., Behye, T., & Moll, H. (2005). Understanding and Sharing Intentions: The Origins of Cultural Cognitions. *Behavioural and Brain Sciences*.

Woolfolk, A., Misra, G., & Jha, A. K. (2010). *Fundamentals of Educational Psychology*. New Delhi: Pearson.

Motivation and Emotion*

Introduction

The study of motivation endeavours to understand the driving forces behind human actions. It includes explorations of questions like, why some people work harder than others, why some people are more aggressive than others, why some people are more altruistic than others and so on. There are different kinds of motives that can propel actions in a particular direction, and alternately, a single motive can also propel actions in varied directions. These motives range from being biological, psychological, social, or political in nature. The activities of this Unit have been planned to enable learners to realise that different motives guide their actions in different ways.

Among these different driving forces or motives, emotions also play a significant role as psycho-social motives. The study of emotions, explains how and why people feel happy, sad, hopeful, excited, and sorrowful. It also attempts to explain the probable actions of people when they experience the various emotions. A general definition of emotions suggests that emotions are internal subjective feelings which include both physiological responses and a cognitive analysis of the situation. However, there are different views about what comes first: cognitive appraisal or physiological responses. Learners thus need to be acquainted with different, perspectives to understand emotions. This is an important issue that needs to be highlighted in the classroom discussions.

Motivation and Emotions are usually discussed together as one unit in books of General Psychology. This is probably because they both try to understand the internal subjective state of a person.

---

* Vishakha Kumar and Rashmi Malhotra

Secondly, there is a close relationship between motivation and emotions. Motives assign direction to behaviour and in the course of pursuing a particular goal, a person may experience several emotions. For instance, a person driven by an affiliation motive may experience joy in working for someone she/he cares for and may become despondent in case of rejection. This Unit will enable learners to reflect on the various forces that drive their actions and likewise what forces or factors affect the way they feel. The teacher must make an effort to help learners express their emotions either verbally, pictorially, dramatically, or through any other channel. The teacher must also give space to learners to deliberate over the various suggested activities and discuss their ideas freely.

ACTIVITY 1: NATURE OF MOTIVATION

Route: The teacher can write five situations in which different people are engaged in varied acts. She can ask learners to give reasons that explain why these people may be engaged in the respective activities.

- A 6-month-old baby is wailing.
- A 14-year-old girl walks 7 kilometres every day to reach her school.
- A 16-year-old takes a sick leave to attend a wedding.
- A 23-year-old is going for her first job interview.
- A 26-year-old saves money to gift her mother a car.

After the learners speculate about the purpose of these actions, the teacher may direct their attention to the term 'motive', which is the underlying reason for every action that one performs. A 6-month-old baby may be crying because she/he feels cold or is hungry. Similarly, a girl who walks 7 km to reach her school every day may be because there is no other school near her house, or because she is interested in studies, or wants to meet her friends. Each one of these situations can have multiple explanations. The teacher should allow learners to come up with as many responses as they can.

Synthesis: Motivation is an important determinant of behaviour. Motives explain the everyday action of a person and thus also enable prediction of behaviour. A need is a lack or deficit of something. This lack of something leads to a kind of tension referred to as 'drive'. When some action in the direction of accomplishing the need takes place, it facilitates drive reduction and a person returns to the balanced state. This process can be explained with the help of the examples stated in the above activity.

ACTIVITY 2: BIOLOGICAL AND PSYCHOSOCIAL MOTIVES

Route: The teacher would ask the learners to imagine that they are on a ship and there is a shipwreck. If they are able to carry only 10 things with them, which things would they choose to carry for their survival. After the learners share their list, the teacher would tell the learners that due to paucity of space, they can now take only five things. They will now have to cut out those items from the list which are less essential. The teacher would ask few learners to read their list. After a few learners have shared their views, the teacher would ask them to identify only three things on board that they would like to take with them. The teacher reminds them that besides those three things they will have nothing else, so they must choose carefully.

As they would discuss their list, it may come up that food and clean water are common to most lists. With the help of their responses, the teacher can discuss the concept of biological motives that are important for survival such as food, water and sex.

Synthesis: Biological motives can also be explained in terms of an inborn tendency called instinct. On the other hand, psychosocial motives are those which satisfy needs such as the need for affiliation and power, but, they only become important once the biological needs are taken care of. The teacher can also discuss Maslow's need hierarchy with reference to this activity, in which, at the base are the physiological motives, followed by safety needs, belongingness needs, esteem needs and at the apex, the need for self-actualisation.

ACTIVITY 3: PSYCHOSOCIAL MOTIVES

Route: The teacher would read out the case vignettes given below and ask the learners to identify the dominant need that each case shows. The learners should also list the most evident characteristics of the person mentioned in the case.

Case Study 1: Reena loves to go out with her friends. She enjoys meeting new people and making new friends. Her parents constantly keep asking her to focus on her studies and to maintain a balance between her social life and studies. Despite her parents' advice, she continues to spend most of the time with her friends.

Case Study 2: Shyama is in class XI. She really wants to hold a prominent office in school next year and is working hard for it. She participates in as many activities as possible and also tries to maintain a leader's position. She communicates on a regular basis with her teachers and shares a good rapport with her juniors.

Case Study 3: Arjun is extremely ambitious. He wants to be very successful in life. At his workplace he takes up moderately difficult assignments to prove his mettle. He eagerly awaits feedback from his boss and other seniors and ensures that he incorporates their feedback in his work.

Case Study 4: Afraz likes to read a lot. He is constantly searching for new books and wants to learn more and more. As a child, he always had questions about different things. Earlier he would bombard his parents and teachers with queries, but, now he tries to find his own answers. He is a keen observer and tries to conduct experiments at home.

The teacher can then discuss the responses of the learners. In the above-mentioned cases, Reena's behaviour seems to be predominantly influenced by the need for affiliation; Shyama is primarily guided by the need for power; Arjun is dominated by the need for achievement, and Afraz's behaviour is affected by curiosity and need for exploration. The teacher must allow learners to reason out and discuss their perspective on each of these cases.

Synthesis: Psychosocial motives are divided into four heads that include the need for affiliation, need for power, need for achievement, curiosity and exploration. These motives are usually acquired or learned. Family, friends, and neighbourhood, all play a significant role in the development of these motives.

ACTIVITY 4: FRUSTRATION

Route: The teacher would ask four learners to volunteer for a class activity. The task given to them would be that one of them tries to go from one place to another place in the classroom or outside the classroom, while the other three block his/ her way. The teacher may also set a certain time limit of about 2 minutes depending on the distance she/he has chosen to make it more challenging.

Alternatively, the teacher can ask one of the learners to read aloud, the chapter of Emotion and Motivation from the book. As the learner begins reading, two or three other learners would start interrupting. These learners can be briefed in advance that their task is to disturb the person who is reading and they have to ensure that he is unable to complete his/her task.

As they go ahead doing this activity, the learners may show signs of frustration and they may even try to push or shout at each other. The teacher must step in at this juncture so that the learners do not become violent. She/he can then inform the class that this was planned before-hand to demonstrate how frustration leads to aggression.

The teacher can give examples of road-rage and other violent incidents and can also encourage the learners to introspect. They would be asked to think about two such situations in life where they felt that their goal seeking behaviour was inhibited. They can also be asked to write a few lines describing a situation where they felt very angry and/ or became violent.

Synthesis: Frustration occurs when a desired goal is not attained and the motive is blocked. Most people would have experienced some form of frustration. However, there can be different kind of behavioural and emotional reactions such as aggression, crying, escape, and avoidance.

ACTIVITY 5: NATURE OF EMOTIONS

Route: Learners would be asked to come to the front of the class and enact a situation/ mood while other learners would try to identify the situation. The teacher can either keep a bowl with different situations/ moods written on slips of paper, or she/he can ask the learners to think of any situation and enact it in front of the class. The teacher may also suggest that learners can enact their feelings if they secured the first position in class or if their best friend is upset with them and they don't know the reason, etc.

The teacher can then discuss how emotions are defined in Psychology. She/he can also ask learners to enlist emotions, which they feel would be universally experienced. Then this list can be compared with the emotions suggested by different Psychologists.

Synthesis: Emotions are subjective feelings, which vary from person to person but their expression has been found to be universal to some extent. They include both physiological responses and psychological reactions. Most of the people experience varied emotions throughout the day. But psychologists have identified six basic emotions, i.e. anger, disgust, fear, happiness, sadness, and surprise. Different psychologists have identified different number of basic emotions.

ACTIVITY 6: PHYSIOLOGICAL AND COGNITIVE BASES OF EMOTIONS

Route: In this activity, the teacher would engage learners in an imaginary simulated learning experience. She/he would ask them to close their eyes and relax. She would then read the passage given below:

> *"Your board exams will begin in a week from now. You are preparing for your exam, but nowadays you get cold feet and are unable to focus. You have started feeling as if you will not do well and get stressed about it. Whenever you sit down to study, you cannot focus and feel that everything you are reading is new. You are unable to recall anything that is given in the syllabus. As the time for exams draws closer you start getting more anxious and frustrated. You feel scared to share your feeling with your parents because they have pinned up lots of hope on you. And you know that they will never be able to understand how you feel at this juncture.*
>
> *Two days before the exam, you start sweating profusely. Your heart beat is increasing and you feel as if your BP has shot up. You are neither able to study nor sleep. The moment you sleep, you get nightmares. What do you do? Your friends are busy studying and are not picking up their phone. You are restless. And the examination-day arrives. "*

The teacher would ask the learners to open their eyes and describe their feelings. The teacher would then screen a video about different theories of emotions, and ask the learners to reflect on their feelings and explain them based on different theories of emotions.

Synthesis: There are three important theories of emotions. One of the earliest was proposed by James and Lange in 1884. According to their theory, an external stimulus evokes a physiological response, which a person perceives and then experiences the emotion. Another theory was proposed by Canon (1927) and Bard (1934). According to their theory, the physiological responses and emotional experience take place simultaneously. A third theory, proposed by Stanley Schachter and Jerome Singer (1962) is called as the two factor theory. This theory states emotional experience includes two processes and they are: physiological arousal and cognitive labelling. Physiological responses in most emotions are the same however, a person looks for external cues to interpret the arousal.

ACTIVITY 7: EXPRESSION OF EMOTIONS

Route: The teacher can play a small game of **passing the parcel** with the learners. If there is adequate space in the classroom, then all learners can stand in a circle, otherwise, they can do this activity standing at their seats. A small bag or a cushion can be used in this activity. Each learner has to pass the bag to the learner standing next to him/her and express a particular emotion such as anger, love, jealousy, without using any words. The teacher should ensure that they chose one emotion for one round so that everyone in the class gets the opportunity to express that emotion. This activity depicts that learners express the same emotion in different ways.

Synthesis: The teacher can reiterate that emotions are subjective feelings. Their expression varies from person to person. A person's feelings can only be inferred from their verbal and non-verbal responses.

ACTIVITY 8: MANAGING EMOTIONS

Route: The class can be divided into three groups. Each group will be given one topic i.e. managing negative emotions, enhancing positive emotions, and managing examination anxiety. Each group would be asked to make a short five-minute presentation, wherein they list ways people attempt to manage their emotions. They can create a documentary movie or a poster presentation about their topic. To theorise their findings, they can be guided by the teacher and other reference books.

Synthesis: The discussion should bring out the significance of enhancing self-awareness, appraising the situation in an objective manner and by persons constantly monitoring their own actions. The teacher must also discuss how positive psychology shifted the focus from managing negative emotions to enhancing positive emotions.

Recent Trends

The study of emotions from a cognitivist perspective was quite popular in the 1950s and 1960s in the works of psychologists like George Kelly, Ulric Neisser, and Schachter & Singer (1962). However, there have been many shifts since then, like, in the 1960s and early 1970s Magda Arnold brought human emotionality to the centre of psychological research. With the gaining popularity of the phenomenological-existential perspectives, the understanding and research about emotions as independent of human cognition and as a 'subjective experiential reality', also gained popularity. The recent way of understanding how emotions take place is to perceive emotions as independent, but inter-connected with cognition. Advanced learners may be asked to make a project around the research trends about emotions. They may also be asked to learn more about the research on emotional intelligence by Daniel Goleman. Further, various indigenous perspectives have their own independent way of understanding emotions, like the *Rasa* and *Bhava* theory in Indian context. These may also be explored for a more culturally rooted understanding of emotions.

Web-links and Readings

Arnold, M. B. (1970). Perennial problems in the field of emotion. In *Feelings and Emotions: The Loyola Symposium* (pp. 169-186). New York: Academic Press.

Cannon, W. B. (1927) The James-Lange theory of emotion: A critical examination and an alternative theory. *American Journal of Psychology*, 39, 10-124.

Fosbender, L. (2013). Psychology 101: Theories of Emotion. Retrieved February 2, 2016, from https://www.youtube.com/watch?v=_Al3wGg2hp8&list=PLGzIp7LJjslSOnQ18L_4oDvCcwSnpQVVC

Goleman, D. (2006). *Emotional Intelligence: Why it can matter more than IQ*. New York: Bantam.

Gorman, P. (2004). *Motivation and Emotion*. Psychology Press. Retrieved from https://books.google.com/books?id=6DGP-e3xMq0C&pgis=1

James, W. (1884). What is emotion? *Mind*, 9, 188-205.

Moore, A. (2013). Motivation and Emotion: theories. Retrieved February 3, 2016, from https://www.youtube.com/watch?v=6SBWYepa4ls

Reeve, J. (2014). *Understanding Motivation and Emotion* (Vol. 3). New York: John Wiley & Sons. Retrieved from https://books.google.com/books?id=zfOyBwAAQBAJ&pgis=1

Schachter, S. & Singer, J. E. (1962). Cognitive, social, and physiological determinants of emotional state. *Psychological Review*, 69, 379-399.

Learning and Cognition*

Introduction

Learning has been considered as an important aspect of human life, for study by psychologists. The point that can be discussed while teaching this unit is that there are multiple perspectives to understand learning, which are rooted in different schools of psychology, namely behaviourism, cognitivism and social learning perspective. The teacher should try to convey that each perspective offers a different explanation of the same phenomenon and, yet, none of the perspectives are complete in themselves. Each theory or perspective has answered some questions and has left many others, unanswered. A new perspective typically emerges as a response to the unanswered questions.

Various experiments have been conducted to understand how human beings learn. This unit provides space to conduct some simple classroom experiments to understand the processes involved in learning and the factors affecting it. The learners will also be able to relate more with the subject matter of learning because they are constantly engaged in the process of learning themselves. Understanding this unit can therefore be a reflective process. The teacher can also encourage learners to do small micro studies in groups, wherein they can study any one of the phenomena discussed in this unit, such as transfer of training, instances of operant learning, effects of reinforcement, social learning, etc.

The teacher should also try to make linkages of learning with other areas of study in Psychology, such as Human Development. There are several theoretical positions that inform the conceptualisation of both learning and development. The nature

---

* Vishakha Kumar and Vikas Baniwal

of relationship between the two is one of the contentious areas in the history of Psychology. Various theorists and psychologists have taken different positions. To elucidate the point, the teacher can discuss the theories proposed by two eminent psychologists, Jean Piaget and Lev Vygotsky. This debate has wide educational implications and sets the ground for the teacher-learner relationship. By introducing learners to debates in Psychology the teacher can help learners understand that there is no fixed body of knowledge. Every area is open to changes in the light of new developments in research.

ACTIVITY 1: NATURE OF LEARNING

Route: The teacher may ask the learners to recall some old memories, such as, recite a nursery rhyme or a folk song that they might have learnt when they were young. Then she/he may ask a few learners to volunteer to show any one exercise or yoga asana to the class. The teacher may also ask some learners to reflect and explain about the nature of Psychology, as they have already studied about it in previous units.

After learners are able to remember, perform, and explain various things, the teacher will facilitate reflection on the reasons that account for learners' ability to complete the different tasks. Here, the term learning may be introduced in the discussion. The teacher may also have to explain the relation between learning and memory during this discussion. He/she could then focus on the meaning of the term learning. Learners may be asked the following questions:

1. From all the above instances, can you identify which one(s) can be described as learning? Why?
2. Do you think any temporary change in human behaviour can be termed as learning? Give reasons for your answers.

There are chances that learners may say that they learnt yoga sometime back and now they can or can't do it anymore. They may also share that they don't remember everything that they had learnt in the previous class. The teacher must at this point discuss that learning in Psychology is used to denote those changes in behaviour which are relatively permanent in nature and which result from some kind of experience. She/he can explicate the term by using various examples of habits, routine, communication, working on computers, and commuting to known places which illustrate changes in behaviour that are relatively permanent and less prone to changes. They all typify learning.

Synthesis: The teacher must bring the discussion to a point that the learners are able to reflect upon the most accepted definition of learning in Psychology. The teacher must also encourage discussion by citing different instances of learning and distinguishing them from reflexes and changes which are temporary. The relation between learning and memory may also be highlighted and the learners told that they will learn more about it in other units.

ACTIVITY 2: DIFFERENCE BETWEEN HABITUATION AND LEARNING

Route: The teacher may conduct an activity where she/he pairs some act performed by the learners with a verbal cue. One such instance can be that learners are asked to perform some action with their hands or legs, when a particular number is called out. The teacher can demonstrate the action. Such as, when number 1 is said they stretch out their left hand, when number 2 is said they stretch out their right hand, number 3, they stretch their left foot out, number 4, they stretch out their right foot and at number 5, they stretch both hands and legs.

Once the learners have understood this, the teacher will call the numbers in the random manner while the learners perform the desired action. In two or three repetitions they become more adept at the game.

Before starting this activity, the teacher may play some music at a low volume in the classroom. The music would continue during the activity but the songs will change. After the activity, the teacher would ask learners to recollect the song that was playing in the backdrop while they were busy exercising. It is possible that the learners cannot do so since they did not pay attention to the music. They also did not get distracted by it because their focus was on the activity. This phenomenon is referred to as habituation. Basically in this situation, the learners got used to the music and stopped responding to it. They focussed only on the activity that they were doing. The teacher can then ask the learners whether they will term habituation as learning. He/she can then discuss that responses produced because of habituation are not considered learning because they mark only a temporary change.

Synthesis: The teacher would then explain the concept of learning and how it involves a sequence of psychological events. She/he can also highlight that learning is an inferred process as it is very difficult to state all that a person has learnt, unlike performance, which is observable. The teacher can emphasize that whether learning has taken place or not, it can only be inferred by observing the person's behaviour. For instance, from the performance on a given test, the teacher infers how well learners have understood a unit. Even so, it may not be possible for the teacher to know exactly how much each student has actually understood.

ACTIVITY 3: DIFFERENCE BETWEEN LEARNING AND REFLEX

Route: The teacher may also show videos of infants' reflexes to various stimuli. Alternatively, something startling, such as banging on the table all of a sudden, may also evoke a reflexive response from the learners. The teacher would then use the reaction to explain the difference between a reflex action and a learned response.

Synthesis: A loud sound also elicits a response. However, this response is not produced because of previous experience. Instead it is an inbuilt response to some stimuli which may be called as a reflex. Therefore, it is different from learning. Examples of the knee jerk, blinking and closing eyes in a dust storm may be discussed for further clarification.

ACTIVITY 4: CLASSICAL CONDITIONING

Route: The teacher will screen a small video about Pavlov's experiment and findings of his study on dogs. Learners will be asked to discuss about their views about the study and its relevance to the human learning process. If there is no provision to source or show the video, the experiment can be described as a story narration. In addition, the teacher can read out other instances of classical conditioning from books on general psychology to enumerate where all classical conditioning explains learning new behaviour. It is important to link the classical experiments with everyday experiences.

The teacher can cite some instances of classical conditioning to learners and ask them to identify the US, UR, CS and CR. Some examples are as follows:

- Little Albert experiment (Watson & Reiner, 1920)

- Samaira loves eating chocolates. One day she ate mint chocolate for the first time. Though she loved it, she fell sick within an hour of consuming it. She threw up all night and was almost dizzy in the morning. Her parents rushed her to the hospital and then she was hospitalised for two days. Samaira was scared of needles, but, in those two days she was injected several times. Despite the fact that the doctor told her that this is not because of chocolates, Samaira feels nauseous even at the sight of mint chocolates.
- Hussain was infatuated with a particular girl during his adolescence. He liked everything about her: her dressing sense, the way she spoke, and especially her smell. She wore a fairly strong perfume that acted as a signal to her presence. Hussain would get elated the moment he realized that she was in the vicinity. The smell of her perfume signalled her arrival. After many years, he got married and realized that his wife wore the same perfume as the girl he was infatuated with earlier.

The teacher can also use such instances given in different books of general psychology to initiate discussion. Learners can also be encouraged to search for and share more examples that show how classical conditioning is used in everyday life.

Synthesis: According to classical conditioning learning takes place when association between two stimuli takes place i.e. when one stimuli acts as a signal for the presence of another.

ACTIVITY 5: OPERANT CONDITIONING

Route: The teacher can show a video of any of Skinner's experiments and discuss how and what the animals (rats; pigeons) have learnt based on what they saw in the experiment. If the classroom does not have facility to play the video clip, then the teacher can give a hand-out of any of the original experiments that were done by Skinner in pictorial form with textual explanations.

From the inferences shared by learners on their observations, the teacher would then explain the concept of operant conditioning. Operant conditioning results from pairing of some action done by the organism with result of his/her action. The teacher can ask learners to think about things or reasons that make them work harder and excel in their interest areas such as dance, academics, sports etc. The teacher could then compile the responses on the board. He/she can also explain the difference between positive and negative reinforcement from the compiled list on the board.

Synthesis: The teacher must emphasize that according to operant conditioning, behaviour is learnt, maintained, and changed through its consequences. These consequences act as reinforcement for the maintenance, increase, or decrease in the behaviour. Reinforcements can be both negative and positive.

Alternatively

Route: The teacher can read out the following case vignettes to the learners:

> *"Priya is a 7-year-old girl who loves to study. She enjoys reading books and having long discussions about different topics with her friends and teachers. Her reading helps her have more views and a better understanding of different topics. In addition, when she hears her friends commenting about how knowledgeable she is, she feels more encouraged to read."*
>
> *"Rahul enjoys the title of "joker of the class". He loves doing funny, silly things and feels happy when his classmates laugh at his actions. His teachers tell him all the time to stop doing these things."*

Learners will be asked to present their understanding of how the principles of operant conditioning explain the learnt behaviours of the two characters discussed in the case vignettes. The teacher must encourage learners to focus on the consequences of the actions. In the first case, Priya, is hard working and loves reading. The consequence of her action is twofold: one it gives her satisfaction that she is able to discuss so much with her friends and secondly she also wins accolades from her peer group. The second instance indicates that Rahul acts like a joker because his friends enjoy his jokes and laugh at them. Probably Rahul is an adolescent and assigns greater significance to peer approval.

After discussing these two case vignettes, the teacher can ask learners to think of and share instances from their own lives where they felt that learning took place by operant conditioning.

Synthesis: The teacher must emphasize that according to operant conditioning, behaviour is learnt, maintained and changed through its consequences. These consequences are called reinforcers. They can be different for different people.

ACTIVITY 6: IMITATION AND OBSERVATIONAL LEARNING

Route: The learners can be asked to name their role models and discuss why they have developed admiration for them. They can also be asked to identify what they have learnt and have begun to follow from any one of their role models. Alternatively, the teacher can initiate discussion on the preferred choice of dress/look, choice of music and food preferences of his/her learners and asks them to think about where they have acquired the preferences. A finer analysis of these can reveal that most people are influenced by the fashion trends popularised by various celebrities. Adolescents and children imbibe the dress style and mannerisms of influential people by observing them.

Then the teacher can ask learners to recollect how often they have acquired behaviour by observing others. They can be asked the following questions:

1. Do you think your behaviour resembles your parents' behaviour?
2. Why and how did you learn this?
3. Do you have a specific role model? Have you ever tried to be like him/her?
4. Think of any one instance where you feel you have learnt some skill by just seeing someone else perform it?

With the help of such questions the teacher can elucidate the concept of observational learning. The teacher can also share researches, which indicate that viewing and playing aggressive video games lead to increase in aggression amongst children. She/he can also initiate a debate on this topic and ask learners to share their views.

Synthesis: The teacher must give such instances that enable learners to understand that this form of learning is social in nature and it takes place by observing someone's behaviour who acts as a model. The performance of that learnt behaviour depends on whether the model was rewarded or punished.

Alternatively

Route: The teacher can ask the learners to think about the games they had played as children. Once they recall some games, the teacher can use ideas from observational learning theory to draw links between what they observed and what they played, or how they behaved.

Synthesis: The purpose of this activity is to enable learners to think and reflect on how they have learnt some aspects of their behaviour from the movies or games. Such activities also help to connect text with real life instances and help learners draw examples from daily life.

ACTIVITY 7: CATEGORY CLUSTERING

Route: The teacher can conduct a simple classroom experiment. She may ask a few learners to volunteer to participate in the experiment. From among those who volunteer, she can make two groups.

Group 1: This group of learners is asked to prepare a list of 50 words from the following categories: fruits, vegetables, animals and cars. The words from each category have to be mixed up and made into a composite list. The teacher should check the list before handing it over to the next group.

Group 2: There will be two to three learners in this group. One will read out the list, while the other two will remember it in any order. During the recall, one of the learners can be asked to write the list while the other person is reading it. One person can note down the words recalled verbally in the exact sequence in which they were spoken. The teacher doesn't have to wait for completion of the entire list. She can even conduct 3-4 trials and then stop. The recalled lists are read out loudly and learners are asked to analyse the pattern that the particular learner has followed. The upcoming patterns can be used to explain the concept of category clustering.

Synthesis: When the learners are not asked to memorize the list in a fixed order and are allowed free recall, then it is seen that the recall is organized. They organize the information not according to the order in which it is presented; rather they allocate the words to different semantic categories. In this case the teacher had already given these categories to those who were preparing the list i.e. fruits, vegetables, animals and cars.

ACTIVITY 8: CONCEPT LEARNING

Route: The teacher can elaborate on 'concept learning' using the following activity. The teacher may list out a few words on the board and tell the learners that in this list they need to separate out words and phrases which are the same when written either ways (palindromes).

The list is as follows:

> *eye, racecar, tattarrattat, prop, agoraphobia, aibohphobia, summers, rotator, malayalam, transport, 12321, 2345, 464*

The group is then asked to list out what are the rules they followed while finding out palindromes from the given list. Through this they understand the concept of relevant features and what conjunctive concept means. They learn that there are two rules which are followed: first, it has to be a word or a phrase and not a sequence of numbers and second, the word should spell the same, both ways.

The teacher can then ask learners to reflect on the term 'concept' and try to articulate their understanding of it.

Synthesis: The teacher must discuss concept as a category that is used to refer to objects or events. It is defined as a set of features connected by some rule. A set of features connected by some rule are called relevant features. In conjunctive concepts relevant features have to be present and irrelevant ones left out.

ACTIVITY 9: SOCIOCULTURAL THEORY OF LEV VYGOTSKY

Route: The teacher can present a case vignette to the learners and ask them to think of a similar incident that they may have encountered in their life. The case vignette is given below:

'A day out with a friend'

Samaira and Anju are very close friends in school. Samaira visits Anju's home first time since they became friends. It's a Sunday and Anju's family is getting ready to go to Sunday church. Samaira also joins them on the condition that Anju and she will go to the park, after the Sunday mass. Samaira has never been to church. The moment she reaches church she starts taking off her shoes. Anju is unable to comprehend Samaira's behaviour. Samaira tells her that since shoes are not allowed inside a temple so she surmised that she may have to remove her shoes in a church as well. Anju tells her that everyone is allowed to wear shoes inside a church. Samaira finds it strange that everyone sits quietly for an hour inside the church listening to the sermon. She starts thinking that unlike church, in a temple there is lot of hustle and bustle with people moving around the deity, offering flowers, ringing bells, burning incense sticks and lighting oil lamps. In a church they light candles instead of oil lamps. She wonders how different the two ways of worshipping the almighty are.

After church, they play in the park and then reach home. Anju's mother has made chicken curry for them but Samaira tells them that since the festival of Navratri is going on, she cannot eat non-vegetarian food. Anju is curious and asks her friend about this festival. Samaira tells her that the nine days of the Navratri are sacred days for Hindus, during which they are expected to fast, pray and abstain from eating non-vegetarian food. During these days, people worship Goddess Druga and her different forms. Anju compares Navratras with Lent and tells Samaira that they also observe fasting for forty days during which they abstain from eating non-vegetarian food and eat just one meal in a day. It is a way of remembering the suffering of Jesus Christ. The two girls have a long conversation on what is considered sacred and profane in the two religious beliefs.

Do you remember having such a conversation with your friend sometime? Try to analyse what you have learnt and understood about the meaning of cognition and learning with the help of the following questions:

- How do you know what is sacred and profane?
- Do you think development of beliefs, faith, food preferences, understanding of 'self' and 'the other' is also part of learning?
- People's beliefs vary from culture to culture. If you accept the premise that offspring in a particular culture learn those belief structures, then do you think that developmental stages are universally experienced?

The learners may discuss the role of observational learning, operant conditioning and classical conditioning to discuss this example. The teacher should give space to them to think and try to recognize that how human cognition develops with the help of social interaction.

The teacher can scaffold learners to understand that learning not only takes place when there is reinforcement, rather a person is propelled from within to make sense of the world around him/her. Each person is an active agent and social interaction plays an important role in learning as well as development.

If the learners are aware of the theory of Jean Piaget the teacher can discuss the relationship between learning and development with them. He/she can pose a question:

- What comes first – learning or development? The teacher should allow learners to think and discuss the above question. The teacher can then discuss the work of two theorists Jean Piaget and Lev Vygotsky to highlight the debate about the connection between learning and development. Piaget strongly argued that development precedes learning whereas, Vygotsky argued that learning precedes development.

Here the teacher can discuss both theoretical positions.

- The teacher can then raise further questions such as:
- What is the role of a teacher in a classroom?
- Is it possible to accelerate learning?

The teacher can discuss how engaging with a teacher or any person who is more knowledgeable can help learners move from a level where they are unable to complete a task to a level where they can complete the task with assistance. This process begins when two people engage in a problem with different understanding but arrive at a shared understanding. This is an important principle proposed by Lev Vygotsky. For him, the genesis of knowledge was in social interaction. Adult-child interaction and child-child interaction can both be discussed in terms of how they influence the process of cognition. The ideas of zone of proximal development and scaffolding can also be introduced and explained.

Synthesis: The teacher can present Vygotsky's sociocultural theory by comparing and contrasting it with the theoretical position of Jean Piaget. Learners would be well acquainted with the theory of Piaget if they have read the unit of Human Development. Jean Piaget emphasized the biological side of cognitive development. Piaget saw a child as self-motivated and as an active explorer who forms ideas. Lev Vygotsky also saw the child as an active seeker but he laid greater emphasis on social and cultural contexts in the process of development of thinking. Unlike Piaget, Vygotsky emphasized that learning precedes development.

Recent Trends

Constructivist Views of Learning: Constructivism is a broad worldview that recognizes learner as active agent who plays a pivotal role in building understanding and making sense of the information that he/she receives. This perspective gained grounds with the work of Jean Piaget, Vygotsky, Gestalt Psychologists, Jerome Bruner, Bartlett and Rogoff. Thinkers from other fields such as John Dewey, the philosopher and Jean Lave, the anthropologist have also played a role in the development of this perspective. It is important to note here that constructivism is a broad approach and not a theory. There are two central ideas that bind this approach. The first idea is that learner is active in constructing knowledge. The second is, that social interaction is important in this knowledge construction (Woolfolk, Misra & Jha, 2010).

Constructivism can be broadly classified in two forms: psychological and social (Palincsar, 1998). Putting it in simplistic words it can be surmised that psychological constructivism focuses on how the individual uses information, resources and assistance from others to build their mental models and problem solving strategies. It also talks about the centrality of the actors' interpretation of the situation. So the person's self, beliefs, identity and knowledge are at the fore of this theoretical approach (Woolfolk, Misra, & Jha, 2010).

Social constructivism, on the other hand, emphasizes the ability of a person to participate in the activities of the culture. It states that to engage in the process of learning, cultural tools such as language, calendar, social interaction and activity are essential. This approach does not focus merely on individual's knowledge construction; rather it emphasizes learning in a group by participating in social construction of knowledge (Woolfolk, Misra & Jha, 2010).

Most thinkers see Piaget as a psychological constructivist because he studied the individual's knowledge construction. It is however debatable whether Vygotsky was a social constructivist or a psychological constructivist or both. Vygotsky's theory included both the process whereby an individual's learns in a social context, as well as the role of social interaction and cultural context to explain learning. At best he can be seen as someone who tried to bridge the gap between the two forms (Woolfolk, Misra & Jha, 2010).

Situated Cognition: The approach of situated cognition proposes that knowing is inseparable from doing. It argues that all knowledge is situated in activity bound to social, cultural and physical contexts. While situated cognition gained recognition in the field of educational psychology in the late twentieth century, it shares many principles with older fields such as critical theory, (Frankfurt School, 1930; Freire, 1968) anthropology (Lave & Wenger, 1991), philosophy (Heidegger, 1968), critical discourse analysis (Fairclough, 1989), and sociolinguistics theories (Bakhtin, 1981) that rejected the notion of truly objective knowledge.

However, the most recent origin of perspective on situated cognition can be traced to the Piagetian and Vygotskian socio-cultural perspectives in learning. Piaget rejected the Cartesian model to propose that knowledge is situated in action. However, Piaget's theory is context neutral. On the other hand, Jerome Bruner's and Lev Vygotsky's theories propose learning to be situated in the cultural context and situated cognition can be seen as the extension of these theories.

Situated cognition theory shifts the focus from the individual to the sociocultural setting and the activities of the people within that setting. Knowledge accrues through the lived practices of the people in a society. These practices are meaningful actions that have relation of meaning to one another in term of some cultural system. Knowledge as lived practices must be understood in its relation to the social aspect as well as the individual aspect that is generally stressed in other theories of learning (Driscoll, 1994).

Sociocultural Theory of Lev Vygotsky: Lev Vygotsky, a Jew, was born in the Soviet Union in the year 1896. His work remained largely under cover for the rest of the world till the 1970's because of its controversial nature. However, today it is a widely researched area in Psychology and Human Development. Vygotsky was deeply influenced by Marxist ideas and this led him to reject the individualistic notion of a child. Rather he emphasized that mind is socially formed. He theorized that children are born with basic perceptual, attention and memory capacities which develop till the child attains two years of age. The development of language plays a very important role in the development of cognition. According to him, language helps to widen the participation of children in the society by giving them an opportunity to engage with more knowledgeable individuals. Eventually, children start talking to themselves the way they talk to others.

Vygotsky stated that every mental function goes through an external stage. The mental processes are formed when the interpersonal interaction becomes intra-personal (Berk, 2006). An example of this can be the internalisation of guilt that one experiences when one flouts the value system that was given to us by our parents. For example, a child who is warned against stepping out of the house after it gets dark may continue to feel scared of dark even after he/she grows up and starts living away from his/her natal homes or if the child was taught that eating non-vegetarian food goes against their religious norms because it is a form of violence then even if he/she starts consuming it after he/she moves away from home, he/she may feel guilty.

Web-links and Readings

Bakhtin, M.M. (1981). *The Dialogic Imagination: Four Essays by M. M. Bakhtin* (M. Holquist, Ed.; C. Emerson & M. Holquist, Trans.). Austin: University of Texas Press.

Berk, L. (2006). *Child Development*. New York: Pearson.

Buchanan, J. (2013, March 21). *Stop Climbing, Start Swimming: The hidden advantages of dyslexia: Jonathan Buchanan at TEDxWarwickED*. Retrieved January 24, 2016, from YouTube: https://www.youtube.com/watch?v=VIIbeqMGB3o

Cahya, F. (2013, January 4). *Nine Reflexes of Baby*. Retrieved March 12, 2016, from YouTube: https://www.youtube.com/watch?v=KkT7SPr30Fw

Driscoll, M. (2000). *Psychology of Learning for Instruction*. Boston: Allyn and Bacon.

Fairclough, N. (1989). *Language and Power*. London: Longman.

Freire, P. (1968). *Pedagogy of the Oppressed*. New York: Continuum.

Heidegger, M. (1968). *What is Called Thinking?* New York: Harper & Row.

Krantz, J. H. (n.d.). *Psychological Tutorials and Demonstrations*. Retrieved January 25, 2016, from Hanover College: http://psych.hanover.edu/krantz/tutor.html#Learning

Lave, J., & Etienne, W. (1991). *Situated Learning Legitimate Peripheral Participation*. New York: Cambridge University Press.

Leicestershire Partnership NHS Trust. (2013, January 7). *If You Listen, You Will Hear Us*. Retrieved January 13, 2016, from YouTube: https://www.youtube.com/watch?v=Hp4PW17U_h8

Lightfoot, C., Cole, M., & Cole, S. (2013). *The Development of Children*. New York: Worth Publishers.

Marr, D. (1982). *Vision: A Computational Investigation into Human Representation and Processing of Visual Information*. New York: Freeman.

Palincsar, A. S. (1998). Keeping the metaphor of scaffolding fresh: A response to C. Addison Stone's "The metaphor of scaffolding its utility for the field of learning disabilities". *Journal of learning disabilities, 31*(4), 370-373.

The Fletcher Academy. (2008, April 24). *My Life with a Learning Disability*. Retrieved January 24, 2016, from https://www.youtube.com/watch?v=kiqDq0fimXk

The Learning Disabilities Association of Alberta. (2012, October 3). *What Are Learning Disabilities?* Retrieved January 24, 2016, from YouTube: https://www.youtube.com/watch?v=_3ONz6TaKIk

Tulving, E. (1972). Episodic and Semantic Memory. *Organisation of Memory, 381*(4), 381-402.

Watson, J.B. & Reiner, R. (1920). Conditioned Emotional Reaction. *Journal of Experimental Psychology*, 3, 1-14.

Woolfolk, A., Misra, G., & Jha, A. K. (2010). *Fundamentals of Educational Psychology*. New Delhi: Pearson.

Human Development*

Introduction

Human Development is one of the most interesting and engaging areas of study in Psychology. For most of the learners, who get introduced to the discipline of Psychology, this unit comes as a breath of fresh air. The reason for this is the connection that they can feel to the various theories and the personal experiential linkages that they can make with the subject matter. The contents of the unit help them to understand how an individual grows, matures, and develops as a human being in the culture and context in which he/she lives and grows and also builds perspective about the idea that development encompasses physical, social, cognitive, moral and personal aspects.

A discussion of this unit may begin by differentiating development from growth and maturation. Most learners would have heard these terms in other subjects like Economics and Biology. The teacher can thus use their existing knowledge base to build up a basic understanding of growth and development in Psychology. Using classroom discussions accompanied by examples from learners' lives, the teacher can arrive at the various principles of development instead of merely telling the learners about them.

There are two key debates in Psychology that can be introduced to the learners through this unit. The first is the nature - nurture debate. As in any other debate, there are evidences to support the importance of both nature and nurture, and one of the learning tasks assigned to the learners could be to search for evidences to support either of them. The teacher can provide references and the learners can be asked to develop arguments

---

* Vishakha Kumar

in favour of both positions. This can be shared in the class for the benefit of all. The second debate is the continuity - discontinuity debate which examines whether development is a continuous, or a discontinuous process. Learners need to be given space to think freely about such debates so that they can share their informed responses. By introducing such debates, the teacher can familiarise them with conflicting opinions and perspectives in Psychology, which in turn will enable them to understand that there is no fixed body of knowledge in Psychology, nor final words about any question. The existing body of knowledge that constitutes its subject matter keeps on changing and gets modified in the light of new evidences.

This unit gives ample scope for reflection and experiential learning and many sections, such as contexts of development, gender roles and challenges of adolescence, can be best taught through peer interaction. Understanding the changes that the learners themselves have undergone over the years, they can be asked to share narratives of how they experienced and dealt with these changes and also how people's perceptions towards them have changed. The teacher can create connections between these changes and various concepts of this unit. He/she can also use learners' reminiscences of their childhood and their observations of children around them as resources for this unit. Some other suggested activities are as follows:

ACTIVITY 1: MEANING OF DEVELOPMENT

Route: Learners can be asked to collect different pictures of themselves ranging from the time they were born to the present day. They should bring at least five pictures of themselves clicked at different times, with a gap of at least 2-3 years between each of these five pictures such as, when they were:

- A few-days-old
- Two or three-years-old
- Six to seven-years-old
- Eleven to twelve-years-old
- A recent one

The teacher must also have five such pictures, in case learners are unable to gather them. Learners should then be asked to place them in an age sequence and then do the following:

- List out the similarities and differences between the times when they were just a few days old up to what they are at present.
- Think about the things which have changed in them over a period of time, particularly with reference to physical changes, emotional changes and changes in their thought processes, perceptions and experiences
- Try to identify some things which are given and do not change that much. This task can be confusing because it relates to the notion of identity in which, there is an inner sameness and continuity in the person in terms of his/her basic features. A brief discussion of identity can be taken up here and can later be integrated with its theoretical perspective. The sociocultural matrix in which it develops may also be highlighted.

To make the activity more interesting, learners can also be asked to exchange their pictures with their friends and then the same tasks/questions can be given/asked.

The responses given by the learners can be used to discuss the concept of development.

Synthesis: The learning from the discussion will include a definition of development relating to those changes in human beings which are orderly, progressive, and predictable. These changes begin at conception and continue throughout life. They take place in physical, cognitive, emotional as well as social aspects. The physical changes include changes in height, weight etc. Cognitive changes entail changes in thought processes, perceptions etc. Social changes refer to changes in the nature and forms of social interaction. The fact that development subsumes growth and maturation, can also be highlighted.

ACTIVITY 2: LIFE-SPAN PERSPECTIVE OF DEVELOPMENT

Route: The teacher can divide the class into seven small groups. Each group will be assigned a developmental age group, as follows:

- Infancy
- Early Childhood
- Late childhood
- Adolescence
- Adulthood

- Middle years
- Old age

Each group will be asked to write the characteristics of persons who are in the age group, assigned to them. One volunteer from each group can also be asked to enact something characteristic of that age, while others try to guess what the age of the person is.

As the learners read out the characteristics that they have enlisted, the teacher can make the following chart on the board (age wise):

Age group	*Characteristics*
1. Infancy	
2. Early childhood	
3. Late childhood	
4. Adolescence	
5. Adulthood	
6. Middle years	
7. Old age	

These characteristics can be used to explain the underlying life-span perspective of development and its various assumptions. The teacher can draw learners' attention to what they had learnt in the previous class about development being a lifelong process.

Synthesis: As learners enlist the characteristics of each age group, they will themselves be able to comprehend that:

- At every stage there are changes in physical, cognitive and psycho-social aspects. Development is thus multi-dimensional.
- These changes are intertwined with one another. Physical changes influence the cognitive, psychological and emotional changes in a person. For example, as children become more competent to manipulate and make negotiations in their environment, they develop different concepts. They also develop social skills in this process.
- The context influences the process of development. This can be discussed with the help of more activities, some of which are discussed below.

ACTIVITY 3: MY STORY

Route: Learners may be asked to write about their respective lives, in the form of a story wherein they highlight those events which they consider as turning points in their life. They have to reflect back and write about all the factors which they feel have contributed to their growth and development till now. They may be asked to write at least 500-700 words. The teacher can then collect these stories and share some of them in class. Peers may be encouraged to exchange their stories.

This should then be followed with a discussion about factors that influence development. Learners can be asked to discuss and decide on which of the two are more powerful- the genetic factors or the environmental factors in the development of a person. The teacher can then highlight that the nature-nurture debate is an important area of study in Psychology. He/she can also draw the attention of learners to various research studies that have been used to investigate the impact of genes on development. Reference can be made to studies on identical and fraternal twins brought up together and apart, to determine the influence of genes.

Synthesis: The teacher can highlight the interplay of genes and environment in the development of human beings. This will also help learners to acquire a learning base for understanding the importance of the context in the process of development.

ACTIVITY 4: THE CONTEXT OF DEVELOPMENT: URIE BRONFENBRENNER

Route: The teacher can either give a handout to the learners with different concentric circles or he/she can make the circles on the board. The learners can be asked to draw the same in their notebooks and complete them, based on the following instructions:

- Write their name in the centre.
- In the concentric circle immediately surrounding the core, they would be asked to write the names of people or objects and situations, whom/which they interact with at a very personal level and who/which influence their lives deeply.
- Once they have done this, in the third concentric circle, they can be asked to write the names of persons, groups or objects and situations in society which they are not directly a part of, but which affect them nevertheless.

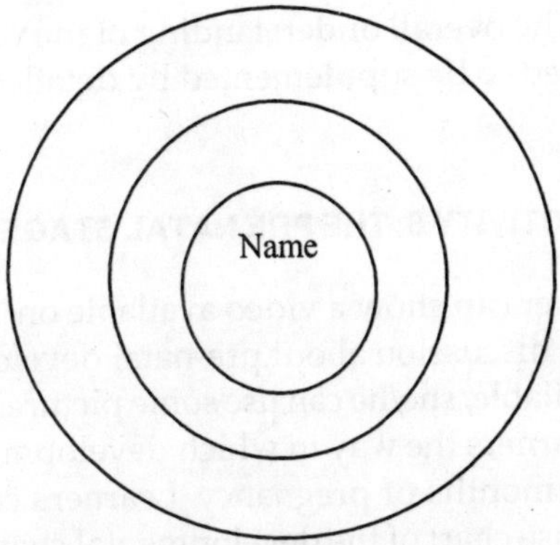

The Context of Self Development

- Then a discussion can be taken up on the data that emerges. This can be used to build understanding of what constitutes the socio-cultural context of development and its impact.
- Each of the circles can then be discussed for its importance and value individually and holistically. The concepts of microsystem, mesosystem, exosystem, macrosystem, and the chronosystem can be discussed.
- Learners can be encouraged to share their own diagram with their peers. The teacher can then ask them to read Bronfenbrenner's model from different sources.

Synthesis: The process of development is embedded in a socio-cultural context. Even though a person is maturing physically, yet it is important to recognise that the social context interprets these changes and assigns them meaning. Uri Bronfenbrenner's model attempts to describe the context of development in a holistic way.

ACTIVITY 5: STAGES OF DEVELOPMENT

Route: Learners can be divided into groups of five or more depending on the class strength. Each group can be assigned a particular life stage. They can be asked to read what their book says about that particular stage, and club this with their own understanding and prepare either a 10-minute role play highlighting the important characteristics of the stage, or locate and show a you-tube video, presenting their understanding alongside. They can also make a power point presentation or a collage about the important characteristics of the stage.

Synthesis: The overall understanding of the various stages of development need to be supplemented by detailed discussion of all the stages.

ACTIVITY 6: THE PRE NATAL STAGE

Route: The teacher can show a video available on YouTube to the class to initiate a discussion about pre-natal development. If, this facility is not available, she/he can use some pictures or ultrasound scans to show learners the way in which development takes place through various months of pregnancy. Learners can be asked to make a month-wise chart of the developmental changes in a foetus before it is born.

Synthesis: What needs to be highlighted is that the pre-natal phase begins at conception and continues for about 40 weeks till delivery. At this stage both biological factors and environmental factors play a role in growth and development of the foetus. Research indicates that maternal health also plays a significant role in the development of the foetus.

ACTIVITY 7: INFANCY

Route: Learners will be asked to observe a child who is under 2 years of age. In case they do not have access to any child in or around the house, then, they can be asked to surf the internet or refer to books on Child Development available in the library. They will be asked to find answers to the following questions:

1. What physical changes take place from the time a child is born to the time he/she turns 2 years?
2. At what age does an infant display a social smile?
3. At what stage does an infant start recognising his mother and other caregivers?
4. At what stage does an infant make an effort to communicate?
5. When does language development start?
6. When do children start playing with other children?
7. When do children start looking for objects that are hidden from them?
8. What does an infant, who is 8 months old, do when he/ she lays his/her hands on a pair of slippers, a toy, a spoon or a pencil?

9. How does a child who is 3 months, six months, one years, eighteen months and 2 years respond to unfamiliar faces?

The teacher should encourage learners to find answers to at least five of the questions given above and discuss them in class. Question number 1 is related to physical development. The teacher can discuss the growth pattern in the first two years and other milestones that unfold as a result of maturation. The discussion must encompass the initial reflexes which a child is born with and proceed to the development of fine and gross motor skills.

Questions 2 to 6 and question 9 are related to socio-emotional development. The development of attachment is an important hallmark of this stage. The relationship with the primary caretaker plays an important role in this regard.

Questions 7 and 8 are related to cognitive development. The teacher can discuss object permanence and sensory-motor development.

Synthesis: The first two years are marked by rapid changes in the physical, cognitive, and emotional aspects of a child. The teacher can introduce the work of Jean Piaget, Lawrence Kohlberg, and Erik Erikson, setting the backdrop of stage theories. If the teacher feels that her learners are ready for more detailed study, then, she/he can give a handout to them from any of the books of general psychology, which describe these theories in a tabular form, like Stubbe, Zeanab, & Mrazek (2015) or Child Development by Laura Berk (2006).

ACTIVITY 8: CHILDHOOD

Route

Task 1: Learners can be shown or asked to view movies like *Udaan* (2010), *Tare Zameen Par* (2007), *Jalparee* (2012) or any other film which has a child/ children as the main protagonist(s). The screening of the movie should be followed by a discussion on the following themes:

- What constitutes the world of a child?
- How does a child think?
- How does he/she understand adults and their world?
- What does morality mean to a child?
- How do children differentiate right from wrong?

Task 2: The teacher can ask learners to discuss the ways in which children of different age-groups will respond to the following questions:

- Plants are living beings. Yes or no? Give reasons
- Aeroplanes are living things or not? Give reasons
- Do Santa Claus and the Tooth fairy really exist or are they fictitious? The teacher can also use locally used names for such characters.
- When one is talking to a three-year-old child on the telephone and she is asked to say hello, she waves her hand. Why do you think this happens?
- If four-year-old children are asked to sort out various shapes, they do so according to colour or shape. Why is this so?

The teacher must introduce the concepts of animism, ego centrism and centration as cognitive constraints evident in a pre-operational child. The discussion should also include how these cognitive constraints are overcome in the next stage which is called the concrete operational stage.

ACTIVITY 9: ADOLESCENCE

Route: The teacher can ask the learners to describe themselves in 500 words. They should be asked to write about their dreams and aspirations, things which irk them the most and where they imagine they will be five years from now. They should also be asked to write a few lines about how they think they have changed from the time when they were 7 or 8 years old.

After this, the teacher can discuss what they have highlighted and also some of their concerns, dreams, and aspirations.

Synthesis: The teacher can emphasise that adolescence is not just a physical transformation; rather it is about very important psychological changes. The discussion should centre on the process of identity development as an important developmental task. Learners may also be asked to find out some adolescent issues depicted in popular movies.

ACTIVITY 10: SUMMARISING THE STAGES OF DEVELOPMENT

Route: The teacher may provide the worksheet given below as a home task to summarize the characteristics of different stages of development. She should encourage learners to use multiple references to complete the table. Alternatively, she can divide the class into groups of four and ask them to complete the table using different references.

Age Group	*Physical Characteristics*	*Cognitive Characteristics*	*Socio-emotional Characteristics*	*Moral Characteristics*	*Other important Characteristics*
Infancy					
Childhood					
Adolescence					
Adulthood					
Old age					

ACTIVITY 11: ROLE OF CULTURE

Route: The teacher can ask learners to study any two or three children who have never had the opportunity to attend school. They can select such children from anywhere in the city of Delhi. They should find out the daily routine of these children. They should try to observe all the activities they engage in during the day and compare them with their own childhood experiences. Some of them may be selling magazines at the traffic lights, begging alms, polishing shoes outside some shop, working in a tea stall, or with a vegetable vendor etc. If possible they can also ask them to perform any one or two Piagetian tasks. The teacher should ask the learners to write a report on what these children could do. He/she should make an effort to direct learners' attention to such skills as marketing, calculating money to be paid, ability to conduct themselves more confidently even in absence of an adult etc. This can be followed by a discussion on the following points:

- How were the children who had never been to school different from those who are in school?
- If they are engaged in some form of work, then what kind of skills have they acquired to fend for themselves?
- How do you think they would have acquired these skills?
- Do you think everyone follows the same pattern of development as Piaget had proposed?
- What are the things that are valued in their culture?

The teacher should then discuss that one of the criticisms of Piaget's work was that it did not take into account, the child's cultural and social milieu. Research indicates that Piagetian tasks have to be modified according to what the culture values and teaches their young ones. A study conducted on Brazilian street children found that they are unable to perform certain Piagetian tasks such as classifying flowers in categories of daisies, tulips and other flowers. But when the task was rephrased to include the concepts they were familiar with, then their responses changed (Saxe,1989).

Synthesis: The teacher can introduce the theory of Lev Vygotsky to highlight the role of culture in the process of human development. This theory places importance on the interaction between a child and more knowledgeable members of the society. Children acquire ways of thinking and behaving, termed as the culture of their community, by social interaction. There can be many such examples such as the emergence of famous singers from different *gharanas* in Indian music, weavers of Banaras who have passed the skill from one generation to another, or the understanding of flora and fauna of the forest by the tribes who have lived there for generations.

Recent Trends

Limitations of Piaget's Theory: Piaget's theory of cognitive development was a landmark in the history of psychology because it changed the notion of children. He argued and presented evidences to support that children's ways of thinking are qualitatively different from that of the adult. Despite its ground breaking claims the theory is not devoid of criticism. Later researchers found that stages as explained by Piaget, were not neat boundaries. Children may acquire a cognitive feat that may not be applicable across all categories. One such example is that of the conservation principle. Children acquire conservation of number much before conservation of volume. Secondly, it also appeared in some studies that development is a more continuous process than was proposed by Piaget.

The second criticism of Piaget was that he underestimated children's ability to think. Heyman & Gelman (2000) demonstrated that children were much more capable than what Piaget had estimated. The theory also fails to take into account that why young people excel in certain domains where adults may be struggling.

For instance, a young chess player may outplay a 20-year-old novice. The final and the main criticism of Piaget's theory was that it underplays the role of culture in cognitive development. When Piaget's tasks were given to children in different cultures it was found that the tasks failed to capture cultural diversity and knowledge. Different cultures place importance on different aspects of thinking and learning.

Vygotsky's Sociocultural Perspective: Today, a number of researchers are working on the role of culture in cognitive development. Researches indicate that cultures that value cooperation and sharing teach these to their children vis-a-vis cultures that value competition. Lev Vygotsky made a significant contribution in emphasising the role of culture in learning and development. We have discussed his theory in the unit on learning as well. According to him, human activities take place in a cultural context and they cannot be understood outside that context. He also proposed that the social interactions lay the foundation of specific mental structures and processes in a person. For him development was the transformation of socially shared activities into internalised processes. At first level, higher mental processes are co constructed through interaction where people direct their attention and thinking in solving a particular problem. People interact and negotiate to arrive at a shared understanding in the quest to solve a problem. Then these processes are internalised by the person who participates in this process (Woolfolk, Misra, & Jha, 2010). A mother sees her toddler howling and throwing things around. She has never seen her child behave in this manner before. She asks her what does she want? does she want a particular toy? Or she wants something to eat? Or she wants to go outside? The child responds by crying even more loudly. The mother picks her up, offers some water and tries to soothe her. In the process the child sleeps. The mother and the child in this process understand that crying was because the child was too tired and needed rest.

Another example can be of a child learning to arrange blocks with her mother. She tries to place a block on top of the other. Her mother directs her attention to different figures such as a car, train or house that can be made from the blocks. Next time when the girl plays with the blocks alone she thinks of different figures she had made with her mother and repeats the same instructions that her mother gave aloud while arranging blocks.

Web-links and Readings

Butterworth, G., & Harris, M. (2014). *Principles of Developmental Psychology: An Introduction.* Sussex: Psychology Press.

Heyman, G. D., & Gelman, S. A. (2000). Preschool children's use of novel predicates to make inductive inferences about people. *Cognitive Development, 15*(3), 263-280.

Prenatal Development (n.d.). [Motion Picture]. Retrieved January 20, 2016, from https://www.youtube.com/watch?v=36DO2R8y1fg

Ranganathan, N. (2000). *The Primary School Child: Development & Education.* New Delhi: Orient Blackswan.

Saxe, G. B. (1989). Transfer of learning across cultural practices. *Cognition and Instruction, 6*(4), 325-330.

Shaffer, D. R., & Kipp, K. (2010). *Developmental psychology: Childhood & adolescence* (8 ed.). California: Cengage Learning.

Stubbe, D., Zeanab, C. H., & Mrazek, D. A. (2015). A psychiatric perspective on human development. In A. Tasman, J. Kay, J. A. Lieberman, M. B. First, & M. Riba (Eds.), *Psychiatry* (4 ed., pp. 101-121). New York: John Wiley & Sons. Retrieved from https://books.google.co.in/books?id=l2KRBgAAQBAJ&printsec=frontcover#v=onepage&q& f=false

Woolfolk, A., Misra, G., & Jha, A. K. (2010). *Fundamentals of Educational Psychology.* New Delhi: Pearson.

Individual Differences and Human Intelligence*

Introduction

Intelligence is one of the most contentious and debated topics in the discipline of Psychology. The history of its development is replete with biases and pre-conceived notions about gender and race. However, over the years, Psychologists have made an effort to develop a more holistic definition of intelligence that is more inclusive. While teaching this unit, teachers must make an effort to dispel myths associated with its common everyday usage. Debates and discussions could form a very significant part of teaching this unit. Secondly, this unit can also be taught by associating the development of intelligence as a unit of study with the development of psychometrics in Psychology. The history of intelligence indicates that the definition of intelligence evolved and underwent change, in light of evidences that emerged from the results of various psychometric tests. The domination and critique of Psychometric tests must both be discussed. The more contemporary approaches to understanding and defining intelligence must also be covered. Students should be enabled to understand the rich evolutionary journey of intelligence and appreciate that all the approaches to understanding and measuring intelligence co-exist.

ACTIVITY 1: INDIVIDUAL DIFFERENCES

Route: Every learner will be asked to write 5 points about herself/ himself, which he/she feels makes him/her different from the

* Vishakha Kumar and Rashmi Malhotra

person sitting next to him/her. Then he/she would be asked to write five points about how he/she thinks the person sitting next to him/her is unique. Finally, every learner would be asked to write about the ways in which he/she thinks these differences can be measured.

The teacher would then take up a detailed discussion on what the learners have written about themselves. From the points that emerge, the teacher should arrive at the notion of psychological attributes such as learning, intelligence, perception, thinking etc., that are present in all persons in different degrees and forms of representation. He/she can then introduce the concept of individual differences and link these differences to the concepts of variation and diversity. This will help the learners to build perspective about the nature of individual differences and appreciate diversity.

Synthesis: Every learner needs to recognise that each one of them is unique. The variations and distinctiveness among their characteristics and behaviour patterns are what are known as individual differences. Individual differences are usually studied under the broad categories of intelligence, aptitude, interest, personality, and values.

ACTIVITY 2: INTRODUCING INTELLIGENCE AND PSYCHOMETRICS

Route: The teacher would ask the learners to answer the following questions:

1. Who is the most intelligent person according to you and why?
2. Why do you think that a particular person is intelligent?

The task may be done through verbal discussion or by requesting learners to write their responses. The teacher should encourage learners to think and come up with varied responses. In their responses to the first question, learners may indicate that someone with high scores is intelligent or someone who is quick witted is intelligent and so forth. The teacher must probe further with the help of following questions:

1. Do you think an intelligent person performs better on different kinds of tasks?
2. Do you think that an intelligent person is able to solve everyday problems in a better way?
3. Do you think that an intelligent person is creative?

The first question can help in discussing what learners consider the characteristics of an intelligent person to be. The teacher can share the historical story of how Alfred Binet, in France, was entrusted with the task of segregating intellectually superior children from slow learners. He constructed the first intelligence test based on the premise that intelligence is one set of similar abilities which can be used to solve any problem which was called general mental ability. His theory was countered by Charles Spearman's proposition that intelligence has some general factors as well as some specific factors.

The second question must lead to how psychometric tests try to measure intelligence. Most students may report that according to them the most intelligent person is decided on the basis of scores in exams or some other performance. Then the teacher can prompt them to think about how tests in Psychology have developed. The learner's imagination can be helpful in making them understand what a psychometric test is after this task.

Synthesis: After the discussion, the teacher can introduce learners to the formal definition of intelligence. At this stage the teacher must discuss with learners, the entire evolutionary journey of defining and measuring intelligence. This may be done through narrating the historical landmarks that mark the conceptualisation of intelligence. For instance, Binet first defined intelligence as an ability to judge, reason and understand well. Wechsler modified it by stating that it is a global and aggregate capacity to think rationally, act purposefully and to deal effectively with one's environment. However, at present, psychologists, like Howard Gardner and Sternberg, consider that an intelligent person not only adapts to his environment, but is also capable of modifying or changing it. The teacher at this stage can also highlight the two broad approaches, under which the theories of intelligence are studied, namely, psychometric approaches and information processing approaches. The role of culture and context can also be highlighted. The important learnings from the classes should be that there are varied ways of defining and measuring intelligence and they all co-exist. Further IQ is only a measure of intelligence and not a substitute term for it. The difference between intelligence, academic performance and achievement should also be highlighted.

ACTIVITY 3: HOWARD GARDNER'S THEORY OF MULTIPLE INTELLIGENCE

Route: Students will be given the following activity.

Imagine that you are the Principal of a leading private school. You receive applications from six students for admission to class 7. You can select only one of them since you have a single vacancy. You don't want to judge the students through a test. You have thus invited parents to submit applications describing their child. After reading the six case descriptions, you have to make your decision. Whom will you select and why?

Case 1: *Reyan is a twelve-year-old boy who is visually challenged. He was born blind. His parents initially placed him in a blind school where he learnt braille. He enjoyed listening to music and insisted that he wanted to play some instrument. His parents bought him a casio. He started playing it on his own. His parents saw his eagerness to learn and enrolled him in a music school. He is now not only adept in playing both the guitar and piano, but is a wonderful singer too. He can now navigate his way through a very crowded place, dress himself, arrange his almirah and read with the help of braille. He mingles with people easily and is very good at making friends. His parents want him to be in a regular school.*

Case 2: *Aradhana is a twelve-year-old girl who is very good in studies. She reads on her own the entire day and always secures first position in her class. However, she is unable to communicate with other children and prefers to stay aloof. She feels that talking to people is a waste of time. When others try to make friends with her, she snaps at them and later feels guilty about her actions. She has no friends. But everyone in class respects her ability to top the class consistently.*

Case 3: *Sameer is a twelve-year-old boy, who belongs to a low socio economic group family. His father is a rickshaw puller and mother is a domestic help. He goes to a nearby school. Sameer gets additional help in studies from the lady who has employed his mother. He works part time with a vegetable vendor and impresses him with his ability to sell vegetables. He calculates the amount of money to be paid by a customer in a fraction of a second. He is able to remember the name and house number of any person who visits him even once. Further, despite the fact that he does not get much time to study because he also helps his mother with domestic chores and takes care of his younger siblings, he always completes his school work. He also manages to read some extra books, which his mother's employer gives him. Now he wants to study further and aspires to be in a good school.*

Case 4: *Ruchira is a twelve-year-old girl who is very fond of reading and writing. She does not score high marks on scholastic tests but has a great flair for language. Since the age of nine, she has been composing poems. Recently she has written a few short stories, which got published in a magazine. She is a voracious reader and aspires to be a writer, someday. She writes plays for her class and helps in theatre activities too. She has won accolades for her debating skills as well.*

Case 5: *Aman is a thirteen-year-old boy, and hails from Meghalaya. He is a budding footballer. His scholastic performance is average but he is a very good athlete. He has been playing varied sports since he was seven years old. He is self-motivated and practices for hours on his own. Even though his family could not afford his sports training, he managed to finance it on his own by doing small errands. He now wants to move out of his home-town and study in a school that can nurture his potential.*

Case 6: *Shagufta is eleven years old. She feels very concerned about preservation of the environment and pursues this with great zeal and passion. She designed an awareness campaign in her school on saving the environment and minimising the role of plastic in everyday life. She writes articles on various environmental issues, such as the harmful effect of burning crackers on Diwali and during the wedding season which she publishes in children's magazines and her own school magazine. Since the age of nine, she has been planting ten trees, every year, on her birthday. She has recently joined an NGO that works towards saving the environment. She also insisted that her parents make some space for plants in their home. In her spare time, she takes care of the plants.*

Based on these six case vignettes, the teacher must engage learners in an open-ended discussion and prompt the learners to think with the help of the following questions:

1. Who would you select among them and why?
2. Why would you not select others?
3. Do you think all of us in this class are similar?
4. How are we different from one another?
5. What you understand by the term intelligence?

There is a deliberate attempt to introduce case vignettes of learners from diverse backgrounds, so that the learners can appreciate that intelligence cuts across social class and gender.

Synthesis: The teacher should be able to discuss the following concepts with the help of this activity:

- *Individual differences*: This refers to the distinctness and variations among people's characteristics and behaviour patterns. People vary with respect to their intelligence, aptitude, interests, values and personality.

- *Intelligence*: The teacher should dispel the myth that intelligence is equated with scholastic achievement. The learners can be prompted to think that intelligence also encompasses other facets such as capacity to understand the world, think rationally, and deal effectively with challenges.
- Intelligence is contextual.

Howard Gardner's theory of multiple intelligences also supports this. Each case indicates a different type of intelligence such as linguistic intelligence, logico-mathematical intelligence, musical intelligence, etc.

ACTIVITY 4: MULTIPLE INTELLIGENCES

Route: The teacher would ask learners to identify a famous personality from any walk of life, like, literature, dance, music, science, and sports and then ask learners to discuss who amongst these personalities, in their view, typifies an intelligent person.

The teacher can take discussion forward by asking learners to identify what makes these people famous. They can also be encouraged to find out what their personal characteristics are that have helped them become frontrunners in their respective professions. They can further be asked to discuss whether we can call each one of them intelligent in their own right, and why.

Synthesis: The teacher can discuss Howard Gardner's theory of multiple intelligences. Each case indicates a different type of intelligence such as linguistic intelligence, logico mathematical intelligence, musical intelligence, etc.

ACTIVITY 5: DEBATES RELATED TO INTELLIGENCE

Route: The teacher can divide the class in four groups and give each group, one of the following statements to discuss:

(a) People are born intelligent.
(b) People born in certain regions of the world are more intelligent.
(c) Boys are more intelligent than girls.
(d) People who go to school are more intelligent than those who have never been to school.

Each group has to note down points both in favour of and against the topic. Then the discussion points will be shared with the rest of the class.

Synthesis: In the end, the teacher can share studies, which indicate that intelligence has a genetic component. In Psychology, studies of fraternal and identical twins are used as an effective method to determine the effect of genes. On the other hand, gender and race differences in intelligence are now considered as myths, whereas, the initial research findings reported that men are more intelligent as compared to women and on the same lines, whites were tested to be more intelligent than blacks in America. Later it was found that these results were biased because the tests designed to measure intelligence were standardised on a certain group of people and used on some other groups. Thus, these tests were culturally biased and did not take into account cultural variation. This was one of the important reasons why some sections of society such as blacks and women were seen as less intelligent. Secondly, the tests only confirmed the social bias that was prevalent at that point. It would be a good idea to discuss the issues and concerns related to the development and use of intelligence tests in Psychology.

ACTIVITY 6: STERNBERG'S TRIARCHIC THEORY OF INTELLIGENCE

Route

Step 1: The teacher will show an audio-video presentation to the learners, like Mercury, 2016. After the presentation, learners will be asked to read the following job descriptions. They would be asked to identify the type of intelligence that will be required in these cases:

Case 1: An international firm specialises in bringing out reports on economic status of different countries. They are looking for a financial analyst who can lead a team of twenty people to research markets and present reports. The person should be able to formulate plans to address economic problems related to production and distribution of goods and services. The person should be adept at analysing economic and statistical data and come out with forecasts to recommend action.

Or

An agency which conducts exit polls is looking for a Psephologist, who can head a team of people for the upcoming state elections. He/She has to oversee the sampling, tools for data collection and also the training of the data collection team. Finally, he/she has to analyse the data and bring out a report at the time of polling.

Case 2: ONM is an advertisement agency. They are looking for a young copywriter who can think out of the box. They want someone to work on the fast moving consumer good (FMCG) sector and come up with ideas which attract the common man.

Case 3: A software development firm is looking for a marketing executive. He/she should have an understanding of market trends and also possess effective communication skills. This person should be able to manage production of marketing material, organise events, seminars, communicate with the larger audience and manage customer relationships. The person should also be quick in identifying crises situation and manage the expectations of the customers.

Or

A company launching a new line of cosmetics is looking for sales executives who can tap the existing customers as well as attract potential customers. The person should be young, smart, impressive and quick witted. He/she should have negotiating skill and the ability to convince people. The person will be required to make phone calls and communicate via emails. They should be good listeners so that they can cater to the customers according to their requirement.

The teacher can ask the learners to write 4-5 points on why they think that a particular type of job requires a person with either componential, experiential and contextual intelligence. The first type of profile will require someone with high componential intelligence because the person should have analytical ability. He/she should be efficient in all three components of this type of intelligence which includes the ability to understand new information, plan and organise the thinking process and perform.

Step 2: To know what learners have understood about the three types of intelligence the teacher can ask them to make a table in which they identify certain job profiles, which will be most appropriate for the people with these types of intelligence. They must also give reasons why certain jobs would be more appropriate for them and why others would not be so appropriate:

	Job profiles which are appropriate	Job profiles which are inappropriate	Areas of overlap
Componential intelligence			
Experiential intelligence			
Contextual intelligence			

Synthesis: Robert Sternberg defined intelligence as an ability to adapt, shape, and select the environment to accomplish one's goals and those of society and culture. He categorised intelligence into three different types which include componential, experiential, and contextual. With the help of the obtained responses, the theory can then be discussed.

Even if showing the film is not possible, the situational vignettes can be used to build up the discussion.

ACTIVITY 7: EMOTIONAL INTELLIGENCE

Route: The teacher would begin the class by asking learners a set of questions, which are related to their feelings and their reactions to emotional situations. Then three sets of tasks would be taken up: A, B and C.

Part A: The teacher will divide the class into groups of 5-6 learners each. They will be asked to collect as many photographs as possible of people showing different emotions. These photographs would then be shown in the class, the emotions portrayed within them would be identified and an exhaustive list of emotions would be prepared. The teacher can then draw from the list and discuss basic emotions and mixed emotions.

Part B: Learners will be asked to respond to the following questions:

- What do you do if you are upset?
- What are your immediate thoughts when you see a road accident?
- What do you do when you see that your close friend is happy and wants to celebrate?
- What do you do when you see that your mother is angry?

Part C: Learners will be asked to share their views about the following:

- How do you respond when you are ill-treated by someone?
- Think of the time when you misbehaved with someone. Why did you behave like that? Given a choice, how would you act if the same conditions are repeated?

The teacher should allow the learners to think and write answers to these questions.

Synthesis: Depending on the responses of the learners, the teacher can direct the attention of the learners to the concept of emotional intelligence. Emotional intelligence is the ability to monitor one's own emotions as well as the emotions of others. It also encompasses the ability to discriminate amongst the various emotions that one experiences and have the ability to guide one's thinking as well as actions in relation to them, in a more meaningful way. These questions will provide the learners, an opportunity to reflect on some of their actions and think of modifying them in future.

ACTIVITY 8: CULTURE AND INTELLIGENCE

Route: The learners can be asked to make a set of questions that probe the concept of intelligence, to be asked to 3 people from different cultural contexts and in their native languages. They can also seek responses to these questions from people belonging to different socio economic backgrounds. They should be careful to note the words that are used for 'intelligence' and 'intelligent person' in the different languages. The questions may be from among the following:

- Who is an intelligent person?
- Do you remember any story that you heard in your childhood, which described an intelligent act or an intelligent person?

- Are there any prototypes/ reference points of an intelligent person for you?

Responses to these questions will indicate how culture influences the notion of intelligence. Learners may come across words such as, *'samajhdar'*, *'buddhiman'* especially in Hindi speaking areas. If learners bring such terms to class, the teacher should discuss their meaning and relate them to how *'buddhi'* is defined in that specific context. It would be of value if the exact meaning of these terms is discussed in class. Some of these words may not have exact counterparts in the English language, but the general ideas within them can be discussed.

References to the literature that the respondents use to explain intelligence and other related ideas must be highlighted and discussed by the teacher in the class. If desired, references may be made to the *Panchatantra* or the stories of *Vikram Betaal*. Alternatively, the teacher can also select folklores from any culture that depict the notion of an intelligent person.

Synthesis: The Sanskrit word *'buddhi'* is a more complex term than intelligence. J.P. Das has described it in detail as a more pervasive concept than intelligence. The concept of *'buddhi'* includes affective as well as cognitive components. The intent here is to enable learners to appreciate the local or contextually rooted psychological ideas.

Recent Trends

Five Minds for the Future: Howard Gardner, an acclaimed Professor of Education and Cognition, has revolutionized the understanding about individual differences. His theory on multiple intelligences had a deep impact on the discourse of education and how intelligence is conceptualized. His recent work 'Five Minds of the Future' transcends the individual to enter into a realm where he tries to exemplify the kinds of mind that we should nurture for the future. Gardner carefully describes these five minds in his framework that according to him form the bedrock for survival in future; these include the disciplined mind, the synthesizing mind, the creating mind, the respectful mind and the ethical mind. His carefully synthesized book provides an example of how one can move towards synthesizing knowledge from several disciplines in order to create a more meaningful whole. Instead of arranging the five minds in a hierarchy, Gardner conceptualizes the five minds in an epigenetic mode.

Gardner describes that a *disciplined mind is a result of several years of training the mind to think in a certain way about the world.* A disciplined mind is the key to professional success. He clearly distinguishes between individuals who have a lot of factual knowledge and those who have learnt to think in a disciplined way. A psychologist has a discrete way of approaching a problem from that of a physician, a historian and a sociologist. Closely related to the disciplined mind, yet stretching its limit is the synthesizing mind. Gardner (2010, p.46) defines a synthesizing mind as 'the ability to knit together information from disparate sources into a coherent whole'. Citing several examples, including that of the 'Bible,' Gardner emphasizes that synthesizing all the accumulated knowledge is a natural propensity of the human mind. Human beings crave for coherence and integration. Syntheses aids in creating a larger picture and look beyond details. The third type of mind that Gardner describes is the creative mind. He states that creativity is not just an inborn gift that only some have received. Rather, it can be inculcated. This model explains creativity as the product of interaction of an individual with his cultural domain and the social field. The cultural domain is his work place and the social domain is the larger community that either endorses or rejects a work that is deemed creative. Another acid test of creativity is the impact that it has had in its relevant area.

Gardner deftly weaves together the issue of respect and ethics along with the three types of minds. Making groups and differentiating one's own group from another is almost instinctual to human beings. A simple suggestion by Gardner is that these differences should be accepted and we must inculcate respect for the other in our young ones. Finally, the ethical mind steps back from the daily rigmarole and contemplates about the nature of work he is doing, as well as about the nature of society he dwells in. This contemplation includes deliberation on one's own responsibilities and commitments. The ethical mind is more abstract in comparison to direct inculcation of respect and tolerance for those who are around.

Web-links and Readings

Ang, S., & Dyne, L. Van. (2015). *Handbook of Cultural Intelligence*. London: Routledge. Retrieved from https://books.google.com/books?id=mKBsBgAAQBAJ&pgis=1

Brody, N. (2013). *Intelligence*. California: Academic Press.

Gardner, H. (2010). *Five Minds for the Future*. Boston: Harvard Business School Press.

Mercury, K. (2016, February 6). *Sternberg's Triarchic Theory, simplified*. Retrieved March 30, 2016, from YouTube: https://www.youtube.com/watch?v=1_7YDHtTURI

Plucker, J., & Esping, A. (2013). *Intelligence 101* (Vol. 12). New York: Springer Publishing Company. Retrieved from https://books.google.com/books?id=VRjdAQAAQBAJ&pgis=1

Attitudes, Social Cognition and Pro-Social Behaviour*

Introduction

Studying Social Psychology is quite often an interesting and engaging experience for the learners. After studying the basis of human behaviour and its principles through topics like learning, thinking, memory, motivation, personality, research methods etc. in their introductory course, the learners get an opportunity to apply this knowledge, in Social Psychology, to understand and predict the patterns of behaviour in the social world. Social Psychology is also exciting because the subject matter helps learners understand the behaviour of people in social settings. They also get some insights into their own attitudes, behaviour and biases. As a result, they may feel that finally, they are able to apply what they have learnt so far. Topics such as impression formation, persuasion, attitudes, pro-social behaviour appear easy to comprehend and remember, as with little attention, learners see these phenomena unfolding in their day to day life.

For teachers, this excitement of learners about the area is positive as they are able to channelize their energies in learning through different methods. But, the perception of the learners that the topics are relatively easy- which is mostly misplaced- can act as an impediment to learning. The challenge for the teacher, therefore, is to sustain the excitement of learners for hands-on learning and simultaneously, make sure that learners adequately master the theories and research that nourishes the application of these concepts. While some of the classical researches, related to

---

* Anshu Chaudhary

the topics can be introduced through activities and field experiments, the teacher should also encourage learners to read about the classical studies and watch videos about them that are readily available on internet. They can also be encouraged to self-administer some offline/ online psychological tests/measures for enhanced self-awareness. These activities will also help learners appreciate the vast research base that informs the practice of Social Psychology as a field and differentiates its knowledge from common-sense or folk wisdom.

Since, the topics like attitude change, persuasion, impression formation etc. have applications in marketing, advertising, politics, social work, and mass media etc., the teacher should encourage learners to analyse advertisements, political campaigns, and social campaigns to uncover the psychological strategies employed by them. Since, prejudice, discrimination, stereotyping, and bystander's effect are significant social problems, learners should be encouraged to analyse newspaper reports, films, advertisements, and public policies that promote, sustain, and challenge these problems. Learners can also be given mini-assignments or projects to bring about public awareness on these issues. Even if the impact is minor, such assignments will help them to see themselves as agents of change. These activities and assignments facilitate their becoming informed consumers, sensitive viewers and critical citizens in the long run.

The purpose of this unit is to equip the teacher with such reference group exercises, projects and assignments so that the basic topics of Social Psychology can be introduced through interactive pedagogy and creative learning resources.

ACTIVITY 1: NATURE OF ATTITUDE: ABC MODEL OF ATTITUDE

Route: The teacher will discuss the definition, components, and features of the ABC model of attitude. Alternatively, a handout may also be provided to the learners about the ABC model of attitude. Then, with the help of the learners in the classroom, a list of probable topics, which can be used as the context to study attitudes of people, will be generated. This list could include topics such as global warming, mental disorders, social networking, religion, women's empowerment, euthanasia, and capital punishment. Each learner would be free to select a topic of his/her choice from this list for the assignment.

Learners would be required to discuss with a friend/ family member/ neighbour about their chosen topic to understand their attitude. They may write down the significant statements that the respondents make during this discussion. In order to facilitate this, a recording of the discussion can be made with the permission of the participant.

Based on the discussion, the learners will be required to complete the following table and discuss with the teacher:

Statements reflecting Attitudes	Component of attitude reflected in the statement (Put a tick mark for the relevant component/s)		
	Affective	Behavioural	Cognitive
Overall assessment of the attitude based on the following features:			
Valence (Positive/Negative)			
Extremeness			
Simplicity/Complexity			
Centrality			

Synthesis: The objective of this assignment is to refine learners' understanding of the various components and features of attitude. The activity is aimed at helping them realize that attitudes held by people can be discerned from the statements they make in their day to day conversations. After the assignment, in the next class, the teacher would encourage learners to share their experiences of working on this assignment and the challenges they encountered (such as social desirability, faking etc. on part of the participants). This discussion can be concluded by referring to the challenges that psychologists face while studying a topic like attitude.

Alternatively

Route: The teacher may ask learners to discuss in class any one issue on which people typically express their opinion readily such as global warming, mental disorders, social networking, religion, women's empowerment, euthanasia, capital punishment etc. The statements generated in this discussion may be recorded on the blackboard by the teacher in a tabular form as follows:

Statements reflecting Attitudes	**Component of attitude reflected in the statement (Put a tick mark for the relevant component/s)**		
	Affective	Behavioural	Cognitive

Synthesis: After the statements are recorded in the table, the teacher can discuss the definition and components of the attitude and help learners see that the statements they collectively shared so far are attitude statements. The learners can also identify the three components of attitudes in the recorded statements. This can be followed by the teacher introducing terms associated with attitudes like valence, extremeness, centrality and complexity. The meaning of these terms can be explained in reference to the generated statements.

ACTIVITY 2: ATTITUDE-BEHAVIOUR RELATIONSHIP AND COGNITIVE DISSONANCE

Route: This exercise is adapted from a classroom activity described by Carkenord & Bullington (1993). The purpose of this exercise is twofold. First, it helps learners to appreciate that the link between attitude and behaviour is a complex one; second, it is likely to make learners' experience and thus, better understand the phenomenon of cognitive dissonance.

For this activity, the teacher should draw a five point Likert scale as follows on the blackboard:

1	2	3	4	5
Strongly Disagree	Disagree	Neutral	Agree	Strongly Agree

Then, he/she will read the following statements aloud to learners and ask them to rate these statements as per the scale above on a blank sheet of paper:

a. Illiteracy is a serious problem that needs attention of the youth.
b. Public awareness and political participation is a must for healthy democracy.
c. Global warming is a serious problem which is likely to endanger our existence on the planet.
d. Exercising and healthy diet should be a part of everyone's lifestyle.
e. Plastic pollution can be life threatening for both animals and humans.

Learners will then be asked to turn the sheet and respond to the following questions as 'Yes' or 'No':

a. Do you frequently participate in literacy programmes run by the school, neighbourhood or NGOs?
b. Do you follow the political developments and debates regularly on television and in the newspapers?
c. Do you prefer using public transport over personal vehicles?
d. Do you exercise regularly and avoid junk food?
e. Do you accept groceries, fruits and vegetables from vendors in plastic carry bags?

After completing this, learners will be asked to compare their responses on both sides of the sheet. If they have agreed or have strongly agreed to the attitude statements, then, the discussion should focus on whether they also engage in behavioural actions in coherence with the attitude statements.

Synthesis: The exercise demonstrates that while most learners may agree with the attitude statements, very few actually translate their beliefs into actions. This observation would follow up with a discussion on complexity of attitude-behaviour link with the above stated examples. Learners can be asked to reflect and respond to the following questions:

- Why do you think there is a discrepancy between your attitude and behaviour?
- How do you feel about this discrepancy?
- Under what conditions does your attitude accurately predict your behaviour?

- Are you going to resolve this inconsistency between your attitude and behaviour? If yes, then describe what are you going to do about it?

This discussion would be followed by an introduction to the theory of 'Cognitive Dissonance'. Festinger and Carlsmith's (1959) classic 20$ study on turning pegs can also be read out in the class as further demonstration. With the help of examples, the discussion would conclude on the strategies that people undertake to restore cognitive consistency.

ACTIVITY 3: ATTITUDE CHANGE AND PERSUASION

Route: After the learners have been familiarized with the theories of attitude change and principles of persuasion, the following activity may be planned for the next two consecutive classes.

The teacher would divide the class in groups of 7-8 learners each and assign them a socially relevant issue on which campaigns can be developed, such as Save the Girl Child, Organ Donation, Say No to Plastic Waste etc. Each group will be assigned a different topic.

After the selection of the topic, the teacher would provide the following instructions:

> *"For the next half an hour/one hour, you all will be working along with your team members to develop a campaign on the social issue that you have been assigned. The purpose of the campaign is to create awareness around the issue in focus, highlight the behavioural change required on the part of the learners to make a difference and give compelling arguments to convince them to bring about this change. After the campaign is designed, your group will be presenting the campaign to the rest of the class who will be giving you feedback on the persuasiveness of the campaign. Each group will be given 10 minutes for the presentation. Since, this is an activity based on attitude change and persuasion, in order to develop a successful campaign, remember to use insights from the theories of attitude change, principles of persuasion and factors affecting attitude change. In case you have any questions or problems, please feel free to discuss the same with me."*

While the learners are engaged in developing the campaigns, the teacher would meet each group briefly to discuss the direction of their efforts and help them appropriately, if necessary. The teacher would have to ensure that learners are taking into consideration the concepts studied in the class on attitude change for developing the campaign, as this is the key objective of introducing this activity.

Before the groups make their presentation, the learners would be asked to be attentive and note down their observations on the content, presentation and overall effectiveness of the campaign. They would also be asked to note down the most appealing aspects of each of the campaigns for subsequent discussions.

Each group will be given about 10 minutes for presentation. At the end of the presentation, the teacher can facilitate a feedback session.

Synthesis: After the conclusion of the activity, the teacher would help learners to analyse the effectiveness of each of the campaigns in terms of the attitude change strategies adopted in designing them and the style of presentation. The learners who developed the campaign would also be encouraged to reflect and share the important aspects and features of their campaigns. The issues related to congruence/ incongruence of change, message characteristics- credibility and attractiveness, nature of appeal-emotional or rational, motive activated, mode of presentation, target characteristics- intelligence, self-esteem, openness etc. would be discussed with the help of observations made by learners about the different campaigns.

ACTIVITY 4: ADVERTISING AND PERSUASION

Route: Before the class, the teacher would need to identify several interesting examples of advertisements from television, newspapers, magazines, or internet. These advertisements may depict a variety of products, such as cosmetics, health drinks, eatables, personal hygiene products, automobiles, and insurance. The teacher may also arrange plenty of magazines for the class from the library or may also request learners in advance to bring some from home.

In the first phase of the activity, the teacher would show some of the pre-selected print or video advertisements to the learners with the help of a projector or a display board. Display of each advertisement will be followed by a class-discussion on the following questions:

- What is the topic of the advertisement?

- To which component/s of attitude does the advertisement appeal?
- What is the target group of the advertisement? What are the characteristics of the target group?
- Does the advertisement have rational appeal or emotional appeal or both? How does this influence the overall effectiveness of the advertisement?
- What is the source of information in the advertisement? Is the source credible or attractive? How does this influence the overall effectiveness of the advertisement?
- Do you think the advertisement is effective? Give reasons.

After viewing and discussing 3-4 advertisements, learners will get an idea about how to analyse advertisements in terms of their persuasiveness. This phase is likely to take 15-20 minutes.

In the second phase of the activity, the learners would be asked to practice their newly acquired understanding of advertisements in groups. So, depending upon the class-size, the teacher would divide the whole class into 4-6 groups, provide 5-6 magazines to each group, and instruct them as follows:

In front of you all there are some interesting magazines. There are variety of advertisements in these magazines which you would be paying close attention to in next 10-15 minutes. After flipping through these advertisements, each group would select two interesting, yet different advertisements for further analysis as follows:

- Which product is being advertised and what is the target group?
- What are the strategies of persuasion used in the advertisement?
- How effective is the advertisement?
- What can be additionally done to improve its effectiveness?

Each group will get 2-3 minutes to present their analysis.

Synthesis: With the help of concrete examples of advertisements, the teacher would help learners in identifying the link between attitudes and advertising, i.e. the way media influences formation and change of attitudes. Through analysis and discussion, the teacher should help learners critically analyse the various strategies and techniques of attitude change that advertisers adopt to bring about persuasion. After this exercise, learners will be able to appreciate the application of social psychology in the fields of advertising and marketing.

ACTIVITY 5: STEREOTYPES, PREJUDICES, AND DISCRIMINATION

Route: The objective of the activity is to introduce the concepts of stereotypes and prejudices with the help of examples from our associations of prevalent social groups. It requires learners to associate spontaneously with the social groups so that the stereotypical images are elicited. Hence, it could be used as an introductory activity to the topic. The learners should not be briefed that this is an activity on stereotypes, prejudices and discrimination.

For this activity, the teacher would need to prepare flash cards in advance. Each of these cards would feature a social group prone to stereotypes with which the learners are going to associate. The teacher can select social groups that are most relevant to the learners. The number of cards prepared should be as per the class size. Cards may be cut from a sheet prepared as follows:

Politician 1.	Model 1.	Rock Band Member 1.
Resident of North-east India 1.	Muslim Boy 1.	Christian Girl 1.
NRI 1.	Grandmother 1.	Soldier 1.
Punjabi 1.	Single Parent 1.	People who wear glasses 1.
Villager 1.	South Indian 1.	Wheelchair User 1.

The teacher would divide the learners in pairs and randomly distribute the cards to them. Each pair would get one card. They will then be instructed to work together and come up with three characteristics that people associate with the person mentioned on their card. They would be asked to respond quickly so that their spontaneous associations are elicited.

Once these characteristics are recorded, the teacher would reconvene the pairs and let the class play a small guessing game.

Each pair would be asked to describe their card to the rest of the class in terms of the characteristics that they have listed. They may begin like, *'Some people might believe that this person is...'* and let the rest of the class guess the card.

At this point, the learners are likely to come up with their implicit stereotypes through these statements. The teacher should also categorize each of these cards as positive or negative associations on the black board as per the feedback from learners.

Picking up examples from the stereotypical description of social groups by learners, the teacher would discuss the following:

- Why do we describe certain social groups in certain ways? (Discuss the concept of schemas and stereotypes.)
- Is this generalization helpful? (Discuss the negative effects of stereotyping and labelling.)
- How do we form these images? (Discuss the influence of media-TV, films, ads, news, etc.)
- Are there any exceptions to these stereotypical descriptions? Can you give examples? (Probe: Are all grandmothers old? Are all villagers uneducated? Are all people who wear glasses intelligent?)
- Why do we attribute negative characteristics to certain groups while positive characteristics to others? (Introduce the concept of prejudices and discrimination.)
- Will knowing someone personally make a difference?

Synthesis: The above activity can be further extended to include a discussion on 'social identities' and how they are formed. The propositions of social identity theory can be discussed along with the 'in-group' and 'out-group' biases with examples. In order to make learners see the negative side of these biases, the teacher can situate the discussion in the problem of communal violence and intolerance by presenting examples from real incidents of communal violence or riots.

ACTIVITY 6: GENDER STEREOTYPES IN ADVERTISEMENTS

Route: The objective of this activity is to sensitize learners to the role of media, particularly, advertisements in promoting gender stereotypes in our society. It is a documentary screening activity where the teacher can screen 'Killing us softly' by Jean Kilbourne. Using advertisements as data, this documentary presents a compelling research based analysis of the image of women as portrayed in the advertisements. This documentary was first released in the year 1979 and has been revised and updated three times in 1987, 1999 and 2010. Any of these versions can be screened for this activity. There is also a book and an article on the same theme by Kilbourne (1993;1994).

After the screening, a follow up brainstorming session can be facilitated by the teacher where learners would be encouraged to reflect on the implicit and explicit gender stereotypical images and values that they receive from the mass-media. The learners should also be made to reflect on the reasons for this kind of portrayal of men and women in media.

The teacher should expand the discussion to include the portrayal of the other minority groups such as persons with disability, mental illness, racial and ethnic minorities, etc.

Synthesis: Through this activity, the teacher has an opportunity to turn learners into critical consumers of media rather than as passive recipients of the stereotypical images. After this activity, the learners can also be given a follow up home assignment where they can be asked to identify, analyse and prepare a short report on any two advertisements, one that promotes gender stereotypes and one that challenges the gender stereotypes.

ACTIVITY 7: ATTRIBUTION OF RESPONSIBILITY

Route: This exercise has been adapted from a class-room activity presented by Lucas (2008, p. 259). It will help learners understand the process of internal and external attribution with the help of a short story.

The teacher would read out the following story aloud in the class as learners read it along, from their handouts or through projection:

As he left the palace for a hunting expedition, the jealous king warned his beautiful queen, "Do not step out of the palace while I am away, or you will be punished severely upon my return." But as the hours passed, the young queen grew sad and restless. So, despite the king's warning, she decided to visit her lover in the outskirts of the town nearby.

The palace was situated on an island on a wide, fast-flowing river. A drawbridge connected the palace to the mainland at the narrowest point in the river. "Surely the king will not return before dawn," she thought to herself and ordered gatekeepers to lower the drawbridge. She instructed them to leave it down until she returned. After spending time with her lover, in the evening when the queen returned, she found the drawbridge blocked by the general with sword in his hands. "Do not try to cross this bridge or I will have to kill you as per the order of the king," he cried.

Fearing for her life, the queen returned to her lover to ask for help. The lover refused the help saying that "our relationship is only a romantic one, I cannot risk my life for you." The queen came back to the river and approached a boatman. She explained her plight to him and asked him to take her across the river. The boatman demanded a hefty sum for the ride as after all, he was risking the wrath of the king. "But I have no money with me!" the queen cried. "That's unfortunate! No money, no ride," the boatman refused her bluntly. As her final resort, the queen ran to her childhood friend who lived nearby. Explaining her desperation to the friend, she begged her for money. To this her friend said, "If you had obeyed the king, all this would not have happened. I will not give you money." With dawn approaching and her last resource exhausted, the queen returned to the bridge in desperation. As she tried crossing the bridge, she was slain by the general.

The teacher would instruct learners to arrange in rank order, the six characters (king, queen, lover, general, boatman and friend) in terms of their responsibility for the queen's death.

Then, one by one, each character can be selected and learners who have selected that character as most responsible for the queen's death can be called upon to explain the reasons for their choice. Most likely, the learners would blame the queen for her own death i.e. an internal attribution- "she was bad and she got what she deserved."

At this point, the teacher can raise the question that "If the queen was visiting her ailing mother whom the king forbade her from visiting, who would be most responsible for her death?" After this change in scenario, many learners may revise their position and blame the king for the queen's death, which is an external attribution. The teacher can probe learners' views on the reasons for change of attribution and help them to see that despite the behaviour being the same, the intent shapes the attributions.

The teacher can consider making the two versions of the same story, one with the lover and the other with the ailing mother. These two different versions then can be circulated in the class to see how the story shapes the internal and external attribution of the learners.

Synthesis: After the activity, the teacher can also help learners reflect critically on their choice of blaming the queen for her death, which is quite similar to the general trend of 'blaming the victim' for his/her condition. The learners should understand how social roles tend to be taken for granted and anyone who transgresses the defined boundaries, is held responsible for the consequences. For e.g., the queen was blamed for overstepping her role as a virtuous wife but the king and general were not blamed for their jealousy and violence as it was consistent with their role.

The learners should also be able to reflect on how these attribution biases and blind acceptance of social roles lead to a rape victim being blamed for her fate or a poor boy being held responsible for his condition.

ACTIVITY 8: BIASES IN ATTRIBUTION

The purpose of these activities is to demonstrate attributional biases with the help of situational examples.

1. Actor/Observer Effect and Fundamental Attributional Error

Route: The teacher would ask learners to think of a specific occasion when someone in a social situation, such as a party or wedding, was rude to them and the reasons thereof. Most of the learners are going to attribute misbehaviour to dispositional factors rather than the situational factors. The teacher would record the ratio approximately.

Next, the teacher would ask learners to think of a similar social situation where they were rude to someone else. They should also respond on why they think they were rude to the other person. In this case, most of the attributions will be situational rather than dispositional. Again, the teacher would roughly record the ratio of responses.

The difference in the ratio on the above two occasions are going to clearly establish the actor/observer effect and will also give ample evidence for fundamental attribution bias.

2. Self-Serving Bias

Route: The teacher would ask learners to think of something at which they succeeded and at which they failed in the recent past and make a note of it. They would also be told to record the reasons for their success and failure, respectively.

The teacher would ask the learners to share their responses which would be recorded on the blackboard as follows:

Dimensions	Reasons for:	
	Success	Failure
Internal		
External		
Stable		
Unstable		
Controllable		
Uncontrollable		

As predicted by models of attribution, the learners are likely to attribute their success to the Internal/ Stable/ Controllable factors and their failure to the External/ Unstable/ Uncontrollable factors. Apart from teaching the self-serving bias, the activity can also be employed for teaching Heider's Theory of Attribution.

Synthesis: Subsequent to this activity, the teacher should explain the different biases involved in the process of attribution. The roots of these biases should also be discussed with reference to different models and theories of attribution.

In order to promote reflection and self-awareness, as an extension activity, the learners can be asked to observe their own attributional process in everyday life for a week and record the instances where they could identify different attributional biases in a diary. These observations can be discussed in the class a week later.

ACTIVITY 9: IMPRESSION FORMATION- PRIMACY EFFECT

Route: This simple activity demonstrates the power of first impressions. According to Asch (1946), the order in which one is exposed to the different character traits about the target, influences the overall impression formation by the perceiver. This activity is designed to replicate this effect in the classroom. The activity would be carried out before introducing the concept of impression formation.

While planning for this activity, the teacher would prepare the following handouts for distribution in the class:

Handout A

You have just interviewed two candidates for the position of an assistant for the summer camp of the school. Presented below are your notes from the interview session based on which you are required to give hiring recommendations for both the candidates.				
Sonia is intelligent, kind, and loves children. She is also a skilled tennis player. She is emotional and talkative. She reported being stubborn, and somewhat sloppy. Give your recommendation for hiring her on the scale below:				
1	2	3	4	5
Definitely don't hire				Definitely hire
Varun is a natural leader. He is athletic and loves kids. He is also confident. He has an offbeat sense of dressing. He is arrogant, awkward, and impatient. Give your recommendation for hiring him on the scale below:				
1	2	3	4	5
Definitely don't hire				Definitely hire

Handout B

You have just interviewed two candidates for the position of an assistant for the summer camp of the school.

Presented below are your notes from the interview session based on which you are required to give hiring recommendations for both the candidates.

Sonia reported being stubborn, and somewhat sloppy.

She is emotional and talkative.

She is also a skilled tennis player

She is a kind woman who loves children.

She is intelligent.

Give your recommendation for hiring her on the scale below:

1	2	3	4	5
Definitely don't hire				Definitely hire

Varun is arrogant, awkward, and impatient.

He has an offbeat sense of dressing.

He is athletic and loves kids.

He is confident.

He comes across as a natural leader.

Give your recommendation for hiring him on the scale below:

1	2	3	4	5
Definitely don't hire				Definitely hire

The teacher should randomly distribute handout A to half of the learners and handout B to the other half of the learners. She will instruct the learners to quickly complete the exercise.

The handouts are identical except the order in which the traits are presented to the learners. In handout A, the positive traits are given first followed by the negative traits, while in handout B, the negative traits are given first followed by the positive ones.

The teacher should collect the handouts from the learners once they have completed the activity and review their responses. If the learners in handout A have rated both the candidates more favourably as compared to handout B, the primacy effect as proposed by Asch is replicated.

If time permits, the teacher can also calculate Sonia's and Varun's average rating on handout A and compare it with the average rating of Sonia and Varun in handout B for a clearer demonstration. The ratings in handout A will be better as compared to ratings in handout B.

Synthesis: The teacher would encourage learners to think about the effect of primacy in their day to day life and come up with examples. They would also be encouraged to apply this understanding for better impression management.

ACTIVITY 10: ROLE OF CENTRAL TRAITS IN IMPRESSION FORMATION

Route: This activity is primarily designed to help learners understand the role of 'central traits' in impression formation as proposed by Asch (1946). Thorough this activity, the learners will be able to appreciate that impression formation is a complex process, where each bit of information about a person is processed in reference to other bits of information.

For the purpose of this activity, the teacher would design two handouts to be distributed to the class as follows:

Handout A

<table>
<tr><td colspan="7">You have recently met Vaibhav and he is known to have the following set of traits:
Intelligent, resourceful, hardworking, warm, determined, practical, cautious</td></tr>
<tr><td colspan="7">What do you think will be your overall impression of Vaibhav?</td></tr>
<tr><td>1
Very unfavourable</td><td>2</td><td>3</td><td>4</td><td>5</td><td>6</td><td>7
Very Favourable</td></tr>
<tr><td colspan="7">How likable or unlikable do you think Vaibhav will be?</td></tr>
<tr><td>1
Very unfavourable</td><td>2</td><td>3</td><td>4</td><td>5</td><td>6</td><td>7
Very Favourable</td></tr>
<tr><td colspan="7">Are you likely to be friends with Vaibhav?</td></tr>
<tr><td>1
Very unlikely</td><td>2</td><td>3</td><td>4</td><td>5</td><td>6</td><td>7
Very Likely</td></tr>
</table>

Handout B

You have recently met Vaibhav and he is known to have the following set of traits: Intelligent, resourceful, hardworking, cold, determined, practical, cautious
What do you think will be your overall impression of Vaibhav? 1 2 3 4 5 6 7 Very unfavourable … Very Favourable
How likable or unlikable do you think Vaibhav will be? 1 2 3 4 5 6 7 Very unfavourable … Very Favourable
Are you likely to be friends with Vaibhav? 1 2 3 4 5 6 7 Very unlikely … Very Likely

The teacher will distribute Handout A to half the class and Handout B to the other half, randomly. The only difference in handout A and B is of the traits 'warm' and 'cold'. According to Asch's theory, this is a central trait and therefore, is likely to have a powerful influence on the overall positive or negative impression of Vaibhav in the two handouts.

After the learners have completed the handouts, the teacher should collect the handout and compare the difference in ratings on the two handouts. If time permits, the average rating of Vaibhav on three scales on each of the handouts may be calculated with the help of the learners. Most likely, the impression of Vaibhav will be more favourable on handout A than handout B. On handout A, he is also likely to be rated better on likability and friendliness.

The teacher should show both the handouts to the learners and share the findings/observations from this exercise.

Synthesis: After demonstrating the effect of central traits on impression formation, the teacher can introduce Asch's study on central traits and discuss the various factors that influence our impressions of others. The learners can also be asked to come up with traits that they think are also central traits.

ACTIVITY 11: PRO-SOCIAL BEHAVIOUR-REPLICATING THE BYSTANDER'S EFFECT

Route: The purpose of this simple field experiment is to give a first-hand experience of bystander's effect to the learners. After teaching the topic on bystander's effect and factors influencing pro-social behaviour, the teacher can ask learners to conduct a simple field experiment to observe the effect in real life scenarios. The activity is quite flexible and can be adapted by the learners. The following broad instructions can be given to the learners:

"Walk through the school corridor/library/shopping mall/local market with a pile of books/shopping bags/grocery bags. At a convenient point, where only one person is present, drop the stuff that you are carrying and pretend as if it has fallen accidentally. Now observe the following:

- *What is the bystander's reaction?*
- *Did you receive help?*
- *Did the bystander help you immediately or was there a delay?*
- *Did the bystander hesitate in extending help?*

Now, repeat the whole act at another convenient location where there is more than one person present, preferably a group of people and observe the following:

- *What is the immediate reaction of the bystanders?*
- *Did you receive help? If yes, how many people came forward for help?*
- *Did the bystanders help you immediately or was there a delay? In case there was a delay, what do you think was the reason for it?*
- *Did the bystanders hesitate in extending help?*

Record your observations and bring them to the class for discussion."

Alternatively, a field experiment can also be carried out in small groups (3-4 learners each) where one person can enact a situation requiring help from bystanders and the others can blend in the background and observe the reactions of the bystanders and note it down.

Synthesis: Through their recorded observations, the teacher would help learners discern the factors that influence bystander behaviour with special focus on the number of people present. The concepts of 'diffusion of responsibility' and 'de-individuation' should be introduced in this discussion along with their harmful effects.

Moving towards the solution, the teacher would stimulate a brainstorming session through which learners will come up with strategies to promote pro-social behaviours in public situations. Through this exercise, the learners should assume responsibility of enhancing their own helping behaviour.

As an extension of this activity, learners can be asked to select, analyse, and prepare a write-up on any two newspaper reports where a person in need received the help and where such help was not received. Learners should analyse these reports keeping in mind the factors affecting pro-social behaviour and bystander's effect.

Some Concepts for Advanced Learners

Social Identity

This encompasses "the social definition of who you are" and "who you are not", i.e. a "circle that includes us and excludes them" (Myers, 2005, p. 43). Social identity includes one's gender, ethnicity, race, religion, nationality, age, occupation, political affiliations, ideological positions etc. When we belong to a minority group, which happens to be surrounded by a majority group, we become more aware about our social identity.

Social identity guides conceptualization and evaluation of our sense of self. While forming social identity, we tend to identify with the positive attributes of the group that we are part of and dissociate with their negative qualities. At the same time, since we engage in a constant social comparison, we tend to highlight negative attributes of the groups we are not associated with and undervalue their positive qualities. This is facilitated by *'social categorization'*, our tendency to divide the social world in two distinct categories- us (in-group) and them (out-group) (Baron & Byrne, 2004, p. 222).

How do we perceive members of 'in-group'? How do we form an image for members of 'out-group'? How accurate are our perceptions of the members of the other social group? What are the biases that are at work as we engage in prejudices and discrimination? These are some significant questions that have been explored thoroughly by Turner and Tajfel in their seminal work in the form of 'Social Identity Theory' (Tajfel & Turner, 1979).

Gender Identity and Gender Roles

"Gender identity is a key part of our self-concept involving a person's identification as a male or a female" (Baron & Byrne, 2004, p. 185). A child acquires gender identity through the process of socialization at about two years of age. In every culture, socialization takes place as per the acceptable ideas of how females and males should behave. Such behavioural expectations or norms of maleness and femaleness are called as gender roles (Myers, 2005, p. 196). These gender role expectations define the image of ideal male or female in a particular culture and these images dictate our ideas of masculinity and femininity, giving rise to gender stereotypes. The extent to which a person identifies with the traditional gender roles prevalent in one's culture is termed as gender-role identification. Various psychological inventories and tests have been designed to assess gender role identification in different cultures. One such example is Bem's Sex Role Inventory.

Sexism

Sexism is prejudice based on gender, rooted in gender stereotypes. Sexism often takes the form of gender discrimination, negatively affecting the lives of both males and females. Unlike other prejudices which are marked by negative attitudes and antipathy, sexism is marked by deep ambivalence due to the intimate relationships that men and women share (Glick & Fiske, 1996). Sexism is multidimensional and encompasses two sets of attitudes: hostile and benevolent. Hostile sexism is a negative attitude towards women where it is believed that women are inferior to men, have many negative traits and should be controlled. Benevolent sexism is an attitude that suggests that women are superior to men in various ways, are indispensable to men and should be protected. Though, benevolent sexism appears positive on face value, it is not so in reality, as it promotes stereotypical gender roles and the power dynamics between both genders still operates.

Web-links and Readings

Asch, S. E. (1946). Forming impressions of personality. *The Journal of Abnormal and Social Psychology, 41*(3), 258.

Baron, R. A., & Byrne, D. (2004). *Social Psychology*. Delhi: Pearson Education.

Carkenord, D., & Bullington, J. (1993). Bringing cognitive dissonance to classroom. *Teaching of Psychology, 20*(1), 41-43.

Festinger, L., & Carlsmith, J. M. (1959). Cognitive consequences of forced compliance. *The Journal of Abnormal and Social Psychology, 58*(2), 203.

Glick, P., & Fiske, S. T. (1996). The ambivalent sexism inventory: Differentiating hostile and benevolent sexism. *Journal of Personality and Social Psychology, 70*(3), 491-512.

Kilbourne, J. (1993). Killing us softly: Gender roles in advertising. *Adolescent Medicine (Philadelphia, PA.), 4*(3), 635–650.

Kilbourne, J. (1994). Still killing us softly: Advertising and the obsession with thinness. In P. Fallon, Makatzman & S.C. Wodey (Eds.). *Feminist Perspectives on Eating Disorders*, 395–418. New York: The Guilford Press.

Lucas, S. (2008). *A Guide to Teaching Introductory Psychology.* Oxford: Blackwell Publishing.

Myers, D. G. (2005). *Social Psychology.* New York: McGraw Hill.

Tajfel, H., & Turner, J. C. (1979). An integrative theory of intergroup conflict. *The Social Psychology of Intergroup Relations, 33*(47), 74.

Social Influence and Group Processes*

Introduction

Personal experiences play a very important role in the teaching-learning process. This is reflected in the expanding discourse of 'experiential education'. Some psychology teachers have shared that teaching social influence and group processes through group activities is effective and engaging for the learners. It is effective as learners not only understand the concept theoretically, but also develop a personal insight while participating in the group and can on the basis of their experience, reflect on group dynamics. Once the learners have experienced the phenomena of social loafing, group polarization, or in-group favouritism themselves, they come face to face with their own implicit tendencies and biases. When such activities are followed up with a discussion, the learners get a space to reflect critically on their own behaviour and thus, become more self-aware. Subsequently, equipped with this experience, they are able to identify these implicit tendencies and biases in others. Considering that groups are ubiquitous and exist in every aspect of life and that we all participate and function through aggregates such as groups, this kind of an exposure for learners of Psychology is crucial.

The purpose of this unit is to delineate group based activities, which teachers can use to engage learners with the ideas like social influence and group dynamics. Since, most activities require pre-planning, the unit provides detailed guidelines to the teacher for the pre-planning, execution, and synthesis of the activities.

---

* Anshu Chaudhary

ACTIVITY 1: DEFINING GROUPS

Route: The aim of this activity is to facilitate learners to arrive at a definition of 'group' and its characteristics. It will help learners to differentiate 'group' from other aggregate terms such as teams, audience, and crowd, with the help of commonplace examples.

The teacher would prepare a sheet, prior to the class, depicting examples of aggregates from day to day life, such as:

S. No.	Aggregate	Rank	Category (G, T, A, C/?)
1	All learners in the class		
2	A mob of rioters burning public property		
3	All people who live in the same residential complex		
4	Members of a football team		
5	Spectators of a cricket match in a stadium		
6	All people who are friends with a single person on Facebook		
7	All members of a college union		
8	All members of a music band		
9	All people standing in a queue for billing in a grocery store		
10	A collective of people taking part in a demonstration on the issue of 'LGBT rights'		
11	Two friends going out for shopping together		

12	Friends travelling together for a holiday		
13	All people gathered on a sidewalk to watch a street magician		
14	All learners who are working together on this sheet at the moment		
15	Roommates		

The teacher will divide the class into smaller groups (with around 5-6 learners per group) for the purpose of this activity. Each of the groups will be assigned one sheet and be instructed as follows:

> *"As you can see, there is a sheet in front of you. This sheet depicts various examples of aggregates we are part of in our daily life. The purpose of this exercise is to place in rank order these examples, in terms of their 'groupness' i.e. the extent to which you would call them as a group. All of you are required to work together to arrange these examples from most group like (rank 1) to least group like (rank 15). Also, try to categorize each response as Group (G), Team (T), Audience (A) and Crowd (C) or put a question mark (?) if you are not sure. You should have points ready to justify the ranking. Also, try to identify and note down the defining features for each of the categories i.e. Group, Audience and Crowd for the purpose of the post activity discussion."*

After the learners complete the sheet, the teacher should give each group an opportunity to present their ranking along with the characteristics that they have listed down for each category of aggregates.

Synthesis: This activity helps learners to explicate their understanding of a 'group'. Learners will be free to question the priority assigned to these aggregates. After the brief presentation and discussion with all the groups, the teacher would summarize the discussion by helping learners differentiate between groups, teams, audience and crowd in terms of:

- Size
- Duration

- Cohesiveness
- Motive
- Roles and norms
- Identity

This discussion can be concluded by learners by formulating a working definition of 'group' which can be compared and analysed in reference to the definition given in the textbook(s).

ACTIVITY 2: SOCIAL LOAFING

Route: The purpose of this simple exercise is to demonstrate how a sense of complacency sinks in when people come together and work in a group. This exercise has been adapted from a classroom study carried out on social loafing by North, Linley, & Hargreaves (2000). Through this exercise, the impact of group size on social loafing in the context of a word building task, will be demonstrated.

This activity should be introduced before teaching social loafing in the classroom. For rolling out this activity, the teacher should divide the class randomly into four groups of three students each and four groups of eight students each. The number of groups may be increased or decreased depending upon the class size. In a mixed gender classroom, the teacher may want to ensure that the girls and boys are equally represented in all the groups. After dividing the students in the groups, the teacher may instruct them as follows:

> *"Each group is required to work together to generate as many words as possible with letter T-O-N. In a word, the letters T-O-N should occur in the stated order and other letters could be interspersed between them. Proper nouns would not be accepted. Each group should appoint a member to keep a count and write down the generated words. The time assigned for this activity is 15 minutes."*

The teacher may want to make sure that all the groups work in different spaces to avoid interference and overhearing from other groups. This is crucial for avoiding contamination of results. After the activity is complete, the groups should reconvene and the teacher may ask each group representative to read the words aloud in the classroom. The erroneous words may be excluded from the total count of each group.

The results from the activity may be tabulated as follows to calculate the number of words generated per student in groups, with three members and groups with eight members:

		Total Words Generated per group	Total Words Generated by SET A	Total Number of Students in SET A	Average number of Words Generated by each student (Total number of words generated/ total number of students in a SET)
SET 1 Group Size = 3	Group A			3*4=12	
	Group B				
	Group C				
	Group D				
SET 2 Group Size = 8	Group A			8*4=32	
	Group B				
	Group C				
	Group D				

The average number of words generated by each student in each group indicates the productivity of the student in each group. If the average number of words per student in SET A, i.e. the smaller group, is higher than the average number of words per student in SET B, i.e. the larger group, the social loafing effect is quantitatively established. Social loafing predicts that people are likely to work harder and be more productive in smaller groups as compared to larger groups.

Synthesis: After the activity, the teacher should encourage the students to reflect on their experience. They can be asked to discuss the following:

- What do you think is the reason behind the smaller groups generating more words as compared to larger groups?
- Do you think everybody working in the group gave their best to the activity?

- What are the challenges of working in large groups?
- What are the challenges of working in small groups?
- What are the challenges of working alone?
- Would you prefer working on an important assignment in a large group, small group or alone? Why?

After this discussion, the concept of social loafing can be introduced along with the diffusion of responsibility. The discussion should conclude on students' brainstorming about the strategies with which social loafing can be minimized.

ACTIVITY 3: GROUP POLARIZATION

Route: This simple exercise demonstrates the fact that when people get together as a group, they are more likely than as individuals, to express an extreme opinion or take an extreme decision.

For this exercise, teachers can ask learners whether they hold a positive or negative opinion about a controversial topic such as capital punishment, euthanasia, brain drain etc. Based on the opinions expressed by the learners, the teacher can divide the class into two parts: those who have expressed a positive attitude and those who have expressed a negative attitude. Those undecided, can be divided equally in both the groups. Subsequently, the teacher can instruct the learners as follows:

> *"Today, we are exploring the attitudes and opinions you all hold about capital punishment/ euthanasia/ brain drain etc. For this exercise, I have divided you all into groups. For the next 10 minutes, all of you will be discussing this topic along with your group members. Think of as many reasons, examples and arguments as you can, in order to justify the opinion of your group. Your representatives would be defending the position of your group in a debate afterwards."*

The teacher should reconvene the class after 10 minutes and let each group debate on their respective position. Each group gets about 5 minutes to debate.

After the exercise, the teacher can ask learners to raise their hands in case their opinion has become less extreme, has remained the same, or has become more extreme. Most likely, more learners will raise their hands for the third condition wherein their attitude has become more extreme after group participation with like-minded people. This demonstrates the group polarization effect.

Synthesis: After introducing the concept of group polarization and bandwagon effect, the teacher can facilitate a discussion on the reasons for group polarization. Some examples and applications of polarization effect from real life group situations can also be taken up by the teacher for further deliberations. The difference between group think and group polarization may also be discussed, as learners sometimes confuse these two concepts.

ACTIVITY 4: DEINDIVIDUATION

Route: Through a thought experiment, the teacher can demonstrate the effect of deindividuation in the classroom. This study has been adapted based on the paper titled 'Robbers in the classroom: A Deindividuation Exercise' by Dodd (1985). Since this is a demonstration of the effect of deindividuation, this exercise should be done before teaching the concept of deindividuation.

The teacher would ask the learners to respond anonymously to the question below:

> *"If you were given an opportunity to be completely invisible for 24 hours and you could do anything humanly possible with complete assurance that you would not be detected or held responsible for your actions, what would you do?"*

The teacher would ask learners to respond in two minutes on a blank sheet of paper, assuring them of anonymity of their responses. They will be asked to fold the paper before putting it in a box/ bowl. After the learners have turned their responses in, the teacher would shuffle the papers and read aloud the responses one by one to the class.

The learners may be quite amused by the exercise as most of the responses are likely to have a mischievous or even an anti-social intent to them. The responses can be categorized on the blackboard as antisocial, neutral, and prosocial to establish the deindividuation effect.

Synthesis: This exercise would be followed with a discussion on the following questions:

- Why do you think people gave the kind of responses they gave?
- Do you think the response pattern had to do with the anonymity and lack of responsibility inbuilt into the exercise?
- Why do you think the antisocial responses outnumbered the neutral or prosocial responses?

The discussion should be concluded with the teacher either reading out Zimbardo's prison study or screening the videos available on the prison study. The deindividuation effect and the Lucifer effect can thus be introduced. The learners can also be made to reflect on the ethics of involving human participants in a research like the prison study.

ACTIVITY 5: CONFORMITY

Route: The objective of this very simple and quick exercise is to demonstrate conformity in the classroom. Since, this activity has a component of disguise and learners are required to reflect on their immediate experience, the concept of conformity should only be introduced and referred to upon completion of the activity. The activity is likely to be of no importance, if learners are already aware that this activity is on conformity.

For this exercise, the teacher should send two learners outside the classroom for 5 minutes on some pre-planned task. In the meanwhile, he/she should instruct the rest of the class as follows:

> *"Today we would be doing a small social study on the effect of other people's action on our behaviour. For this study, all of you are required to stand up with your books/notebooks in hand, as soon as both these learners are seated after returning to the class. Remain standing and we shall continue with the class in the same fashion. Pretend as if everything is completely natural. Avoid any kind of eye contact, gesturing or instructions, to give an idea of this arrangement to your fellow learners, who are currently outside the class. Remember to stand only when these learners come back and sit on their seats."*

After 5 minutes of standing up through the class, instruct the learners to sit down and begin with a discussion on the activity.

Synthesis: The discussion can begin by directing the following questions to the learners who went out:

- Why did you stand upon returning?
- How did you feel when everyone around you suddenly stood up? (Probe about surprise, hesitation, self-doubt, etc.)
- Do you think it was possible for you to continue sitting? Under what circumstances do you think, you would have continued sitting?

The teacher may write the significant words and descriptors that are relevant to the concept of conformity on the blackboard, based on the responses of the learners. Subsequently, all the learners of the class can respond to the following questions:

- What do you think was the purpose of this activity?
- Why did I ask 'everyone' to stand up all at 'once'? Why was this significant?
- Subsequent to this activity, the concept of conformity should be introduced, followed by a reading of the Asch's conformity study. The factors affecting the conformity and various examples of conformity in our day to day life, can also be discussed.

ACTIVITY 6: COMPLIANCE: 'FOOT IN THE DOOR' AND 'DOOR IN THE FACE' TECHNIQUES

Route: This field experiment demonstrates the effectiveness of two frequently used complementary techniques, namely 'foot in the door' and 'door in the face'. The learners from outside the class can be included as participants in the study. Since it is field experiment based on techniques of compliance, the learners should be well versed with the concepts and the techniques.

The teacher should divide the class in pairs (preferably a boy and a girl). Each pair of learners are required to approach three different learners whom they do not know well. Each participant learner should be presented with one of the following three sets of requests:

Request A (Control Condition)
"Hi! I am ______ and he/she is ______. We are collecting data for our psychology project. As part of the project, we are administering an attitude questionnaire on learners which takes about half an hour. Would you be willing to fill the questionnaire for us?" • If the learner declines, note down the response as follows and move on. • If the learner asks 'when', then tell them that they can get back to him/her with a list of available time slots in the next week. Then if he/she declines, note down the response as follows and move on. • If the learner accepts, take down his/her email id/contact number and say "In case we do not have enough participants, we will get back to you with a list of available time slots from which you can choose. Thanks!" Note down the response as follows and move on. Name: Gender: Response: Yes/No

Request B (Foot in the door technique)
"Hi! I am ______ and he/she is ______. We are collecting data for our psychology project. Would you be kind to give us a minute of your time and help us by answering a couple of simple questions?" If the participant agrees, ask the question as follows and record responses: Do you think the canteen should stop serving the fast food and aerated drinks for health reasons? Yes/No/Undecided Do you think the legal age of drinking should be brought down to 18? Yes/No/Undecided After the questions, continue with the script as follows: "Thanks a lot for your time. As part of our psychology project, we are also administering an attitude questionnaire on learners which takes about half an hour. Would you be willing to fill the questionnaire for us?" • If the learner declines, note down the response as follows and move on. • If the learner asks 'when', then tell them that they can get back to him/her with a list of available time slots in the next week. Then if he/she declines, note down the response as follows and move on. • If the learner accepts, take down his/her email id/contact number and say "In case we do not have enough participants, we will get back to you with a list of available time slots from which you can choose. Thanks!" Note down the response as follows and move on. Name: Gender: Response: Yes/No

Request B (Foot in the door technique)
Request C (Door in the face technique) "Hi! I am .... and he/she is .... We are collecting data for our psychology project and we are looking for participants who can give us a couple of hours of their time for the study in the laboratory. Would you be willing to help us?" If the learner turns down your request, ask further "Ok, we also have an attitude questionnaire associated with the project which takes about only half an hour. Would you be kind enough to fill it for us sometime next week?" • If the learner declines, note down the response as follows and move on. • If the learner asks 'when', then tell them that they can get back to him/her with a list of available time slots in the next week. Then if he/she declines, note down the response as follows and move on. • If the learner accepts, take down his/her email id/contact number and say "In case we do not have enough participants, we will get back to you with a list of available time slots from which you can choose. Thanks!" Note down the response as follows and move on. Name: Gender: Response: Yes/No

The teacher should distribute the above requests as handouts to each pair of learners. The learners should be instructed that they should only enter the field, after rehearsing the instructions well and follow them as closely, as possible.

The learners should be very clear that each of the three participants should be given different instructions as per the experimental condition. They should also be cautioned against reaching out to known people. The teacher should tell the learners to bring the completed handouts back in the next class.

Synthesis: In the next class, the teacher can compile the data for the entire class with the help of volunteers and present it on the black board as follows:

Condition	Response of the Participant	
	Yes	No
Control (Request A)		
Foot in the Door (Request B)		
Door in the Face (Request C)		

It is expected that more learners are likely to comply with the request of filling in the attitude questionnaire, in conditions where 'foot in the door' and 'door in the face' techniques are used, as compared to the control condition where no persuasion technique is used.

It would also be interesting to see that of the two techniques used, which one has been more successful in eliciting compliance. The effect of gender on compliance can also be observed by including the gender wise comparisons. The discussion on the activity can be further extended to assess the application of these techniques in marketing, particularly by salesmen.

Note: If the teacher does not have the scope to conduct the field experiment with the learners in the class, a simpler in-school experiment or a class discussion may also be good alternatives of this exercise. In this alternative activity, the teacher may either present or read out the three sets of requests given for the field experiment to the learners. Then, the teacher can ask learners, which of the requests they are going to comply with and why.

After this discussion, the teacher can introduce the different techniques that professionals use, to secure compliance from others. The learners can also be encouraged to share their experiences of being targets of any of these compliance techniques in the past.

ACTIVITY 7: OBEDIENCE

Route: Through this popular case study of Jim Jones, the learners are going to explore the extreme outcomes of our tendency to submit to the orders, from an authority figure. Since this is an analytic exercise, it should be used after the learners have grasped the concepts of obedience and conformity.

The teacher should begin by a narration/screening of the case of the Jonestown massacre, where, in November, 1978, around 900 member of the People's Temple church including women and children committed mass suicide in Jonestown, Guyana, following the cult leader Jim Jones. This case study is widely available on internet. There are also documentaries available on the incident. The case and its analysis can also be presented with the help of a reading titled, 'Making sense of the nonsensical: An analysis of the Jonestown' by Osherow (1991).

After the learners have become familiar with the incident, the teacher can facilitate the analysis of the case, on the basis of the concepts of social influence in groups such as obedience and conformity. Some of the following questions can be posed to the learners to stimulate the discussion:

- Why did such a tragedy happen?
- Why do you think people obeyed the orders of Jim Jones even when they knew it meant ending their life?
- What made Jim Jones such an influential leader?
- What were the strategies used by Jim Jones to ensure obedience from the members of Jonestown?
- How did, establishing a different township facilitate Jones' influence on the masses?

Synthesis: During the exercise, the learners are expected to apply their understanding of the principles of group influence, particularly obedience and conformity, to analyse the case of Jonestown. The discussion can also be extended by the teacher to include other extreme examples of mass obedience, for e.g., the

Nazi holocaust and Stanford Prison Study. The concepts related to obedience, such as brainwashing and propaganda, can also be introduced as tools of mass-control. The learners can in addition, be motivated to watch documentaries and movies on Stanford Prison Experiment (Zimbardo, 1971) and Milgram's Study (Milgram, 1963), Jonestown Massacre and Nazi Holocaust. They can also prepare a report on any movie/documentary and submit it for discussion with the teacher.

ACTIVITY 8: SOCIAL IDENTITY AND BIASES

Route: This study is an adaptation of Tajfel and Turner's Minimal Group Paradigm Experiments (1979). The aim is to explore inter-group bias and group favouritism. In order to establish how quickly we tend to form in-group and out-group biases, the teacher can divide the class into two groups on the basis of some arbitrary and insignificant criteria, such as those wearing sport shoes and those not, those who prefer a particular actor over the other, or those who are wearing a pullover and those wearing a blazer.

The teacher should instruct each group to sit in a circle and discuss the reasons why the other group has not worn the sport shoes, or prefers a particular actor over the other, or does not wear the blazer. Each group should be instructed to list as many reasons as possible in 10 minutes and told that the team with the most convincing reasons, would be the winner. In order to make the whole exercise more competitive, the teacher can announce a small reward for the winning team.

The point of the exercise, however, is not the discussion of the reasons but the group dynamics that are going to unfold while learners are completing the task. Therefore, in order to capture these group dynamics, the teacher should identify two observers in each group, prior to the beginning of the activity. The observers will be separately instructed by the teacher to quietly observe the functioning of the group and note down the negative and positive statements being made by the group members about their own group and about the other group(s).

The observer sheet can be prepared as follows:

Indicate the statements made here in reference to the other team:	
Positive	**Negative**

Indicate the statements made here in reference to your own team:	
Positive	**Negative**

At the end of the exercise, the teacher would invite a volunteer from each group to come forward and share the listing of the group. Most likely, learners will come up with reasons that will present the out-group members in negative light as compared to their own group.

The teacher will then reveal the observers and invite them to present their observations. The group favouritism and biases would be further highlighted with the data that the observers from each of the groups. They are likely to come up with many more negative statements than positive statements that in-group members from both groups would have made about the out-group members.

After the completion of the exercise, the teacher can share the actual objective of the activity with the learners. The teacher can also share the real purpose of the reward which was to intensify the competition between the groups. A discussion on the reasons for inter-group conflict can follow.

Synthesis: The purpose of this exercise was to give learners a first-hand experience of engaging in intergroup bias. They would also be able to appreciate that even when groups are formed on the basis of arbitrary criteria, people identify with the groups readily and demonstrate in-group favouritism. Since group participation is such an integral part of our social reality, learners should understand the psychological tendency behind one's identification with groups.

Through this exercise, the teacher can introduce the Social Identity Theory proposed by Tajfel and Turner (1979). The conditions under which the inter-group biases increase, can also be discussed along with the negative consequences that this can bring, in the form of conflicts, prejudices and discrimination. In this backdrop, the examples of atrocities on Nazis in Germany, Blacks in South Africa and inter-religious conflicts reflected in riots, can be discussed.

ACTIVITY 9: INTERGROUP COOPERATION AND COMPETITION

Route: This simple game introduces learners to a condition where common resources are depleted prematurely, due to the insecurity of competition, induced by the intergroup situation. This demonstration is adapted from the exercise proposed by Hardin (1968) in his famous paper titled 'Tragedy of the Commons'.

For this exercise, the teacher would require the following material for demonstration:

- A large transparent bowl
- A collection of commonly available stationary objects such as paper-clips, erasers, pencils, sharpeners (around 20 in number)
- Toffies/ candies (around 20 in number)
- Plastic tokens or coins (around 20 in number)
- A stop-watch
- A medium size table

The teacher should place the bowl on the table and place any 20 objects in the bowl. Then, he/she can invite any four volunteers from the class to come over and play the game. All volunteers should stand around the table in a manner that they are visible to the rest of the class.

The volunteers should be instructed aloud by the teacher so that all the learners can also hear the instructions and follow the game. The instructions are as follows:

> *"The game you four are about to play has only three rules. First, the number of the objects left in the bowl at the end of every round, will be doubled. Each round will be for 10 seconds. Second, the objective of the game is to acquire as many objects as possible. Third, you can only use one finger and thumb to acquire the objects.*
>
> *You would begin, when I say 'Go'. You would start acquiring objects and you would immediately retreat when I say 'Stop'.*

At the end of every round, I would be replenishing the objects in the bowl and the game continues."

The teacher should check with the volunteers and the rest of the class if they have understood the instructions. The teacher should clarify in case anyone has any doubts.

Once the game begins, the teacher should carefully monitor the rounds of the game and replenish the objects in the bowl, till the point when there are no objects left in the bowl. At this point, the game would end. The teacher should also be observant of any strategy that the volunteers are using to play the game.

Most likely, since each volunteer is likely to be anxious to acquire as many objects as possible, soon there would be no objects left in the bowl which would lead to pre-mature end of the game. After the game ends, the teacher should make the volunteers join the rest of the class for a discussion.

After the game ends, the teacher can raise the following questions:

- Why do you think the game ended so soon?
- Why did the volunteers turn the game into a competitive one despite the fact that no such instructions were given?
- Is there a way, we could have kept on going with the game?
- Do you think the volunteers would have benefitted more if the game kept on going?
- What strategies could have been used to prolong the game?
- How could the cooperation between the group members have been enhanced?

Synthesis: This discussion will be followed up by teacher introducing the actual purpose of the game i.e. to demonstrate the problems that occur when people have equal access to resources that are limited. In such a scenario, the learners should understand that rather than cooperating with each other, people start competing with each other out of insecurity. Hence, due to people's greed of maximizing their profit, the resources deplete prematurely.

The teacher should relate the 'tragedy to commons' to the current environment crisis that the world is facing. At the end of this exercise, they should be able to appreciate that self-interest and competition over limited resources makes all of us losers. They should also be able to assess the merit of cooperation over competition.

ACTIVITY 10: PRISONER'S DILEMMA

Route: This exercise depicts a famous social dilemma where the situation unfolds disastrously for both parties involved, if they choose to be in conflict and both parties stand to benefit if they cooperate. But, the catch is each of the parties has to make independent decision of cooperating or not cooperating without awareness of the other party's decision. This exercise should be done as a demonstration prior to the introduction of the topic in the class.

For replicating the prisoner's dilemma in the class, the teacher should narrate the following situation to the learners:

> *"Two people have been arrested by the police after a crime. They have been kept separately and are being interrogated individually. They are guilty but the evidence that police has is insufficient for conviction. Each of these individuals, now prisoners, can choose to confess or not confess to the crime. If neither of prisoners confess, they are not likely to be convicted for the serious crime and would get a minor sentence (1 year in prison each). If both of them confess, they will get moderate imprisonment (5 years in prison each). If one of them confesses and other does not, the one who confesses goes free, while the other receives severe imprisonment (10 years in prison)."*

The choices can be illustrated with the help of matrix below:

Prisoner's Dilemma Outcome Matrix		**Prisoner B**	
		Cooperate	Compete
Prisoner A	Cooperate	Fairly Good Outcome (1 year of imprisonment for each)	Very Bad Outcome for Prisoner A (10 years of imprisonment) Very Good Outcome for Prisoner B (No imprisonment)
	Compete	Very Bad Outcome for Prisoner B (10 years of imprisonment) Very Good Outcome for Prisoner A (No imprisonment)	Fairly Bad Outcome for both (5 years of imprisonment for each)

The teacher can demonstrate the multiple trial prisoner's dilemma by calling over any two learners to play the game as everyone else observes. These learners should be seated across a table in front the class. Each of them will be given 10 chits of paper where they are going to indicate their preference for competition or cooperation. For the purpose of the game, the outcomes can be converted into points that each prisoner earns as follows:

<table>
<tr><td colspan="2" rowspan="2">Prisoner's Dilemma Outcome Matrix</td><td colspan="2">Prisoner B</td></tr>
<tr><td>Cooperate</td><td>Compete</td></tr>
<tr><td rowspan="2">Prisoner A</td><td>Cooperate</td><td>5 points each</td><td>Prisoner B gets 10 points
Prisoner A gets 0 points</td></tr>
<tr><td>Compete</td><td>Prisoner A gets 10 points
Prisoner B gets 0 points</td><td>1 Point each</td></tr>
</table>

For every trial, both the prisoners independently write compete/cooperate on the chit, fold it and hand it over to the teacher who opens the chit and declares the choices. Based on the matrix, each of the learners earn the reward points which can be tabulated by a learner on the black board. After 10 trails, a winner emerges.

Synthesis: This activity may demonstrate that people have a strong tendency to compete even when the best outcome is only possible through mutual cooperation. It is difficult for people to work together to achieve a mutually rewarding goal.

After this activity, the teacher can discuss the determinants of cooperation and competition in groups. The highlights of the Robbers Cave study can also be read out to the class after which they can brainstorm to come up with strategies of conflict resolution.

Some Concepts for Advanced Learners

Social facilitation and Social Inhibition

Mere presence of other people may affect performance of people on tasks in complex ways. Presence of others as audience may sometimes enhance performance (i.e. social facilitation) and sometimes impede performance (social inhibition). The social facilitation effect was proposed by Norman Triplett in 1898 based on his classical laboratory experiment with children. Zajonc (1966) proposed 'drive theory of social facilitation' to reconcile the apparently contradictory effect of presence of others on performance of the individual. The theory suggested that the "mere presence of others is arousing and can either increase or reduce performance, depending upon whether dominant responses in a given situation are correct or incorrect" (Baron & Byrne, 2004, p. 483).

Group Think

With reference to groups, it is observed by researchers that excessive cohesiveness usually does not lead to effective decisions. Janis (1971) coined the term 'groupthink' for "the tendency of the members of highly cohesive groups to assume that their decisions can't be wrong, that all members must support the group's decision strongly, and that information contrary to it should be ignored" (Baron & Byrne, 2004, p. 509). This mode of thinking leads to disastrous effects sometimes as in a cohesive group, congruence-seeking becomes so dominant that the group does not engage in realistic appraisal of the situation and overrides any dissent without due consideration (Janis, 1971).

Indoctrination

In the context of groups, indoctrination is a "process through which individuals become members of extreme groups and come to accept the beliefs and rules of the group in a totally unquestioning and highly committed way (Baron & Byrne, 2004, p. 380). Baron (2000) suggested four distinct stages of indoctrination: softening-up, compliance, internalization and consolidation. At each of these four stages, the attentional capacity of the targets is reduced and they become more susceptible to social influence tactics. Indoctrination is generally considered an antithesis of education and is viewed as a negative and unacceptable process.

Propaganda

Propaganda is a form of communication or messages that aim at persuading recipients by giving them loaded, oversimplified or one-sided messages. Unlike education, propaganda does not encourage independent thinking or debating. The focus is much more on emotional rather than rational appeal. Propaganda is generally believed to be negative as it is communication with an intent to deceive the target group, e.g., propaganda was extensively used by Nazis during the second world-war (Cull, Culbert, & Welch, 2003).

Web-links and Readings

Baron, R. A., & Byrne, D. (2004). *Social Psychology*. Delhi: Pearson Education.

Baron, R. S. (2000). Arousal, capacity, and intense indoctrination. *Personality and Social Psychology Review, 4*(3), 238-254.

Cull, N. J., Culbert, D. H., & Welch, D. (2003). *Propaganda and Mass Persuasion: A Historical Encyclopaedia, 1500 to the present*. Santa Barbara: ABC-CLIO.

Dodd, D. (1985). Robbers in the classroom: A deindividuation exercise. *Teaching of Psychology, 12*(2), 89-91.

Hardin, G. (1968). Tragedy of the commons. *Science, 162*, 1243-1248.

Janis, I. L. (1971). Groupthink. *Psychology Today, 5*(6), 43-46.

Johnson, P. (2015, February 20). *Psychology: The Stanford Prison Experiment - BBC Documentary*. Retrieved March 25, 2016, from YouTube: https://www.youtube.com/watch?v=gb4Q20z0T1Q

Milgram, S. (1963). Behavioral study of obedience. *The Journal of abnormal and social psychology, 67*(4), 371-378.

Myers, D. G. (2005). *Social Psychology*. New York: McGraw Hill.

North, A. C., Linley, P. A., & Hargreaves, D. J. (2000). Social loafing in a co-operative classroom task. *Educational Psychology, 20*(4), 389-392. doi:10.1080/01443410020016635

Osherow, N. (1991). Making sense of the nonsensical: An analysis of Jonestown. In E. Aronson, *Readings about the social animal* (pp. 69-88). San Francisco: W. H. Freeman. Retrieved November 7, 2015, from http://www.psy.cmu.edu/~kotovsky/85102/readings/old/osherow.pdf

Tajfel, H., & Turner, J. C. (1979). An integrative theory of intergroup conflict. In W.G. Austin, & S. Worchel (Eds.), *The social psychology of intergroup relations*, pp. 33-37, Manterey, CA: Brooks/cole.

Zajonc, R. B., & Sales, S. M. (1966). Social facilitation of dominant and subordinate responses. *Journal of Experimental Social Psychology, 2*(2), 160-168.

Zimbardo, P. G. (1971). The power and pathology of imprisonment. *Congressional Record, 15*, 10-25.

Self and Personality*

Introduction

Learners may find this Unit both interesting and abstract, because, like 'intelligence', the term 'personality' is also very commonly used in everyday life to explain someone's behaviour. The everyday experiences associated with these terms makes it challenging for the teacher to teach them from an academic, psychological standpoint. The task of the teacher is to dispel myths associated with them and at the same time enable learners to discuss, deliberate, and reflect upon the various approaches to the study of personality. Secondly, this Unit is also important because it becomes the basis to understand psychological disorders and therapeutic approaches. So, the teacher must give adequate time to learners to understand various theoretical positions that explain the construct of personality.

Moreover, the basic books of Psychology vary in their emphasis on different theories of personality. They may not discuss all major theories of personality in detail; therefore, the onus lies on the teacher to supplement the text with readings for varied sources so that the learners can appreciate how the various personality theories differ from each other. This Unit gives an opportunity to the learners to acquaint themselves with the work of eminent theorists such as Sigmund Freud, Carl Jung, Karen Horney, Alfred Adler, Erik Erikson, Carl Rogers, Gordon Allport, Raymond Cattell, Hans Eysenck and behaviourists who have not just influenced the course of development of Psychology as a discipline, but other disciplines also.

---

* Vishakha Kumar

Another important area closely intertwined with the study of personality is the study of self and identity. Very often these terms are used interchangeably but there is a fine distinction between the two. It is still a matter of debate, whether self is a broader notion with identity subsumed under it or vice versa. An attempt will be made to bring forth these debates as the students progress in this Unit. What needs to be emphasised is that self and identity, are both very important areas of study.

ACTIVITY 1: INTRODUCTION TO SELF AND PERSONALITY

Route: The teacher can give a set of sentences to be completed by the learners, as an introductory activity. The intent of the activity is to make learners reflect upon the extent to which they know themselves.

1. I am ....
2. I think I look ....
3. I think .... is the best thing about me
4. I think .... is the only thing I want to change about myself
5. My friends see me as ....
6. My mother sees me as ....
7. Others think I am ....
8. Two things that people do not know about me ....

After learners have written their responses to these statements, the teacher can ask them to reflect on how they developed these ideas. The discussion should include the influence of significant others as an important aspect of the development of self. It is through these experiences and the meaning we assign to these experiences that we develop our ideas about ourselves.

Synthesis: Everyone has some ideas about who one is and how he/she is different from others. 'Self' can be defined as the totality of an individual's conscious experiences, ideas, thoughts, and feelings with regard to himself or herself. The way one perceives oneself and how one views one's achievements and failures is one's self-concept.

ACTIVITY 2: SELF AS AN OBJECT AND SUBJECT

Route: Learners will be asked to talk/ write about the person whom they see in the mirror (while they are actually looking at their own reflection). The teacher can ask them to read what they have written, if they would like to. The teacher would, then, discuss how self becomes an object when we observe our own reflection and think of it as a third person.

Most of the times, we describe ourselves as performing something or engaged in some form of action such as, I can do this, I have come back from school, I am a student etc. This is when self is a subject and is actively trying to know itself.

Synthesis: Self has a dual status. It is both an object and a subject. When self is a subject, it actively makes an effort to know itself. As an object self gets observed and comes to be known. Even the self-as-the-subject attempts to know the self-as-the-object.

ACTIVITY 3: SELF-ESTEEM AND SELF-EFFICACY

Route

Task 1: The teacher would provide a checklist to learners, in which they will be asked to mark a tick on statements, which they think hold true for themselves. The list is as follows:

- I am a bright student.
- I am a good dancer.
- I am beautiful.
- I am a well-behaved person.
- I am a good human being.
- I am good at my studies.
- I am a social person.
- Usually people like me.
- I am chosen for other co-curricular activities.
- My teachers mostly like me.
- I think I am attractive.
- Any other that you would wish to add.

After they finish marking the statements, the teacher can ask learners to reflect on each of the statements that they have marked. They may write their reflections, or discuss their responses with their peers.

Task 2: The teacher can ask learners to analyse the following situation:

> *There were two friends Rhyma and Amrita. Both of them had similar interests. They always performed well in school and*

both of them had a flair for writing. After school, Amrita did a course in journalism and later went on to become the editor of an esteemed publication. She is now working on her own book, which will be published by an international publisher after the manuscript is complete. Rhyma works for a small newspaper and is still struggling to make her mark and two ends meet.

Q: What do you think could be the probable reasons for such different life trajectories, despite similar interests?

The teacher would ask learners to think of probable reasons of Amrita's achievements and Rhyma's average performance. They would be asked to highlight 2-3 major points, which they think have led to their different positions in life.

Synthesis: Task 1 is similar to questions that are used in a self-esteem questionnaire, whereas Task 2 gives space to discuss self-efficacy. The question in Task 2 is a semi-projective question, which requires learners to discuss what factors contribute to the success and failure of others. People with high self-efficacy will probably see internal causes of success and failure, whereas, people with low self-efficacy may rely more on external factors, such as, destiny and luck.

ACTIVITY 4: SELF-REGULATION

Route: Learners will be asked to write about any one of their habits that they would like to change and also say, why. They will then be asked to formulate a detailed plan to bring about the identified change. The plan must include long term and short term goals. They may also think of some kind of reinforcement or reward for themselves that can motivate them. Learners may discuss their plans with the whole class. The teacher can further probe by asking the following questions:

- Have you ever deliberately changed something about yourself?
- I am sure you must have set some goals for yourself. How did you set those goals?
- Do you feel that you are unable to meet your goals? If yes, where do you think you lag?

The teacher can then introduce the concept of self-regulation.

Synthesis: Self-regulation refers to the ability to monitor and organise one's own actions. Self-observation, self-instruction and self-reinforcement are important aspects of self-regulation and self-control.

ACTIVITY 5: NATURE OF PERSONALITY

Route: Learners will be asked to identify a person who has influenced them. They would then be asked to write a descriptive paragraph about the person, focusing on his/her qualities, which makes him/her distinct and different from others.

They can then be asked to share their descriptions with the class. After a few of them do so, the teacher can ask the class to try to relate the descriptions that they heard, to the term 'personality' and come up with their own definition of the term. They can be told as a starting point to underline all the adjectives that they have used to describe the person, such as, benevolent, charming, social, extrovert, shy, helping, etc. They can then be asked to translate each of the characteristics into the behavioural pattern related to it. The teacher can then link this with the definition of personality.

Synthesis: The most widely accepted definition of Personality is: 'it refers to our characteristic ways of responding to individuals and situations.' Personality has both physical and psychological components. Its expression is unique in every individual and is less prone to change than self. At the same time, it is dynamic and may change due to internal or external demands.

Secondly, this activity can be used to explicate the trait approach to the study of personality. The trait approach tries to unearth the building blocks of our personality. A trait is seen as a relatively enduring attribute or quality on which one individual differs from others. Traits are relatively enduring qualities which are less prone to change.

ACTIVITY 6: TRAIT APPROACH

Route: Learners will be given a tabular hand-out, in which, the left side represents the different professions and the right side is to be filled by them with the different traits that they associate with people of the respective professions.

Hand-out: Which characteristics do you associate with people in the following professions?

Professions	Characteristics
School teaching	
University Professor	
Businessperson	
Administrator	
Actor	
Politician	
Dancer	
Sportsperson	
Social Worker	
Scientist	

Given a choice, which profession would you choose and why? You have to analyse each option and state a few reasons for choosing or not choosing, each one of them.

Synthesis: The teacher would conclude by a discussion of the trait approach as proposed by Raymond Cattell and Gordon Allport.

ACTIVITY 7: TRAIT APPROACH

Route: The teacher can ask learners to read about the trait and type approach. She/he can then ask learners to read different classification systems such as the one proposed by Hippocrates, or the three *gunas,* or Friedman's Type A, B, C and D personality theory, etc. After reading them, the learners may try to rethink the personalities discussed in the previous activities and place them within the different theoretical frameworks. After they are done with this exercise, the teacher can discuss the following questions:

- Do you think your behaviour can be explained with the help of these categories? Give reasons for your answers
- If no, then can you think of any modification for this theory?

Synthesis: The type approach to the study of personality attempts to explain some broad patterns of the observed behaviour characteristics of a person. Each behaviour pattern refers to a type, in which, an individual is placed according to the similarity of his/her behavioural pattern of the given category.

ACTIVITY 8: PSYCHODYNAMIC APPROACH

Route: The teacher can introduce the theory with the help of a classical case-study that was done by Sigmund Freud. She/he may ask learners to surf the internet or visit the library and search for the case-study of 'Anna O' or 'Little Hans'. Alternatively, he/she can prepare a short note on these case studies and distribute it to the class as a hand-out. A sample of the short note on the case study is presented below:

> *"Anna O was twenty-one at the time when she fell ill. She was very bright and intelligent. She was very imaginative and poetic. She indulged in day dreaming which she termed as her private theatre. Her symptoms started appearing during the time she was nursing her sick father. She showed signs of paralysis of the right lower and upper extremities, squint and headaches. She presented two entirely different states of consciousness. In one state, she was aware of things around her and appeared sad. In the altered state, she hallucinated of black snakes and became violent. She would throw things at people around her. Later she also started showing signs of mood swings. One moment she would be desolate and other times she appeared excited. She could not recognise people around her. She could not understand her native language German but could still communicate fluently in English. Dr. Josef Breuer noticed that some of her symptoms disappeared when he enabled her to speak freely. She coined the term 'talking cure' or sometimes as 'chimney sweeping'. She refused to eat or drink at times. She would ask for food and throw it away the moment, it touched her lips. Breuer treated her from 1881 to 1882 and diagnosed that she was suffering from hysteria. Sigmund Freud identified unconscious desires which were threatening as the underlying cause of her problem. He also found that hysteria is a result of painful memories that are pushed away from consciousness.'*

(Rephrased from *The Studies on Hysteria* by Josef Breuer, Sigmund Freud, James Strachey, 1955).

The teacher may provide more details in the case-study from other sources. Learners must read and discuss them in class. The teacher should encourage learners to put questions about the case presented. Terms mentioned in the case-study such as conscious, hysteria, unconscious, and hypnosis can be explained in detail to weave the theory together.

Synthesis: After reading and discussing the case study, the teacher can introduce the concept of the unconscious mind. She/ he can also discuss how Sigmund Freud's theory shifted the emphasis from consciousness to the unconscious mind. He also postulated that several physical symptoms may have a psychological basis. Such disorders may have their genesis in feelings and thoughts which are sexual, which the person pushes away from the conscious mind because they appear threatening.

ACTIVITY 9: INTRODUCTION TO THE PSYCHODYNAMIC APPROACH

Route: The learners will be presented with some situations followed by a few indicative questions.

- You failed or scored less in an examination. When anyone asked you about the result of the exam you said that your teacher never taught anything or she deliberately failed you.
- You avoid participating in debates. However, you try to excel in dance or sport.
- You really like your friend. But you either keep criticizing the person or avoid him/ her.
- Your aunt dislikes her neighbours and never visits them. Instead she always says that her neighbours deliberately try to avoid her.
- You really think that you respect your elder sibling. Yet you dream or fantasise about hitting him/her, which leaves you both surprised and anxious.

Questions for reflection:

- Have you experienced any of these situations?
- Have you experienced anything similar to such situations?
- Think and list some incidents from your life, or from what you have observed around you.
- Do we always act consciously?

- Have you ever been shocked by your own actions?
- Have you ever regretted saying something that you did not want to say and you continue to wonder why you said it?

Synthesis: The Psychodynamic Approach tries to answer such questions by emphasizing the role of the unconscious. The teacher should discuss the concepts related to the psychodynamic approach. Terms like id, ego, super ego will be discussed along with the concept of conscious, sub-conscious and unconscious.

ACTIVITY 10: ID, EGO, SUPEREGO AND DEFENCE MECHANISMS

Route: The teacher can present the learners with three different voices as in the boxes below:

<table>
<tr>
<td>1. I want to stay at my friend's place tonight because there is no one at her place. Her father's bar is very tempting and she has lots of movies.</td>
<td>2. Oh! this is difficult to resolve. Can we strike a compromise? I will tell my parents that we are doing group study. We will have fun after we are done with our work.</td>
<td>3. What are you saying? How could you think of such a thing? No it is not possible, as we have to complete our project.</td>
</tr>
</table>

Learners can then be asked if they have experienced an internal state of conflict as given in the boxes above.

This can be presented as a cartoon strip. Alternatively, the teacher can assign any three learners to play the role of id, ego and superego. The rest of the class has to identify which one is id, ego and super ego. They have to identify the voices emanating from id, ego and superego in the above three boxes.

The next question is, 'What happens when the bombardment from both id and superego does not stop?'

<table>
<tr>
<td>1. I have to go and party with other friends at my girl-friend's place. I don't want to tell my parents anything about the party.</td>
<td>2. ....
....
....
....
....
....
..............................</td>
<td>3. 'No No No' you cannot do this. What if your parents find out about you? They will be devastated. This is very bad.</td>
</tr>
</table>

Synthesis: Id, ego and superego, constitute the primary structural elements of personality. Id is the source of person's instinctual energy. Ego grows out of id and seeks gratification of instinctual needs in a reality oriented manner. The super ego is the moral side of mental functioning. It informs the id and ego about what is morally correct and what is incorrect and recognises all the norms and socially appropriate traditions of the society.

Ego tries to protect itself from anxiety, evoked by the demands of the id and the moral embargo of the superego. In the face of anxiety, the ego unconsciously builds a wall around itself to protect itself from anxiety provoking thoughts. Defence mechanisms are unconscious reactions that reduce the level of anxiety, thereby helping the individual to cope with the situation at hand.

ACTIVITY 11: LEVELS OF CONSCIOUSNESS

Route: The teacher can give a small instance of a dream to the learners. He/she can give them one day to explore the meaning of any particular dream. The instance can be as follows:

'The boy dreams of going inside a cellar where there is lot of garbage. He tries to clean the cellar but every time he washes the filth, it comes back again. He does it several times and finally gets tired of it.' Does this dream convey anything to you?

Think of any two/ three dreams that made you wonder about their deeper meanings. Have you ever tried to analyse them? The teacher can ask learners to think about these questions and try to look for answers in different books.

When the learners come up with some responses, the teacher can discuss the concepts of conscious, subconscious and unconscious with them.

Synthesis: Sigmund Freud visualised the human mind in three levels of consciousness: conscious, pre-conscious and unconscious. The conscious level includes those thoughts and actions about which people are aware. Information at the pre-conscious level can be accessed only when a person pays attention to it. And the unconscious level is that level, about which people are not aware. Dreams, according to Sigmund Freud, are a gateway to the unconscious mind.

ACTIVITY 12: SELF ACTUALISATION

Route: The following case vignette will be presented to the learners:

Rajendra Singh (born 6 August 1959) is a well-known water conservationist from Alwar district, Rajasthan in India. Also known as "Waterman of India", he won the Stockholm Water Prize, an award known as "the Nobel Prize for Water", in 2015. Previously, he won the Ramon Magsaysay Award for community leadership in 2001, for his pioneering work in community-based efforts in water harvesting and water management.

Starting from a single village in 1985, over the years TBS helped build over 8,600 johads and other water conservation structures to collect rainwater for the dry seasons. It has brought water back to over 1,000 villages and revived five rivers in Rajasthan - Arvari, Ruparel, Sarsa, Bhagani and Jahajwali.

He left his job in 1984. He sold all his household goods for Rs. 23,000/- and took a bus ticket for the last stop, on board a bus going into interior of Rajasthan. Along with him, were four friends from Tarun Bharat Sangha. The last stop turned out to be Kishori village in Thanagazi tehsil in Alwar district, and the day was October 2, 1985. After initial skepticism, the villagers of the neighboring village Bhikampura accepted him, and it was there that they found a place to stay. Soon, he started a small Ayurvedic medicine practice in a nearby village Gopalpura, while his colleagues went about promoting education in the villages.

(Pancholi & Soni, 2015)

Analyze the case with reference to the following questions:

- What are the challenges you think Rajendra Singh would have faced when he started his work?
- How do you think he would have dealt with them?
- Why do you think people take up such challenging tasks?
- What do you think motivates such people?
- Can you think of a goal in your life that you want to work towards?
- If yes, then what can be the challenges in moving towards your goal?

Synthesis: Learners' attention will be drawn towards the concept of self-actualization. Discussion on what is self-actualization and what motivates an individual to move towards higher end goals, can be undertaken.

ACTIVITY 13: SOCIAL COGNITIVE APPROACH

Route: Learners will be asked to interview any 6 people around them to gather data on the following questions: (include both boys and girls)

- Do you dance or sing (not essentially classical music)? Where and how did you learn it?
- How do you express your anger? Why?
- What dress do you like to wear? Why?
- How do you spend your free time?
- Who is your role model?
- What do you dream to achieve in the next 5 years?
- How did you decide what you want to do in your professional life?
- Which is your favourite television show and why?

Try and delve deeper into the 'whys' of the answers. Teachers should encourage learners to analyse the answers that they get from their participants, in light of the impact of the cultural environment on them.

Synthesis: Many behaviours are picked up by individuals from their social context. We learn by observing others; be it parents, siblings, neighbours, peers or from media images. The social context not only influences the way people act, but also the reasons that people attribute to those actions. A discussion on Bandura's theory of social learning may follow after the discussion on the survey responses. The detailed theory will be given as a hand-out for students to read and understand. Their questions related to it will be taken up in the class.

ACTIVITY 14: ERIK ERIKSON'S THEORY OF PSYCHOSOCIAL DEVELOPMENT

Route: The teacher would divide the learners into small groups. Each group will be asked to work on a particular age group, to identify the characteristics, challenges, needs and problems related to people of that age. The issues can be identified by using observation, interviews, media resources etc.

Age Groups	Characteristics/ behaviour/ challenges/ needs/ problems
Pre-school	
Kindergarten	
Primary	
Secondary	
Senior Secondary	
College	

Synthesis: Learners will be asked to read the psychosocial stages of development as given by Erikson and find linkages with the issues identified. These issues will then be discussed in class.

ACTIVITY 15: SEARCH FOR IDENTITY

Route: Learners will be asked to write a few lines and draw a picture of themselves on the following three questions:

- Who are you?
- What is it that you want to be?
- Where do you see yourself ten years from now?

The teacher should encourage learners to deliberate on these questions. After the learners have written answers to these questions, the teacher can discuss them with the class. It might be interesting to ask learners if they had thought previously of these issues, or not. After discussion, the teacher can ask learners to read Erikson's theory and his emphasis on identity development.

Synthesis: Erikson gave a lot of emphasis to the development of identity. For him, adolescence is a crucial juncture for the developmental process. Each person goes through an identity crisis during which she/he asks some fundamental questions about her/himself. He further highlights that a sense of purpose and direction gives unity to personality.

ACTIVITY 16: DIFFERENT APPROACHES TO THE STUDY OF PERSONALITY: ANALYSIS OF A CASE STUDY

Route: The teacher can present a case vignette and ask learners to analyse the case. They should try to think of probable explanations and causes of behaviour.

> *Case vignette: Ranjan and Raman are siblings. Ranjan is the elder brother and is in the final year of college. He enjoys adventure sports and outdoor activities. He has several friends and enjoys the company of people. His social skills are par excellence which enables him to interact with people from diverse social and cultural backgrounds. Ever since Ranjan was born, he spent most of the time with his grandparents who stayed in a small town. Raman is five years younger to Ranjan. He grew up in a metropolitan city. He is a very quiet person and does not have many friends. He chose to study Fine Arts after school and is enrolled in the first year of college. He has an interest in music and theatre. He enjoys staying alone and avoids parties. Raman likes to spend time working with street children. He has started an NGO where he conducts art, music, and theatre workshops for children. He works relentlessly in his spare time to educate the children using alternate methods of teaching. He has many plans to take this forward on a larger scale, once he graduates."*

Imagine that you are a researcher and you want to study the differences between siblings. Think about all the theories of personality that you have read and analyse the case from the perspective of:

- Trait approach: Learners may indicate that both brothers have different set of traits. Their source traits are different. One is an extrovert and other is an introvert.
- Psychodynamic approach: The elder brother is more ambitious and is driven by the desire to control his environment. Maybe he was indulged more during the oral stage, which led to his talkative behaviour. The younger brother may be suffering from social phobia. Probably he experienced something unpleasant during his childhood and therefore gets anxious in the company of people. Or, he may be fixated in the oral stage.
- Behavioural approach: It may be possible that gregarious behaviour was reprimanded when Raman was a child. His

parents were working and he spent a lot of time alone at home. He was rewarded for staying on his own, spending time doing art work.

- Cultural approach: The older boy may have grown up in an environment where there were lots of people around. Maybe his grandparents were more social. It is possible that the younger one was alone at home most of the time, while he was growing up. He probably went to a school where there was a lot of emphasis on art and theatre. He might have observed others engage in such activities.
- Humanistic approach: Maybe the younger brother is driven by the desire for self-actualisation. He feels connected to a larger group of people.

The teacher may allow learners to open their textbooks and reference books for a detailed analysis.

Synthesis: When learners discuss the case from various dimensions, they will find that different theories provide different explanations for the same phenomenon. It may be highlighted that usually psychologists are inclined to refer to multiple theories for a holistic analysis.

ACTIVITY 17: ASSESSMENT

Route: The teacher can organise a few activities adapted from the tools for personality assessment. Some such examples are given below:

Task 1: Learners can be assigned a task of completing a nomination for their classroom peers. They can also be asked to fill the names of their classmates, in the following form:

1. Write the names of two learners with whom you would like to study.
2. Write the names of two people with whom you would like to go for an outing.
3. Write the names of two learners with whom you would like to participate in school activities such as dancing, singing.
4. Write the names of two learners with whom you would like to share a seat in the classroom.
5. Write the names of two learners with whom you would like to participate in a classroom activity.

Subsequently, the teacher can ask one or two learners to plot the nominations received and see which characteristics emerged for each learner. For example, if a particular learner was nominated by everyone for participation in an activity, then that is a characteristic of that learner on the basis of which, others identify him/ her. If most people nominate a particular learner for studying together, then that is his/ her dominant characteristic.

No	Name of the learners	Characteristics that emerged
1	XYZ	Good student
2	ABD	Social
3 and so on	....	Outgoing

Further, learners can discuss nomination as a technique for behavioural analysis.

Task 2: The teacher can ask learners to draw an image of a person on a plain sheet. Most learners may draw an image of a person, from their own gender. The teacher can point towards other intricacies, such as, details in the face, length of body parts, etc. These aspects of the drawing are used to assess the personality of a person. The teacher should abstain from interpreting drawings on her own and let learners analyse and interpret them for each other.

Task 3: The teacher can show a photo to learners, from their own cultural context and ask them to write a short story based on that image.

Synthesis: The purpose of these tasks is to familiarise them with various types of tests used for measuring personality and not to test the learners. After completion of these tasks, the teacher can discuss personality assessment and the different techniques used for it.

Recent Developments

Quest to formulate Fundamental Principles for Understanding Personality: Dan P. MacAdams and Jennifer L. Pals have proposed a comprehensive framework for understanding the whole person. In their paper titled, 'A New Big Five', they observe that the last two decades have seen a resurgence of the trait approach (2006). A wide acceptability of the big five personality factors (McCrae and Costa, 1994) is indicative of that trend. However, they argue that personality psychology should provide a comprehensive framework that can help in understanding the whole person. In their paper, they propose a framework of five principles, based on contemporary empirical trends, which can serve this objective. The first principle is that of human evolution which provides the basis for explaining similarity among all human beings. Human beings adapt to their environment in the process of evolution and these adaptations are passed on through genes. Some such adaptions are forming a culture, developing language and understanding the intentions of others.

The second principle is that a broad range of dispositional traits constitute the most stable aspect of psychological individuality. From Allport (1937) to Eysenck (1952), and now to the big five personality factors, traits serve as a basis for explaining continuity and consistency of a behaviour pattern among individuals. It speaks of a person's unique way of responding to his/her environment. The third principle goes beyond dispositional traits to account for variations in social-cognitive, motivational and developmental adaptions. These adaptations are contextualised by the time, place and social role that the person is playing, or expected to play. These can include values, goals, motives, strivings, strategies, etc.

The fourth principle states that human lives vary with respect to personal narratives, which a person constructs to make meaning in the world around him. Narratives have gained formidable grounds in research in psychology in recent decades. This approach implies that people construct their own life stories and these help to direct their behaviour and shape their identity. Narrative identity includes the past as a reconstruction and as an imagined future. It is an on-going process which helps to give meaning to a person's life. The fifth principle emphasises the role of culture in the immediate life of a person. 'Culture' is a very complex term which includes the meaning, practices and discourse about human life that are prevalent in a given society. There is wide debate on how culture influences personality. Some thinkers argue that traits are resistant to cultural influences, whereas other thinkers state that culture affects the expression of traits.

The five principles cover, from the macro level to the micro level, the study of human beings, incorporating the universal, as well as contextualised understanding. Through this essay, McAdams (2006) makes a plea to teach personality as an integrated field. This approach takes psychology to its historical aim of finding an integrative framework to understanding humans, holistically.

Self and Identity: The study of self and identity along with the discourse on human development has seen a movement away from theories that have universal implication towards a more contextualised understanding. Jensen (2015) in her essay, 'Cultural Developmental Scholarship for a Global world: An Introduction', has addressed the need to bridge the gap between the universal and cultural. On one side of the spectrum are the twentieth century theories that are very broad in their attempt to capture the complexity of the human self and its relationship with culture. On the other end, there are theories specific to a culture. Jensen, proposes the conceptualisation of cultural development theories, which capture the essence of both these approaches.

On similar lines, Cheung, Vijver and Leong (2011) review three approaches to the study of personality. They are the cross-cultural perspective, indigenous perspective and a combined approach to the study of personality. The cross-cultural perspective attempts to study the same construct across cultures such as the comparability of personality traits across cultures. One such example provides vast empirical support for McCrae's (2002) five factor personality model that is studied across cultures. The second area is indigenous psychology that began as a reaction to the dominance of western models. In this, cultural concepts and methodologies are employed instead of using the constructs developed in the West. To cite an example, Heine and Buchtel (2009) have critiqued the five factor personality model for using English terms and American samples for arriving at these five factors. Cultures other than America may assign values to different terms.

Another area of research that has gained impetus is the impact of globalisation and technological advances, on the notions of self and identity. Some researchers think that because of changes in technology, transportation and increased use of internet, more people have come in contact. This has triggered changes even in the process of identity formation. The basic assumptions of their paper are summarised below:

Globalisation, Self and Identity: Hubert J.M. Hermans (2015) has discussed the impact of globalisation on the development of self and identity. He has described globalisation as increased contact of people, ideas, products and world-views with other regions, cultures and nationalities. Internet is seen as one of the most revolutionary developments in the process of globalisation. It has helped people connect with other like-minded people, find solutions to their problems, access information sitting in any part of the world, without any form of race, gender or age discrimination. He refers to the work of Larson (2002), who states that internet has given freedom of choice and has empowered individuals. Internet has impacted every facet of human life including social contacts, health and sense of well-being. He also explicates the darker side of internet such as hacking, accessing pornographic material and others forms of deviant behaviour. He goes further to exemplify that internet not just influences a person's relationship with others, but also with themselves. Researchers like Hermans and Dimaggio (2007) state that internet and globalisation are not something outside, but penetrate deeply into the inner domains of the self.

Hevern (2012) argues that with the increased usage of internet, especially the social networking sites, Skype, video sharing, have led to a new type of environment that is now termed as 'Web 2.0'. This phrase indicates that internet is not just used as a means to access information by people, but also as a tool to create their identity and to share their beliefs. He also talks about both the benefits and negative impact of this phenomenon. On the positive side it can lead to exposure to new ideas and customs, social mobility, changes in gender status and opportunities, etc. On the negative side it can lead to greater divides on lines of class and culture, breakdown of traditional values and greater dependence on the English language.

Hermans (2015) has discussed the vast array of complexity that is associated with the term globalisation by citing different empirical studies. He has highlighted how globalisation has also led to insecurity and as a result, people seek protection and affirmation of their self and identity by associating themselves with any group that reduces that anxiety. According to him, people adhere to religion and the idea of nationalism more because of their greater insecurity. On the other hand, globalisation also incorporates the demands of the locality. He presents both sides of the picture and concludes by saying that globalisation as a phenomenon includes both heterogenisation and homogenisation. This has steered towards what he calls hybrid identities, which on the positive side can promote creativity and innovation and on negative side, can lead to identity confusion.

His paper exemplifies how psychological constructs are

dynamic and are influenced by changes in political, social and economic arenas. The teacher can draw learners' attention towards such studies.

Web-links and Readings

Allport, G. W. (1937). *Personality: A Psychological Interpretation.* New York: Holt.

Cheung, F., Vijver, F. J., & Leong, F. T. (2011). Towards a new approach to the study of personality in Culture. *American Psychologist. Advance Online Publication.* Doi: 10.1037/a0022389

Eysenck, H. (1952). *The Effects of Psychotherapy: An Evaluation* (Vol. 16). London: Journal of Consulting Psychology.

Eysenck, H. J. (1953). *Uses and Abuses of Psychology*. Baltimore: Penguin.

Heine, S. J., & Buchtel, E. E. (2009). Personality: The universal and the culturally specific. *Annual review of psychology, 60*, 369-394.

Hermans, H. J. (2015). Human development in today's globalising world: Implication for self and identity. In L. A. Jensen, *The Oxford Handbook of Human Development and Culture.* New York: Oxford University Press.

Hermans, H. J., & Dimaggio, G. (2007). Self, identity, and globalization in times of uncertainty: A dialogical analysis. *Review of general psychology, 11*(1), 31.

Hevern, V.W. (2012). Dialogicalty and the Internet. In H.J.M. Hermans & T. Gieser (Eds.) *Handbook of Dialogical Self Theory*, pp. 185-199, New York: Cambridge University Press.

Jensen, A. L. (2015). Cultural-developmental scholarship for a global world: An introduction. In *The Oxford Handbook of the Human Development and Culture.* New York: Oxford University Press.

Larson, L. M., Rottinghaus, P. J., & Borgen, F. H. (2002). Meta-analyses of Big Six interests and Big Five personality factors. *Journal of Vocational Behavior, 61*(2), 217-239.

Mc Adams, D. P., & Pals, J. L. (2006). A new big five: Fundamental principles for an Integrative Science of Personality. *American Psychologist, 61*(3), 204-217.

McCrae, R. R., & Allik, I. U. (2002). *The Five-factor Model of Personality across Cultures.* New York: Kluwer Academic/Plenum Publishers.

McCrae, R. R., & Costa, P. T. (1994). The stability of personality: Observations and evaluations. *Current directions in psychological science, 3*(6), 173-175.

Psychological Disorders*

Introduction

The preoccupation with psychological disorders and their treatment pre-dates the history of Psychology as a discipline. Studies on the course of human development are replete with examples of people, who departed from the norms of society, were sidelined, killed, or punished. This deviation could be from common perception, thinking, conduct, habits, beliefs, or other mannerisms. It would be interesting to teach this Unit starting with the history of how this area of Psychology developed over centuries. The teacher should use multiple reference books to discuss the history of Abnormal Psychology. He/she can also plan a class with other teachers of History and English to discuss the socio-political context of mental illness during the ancient and medieval times. English teachers can in addition, discuss how the depiction of abnormality in literature has developed over time.

A discussion on the term abnormality with the learners would help to explicate their ideas on the term abnormality and psychological disorders. In all probability, they would describe someone with whom they have already dealt with directly, or known through the mass media. The teacher must give learners time to share the notions, beliefs, and stigma that they know to be associated with this word. He/she can then dispel their myths and misconceptions. She/he can elaborate that psychologists have arrived at four common features that help in understanding abnormal behaviour, namely, deviance, distress, dysfunction, and danger. Psychology now defines abnormal behaviour from the standpoint of adaptability. As discussed in earlier Units, each person has to face numerous life challenges and so adopts suitable coping strategies. These vary from person to person and across contexts. In this regard, abnormal behaviour may be seen as the inability to adapt appropriately or cope with the life challenges.

---

* Vikas Baniwal

All coping and forms of behaviour involved in making adaptations must ensure one's own well-being and that of others as well. The term 'well-being' is a holistic concept which encapsulates growth and the actualisation of potential. Abnormality is thus perceived in contemporary times not as affliction with diagnosed symptomatic illness, but as transient departure from wellness that can be worked upon with help and support. The potential of the person to return to wellness is what guides clinical practice. With the recent thrust on the human rights of all and social inclusion of all persons, clinical patients and persons with psychological disorders are also very significant. This attitudinal thrust must be communicated to the learners by the teacher.

This Unit discusses the classification of psychological disorders; general factors that lead to abnormal behaviour, and the major psychological disorders. The beginning learners of psychology have a tendency to extrapolate from the description of each disorder to others and analyse their own behaviour as abnormal, and so, here, teachers have to play a very important role. They must discuss how most behaviours, discussed as abnormal, may be seen in normal people, but that there is a difference in the degree and frequency that makes them distinct. Most learners find this unit intriguing and interesting.

ACTIVITY 1: CONCEPT OF ABNORMALITY

Route: The teacher will show the learners a few pictures which depict people engaged in unusual activity. Some examples are given below:

He/she can then ask the opinion of learners about these pictures. Slowly, the teacher can steer the discussion towards analysis of terms like, 'socially approved', 'maladjusted', 'normal' and 'abnormal'. She/he can develop the discussion further with the help of following questions:

- What are your views about the people in these photographs?
- How would you describe the behaviour depicted in these pictures? Give reasons for your answers.
- Have you ever felt that any particular person or behaviour is somewhat abnormal? Why.
- How do you view the 'different' or 'unusual' behaviour of others?

Synthesis: The teacher can discuss that psychologists have arrived at four common features that help in understanding abnormal behaviour. They are deviance, distress, dysfunction, and danger. These terms emphasise that disorders refer to behaviours that are extreme, unusual and bizarre. They can upset the person or inhibit his/her normal day to day functioning. They can also be life threatening.

ACTIVITY 2: DIFFERENTIATING ABNORMAL FROM NORMAL

Route: The teacher would develop a list of discrete forms of behaviour and ask learners to classify them into two categories: category one would indicate behaviour considered to be abnormal and category two would be behaviour considered to be normal. The teacher would ask one of the learners to tabulate the number of items classified as abnormal and normal. The list may consist of the following items:

• Homosexuality	• Washing hands repeatedly	• Staying away from people
• Killing an individual	• Believing in ghosts	• Faith without doubt/ blind faith
• Self-medication	• Talking to an imaginary friend	• Arguing with everyone
• Road rage	• Throwing acid one someone	• Questioning everything
• Talking to oneself	• A man lying on the footpath	• Getting stressed before exams
• Backbiting	• Not talking to your parents	• Believing that people want to harm me

The teacher will display the tabulated data and then ask the learners to explain why they believe that a particular description was classified as abnormal behaviour. The teacher has to explain that a behaviour may be considered normal or abnormal depending on a number of factors, such as, whether they are causing distress to the person, or whether the person's behaviour is influencing their daily life, or whether it is dangerous for the other person, or if that particular behaviour is a social norm, etc.

The teacher can also discuss various myths around disorders such as: disorders are more prevalent in lower socio-economic status; there is nothing like depression, it is just a mood swing which we all experience. Some people may also believe that if a person is diagnosed with some abnormality there is only a little chance of improvement. The word homosexuality may also be seen as an abnormality in some societies.

Synthesis: The teacher should discuss the two broad approaches that explain abnormality, the first approach views abnormal behaviour as a deviation from social norms. Abnormal behaviour includes those actions, thoughts or feelings that are significantly different from societal expectations and beliefs. The second approach describes abnormality as maladaptive behaviours. The important aspect, according to this definition, is the well-being of the person. This term has a wider meaning that encompasses growth and the actualisation potential of a person along with his/her survival. This approach may also visualise a conformist as abnormal, if conformity is impeding the person's growth. The teacher can discuss such examples and enable learners to review their present beliefs about abnormality. At this stage, learners may have a lot of questions in their mind and the teacher must address their queries.

ACTIVITY 3: FACTORS UNDERLYING PSYCHOLOGICAL DISORDERS

Route: The teacher tells the learners to imagine that they are interning with some reputed psychologist. As an initial task, they are asked to find out more about a lady who is reportedly scribbling on the city's walls. The brief given to them by the psychologist is: 'One-day people discovered that many walls in the public spaces had something scribbled on them. Later someone reported seeing a woman in her fifties, dressed in old faded clothes, being responsible for those writings. She writes dates, geography concepts, and names on the walls. Her father died when she was very young and then she started caring for her ailing mother. She took her mother to some distant town for treatment but she believes that the doctor there was a bad man. Some people have said that she was a very bright student and later worked as a geography teacher in a reputed school.' (Times of India, Aug 19, 2014)

The psychologist wants you to gather information, analyse and draw inferences about what factors could have led to such behaviour.

Synthesis: The teacher can give this as a classroom assignment or as a home task. The learners are free to refer to any of the books in Psychology. They have already discussed different approaches to studying personality. The teacher should tell them to think of probable reasons that psychoanalysts, behaviourists, social cognitivists would have assigned to her behaviour. Finally, the teacher can discuss that different schools of thought, explain personality in different ways. The psychodynamic approach will focus on the role of guilt, early childhood memories that were triggered by stressful conditions or that she was abused by the doctor. Behaviourists can state that since most behaviours are learnt, this form of behaviour would have also resulted from pairing of these responses with some consequences that are rewarding. Cognitivists on the other hand may say that this could be due to some cognitive problems. She may be holding irrational beliefs about her own self. Humanists may say that her growth tendencies were inhibited and therefore she is facing problems. Along with all these approaches, the teacher must also discuss the role of genetic and physiological factors in psychological disorders.

ACTIVITY 4: PSYCHOLOGICAL DISORDERS

Route: The teacher reads out case studies and asks the learners to identify the symptoms that indicate that the person may need help from a psychologist.

Case Study 1: *Rahima is scared of closed spaces. She gets so scared that she doesn't take the lift, no matter which floor she has to go to. Even the thought of going in a lift gives her shivers and she starts sweating. She doesn't like to play any games in closed spaces and avoids rides where she has to sit in a small compartment.*

Case Study 2: *Raman is a class XII student in a reputed public school. He prefers to walk to school instead of taking the school bus because he fears that he may meet with an accident on his way to school. He feels anxious in school and avoids playing any form of sport. He is over cautious* *when he takes the staircase. He feels that someone may steal his books and notes, so he avoids bringing them to school. He keeps a copy of all his notes. Raman does not go out with his friends because he fears that he will waste time and will not be able to complete his work. When he starts studying, he fears that he may not be able to pass the exam and is unable to concentrate.*

Case Study 3: *Mahima is a twenty-year-old girl who works in a travel agency. One day she was harassed by her boss and she barely managed to escape from him. She left her job and decided to go for further studies. After one year, one of her friends discovered that Mahima has been telling them about a boy who never existed. According to Mahima, he comes to meet her on weekends. One Sunday her friend found her sitting alone on a bench in a park talking to herself. Slowly, she started talking of things which seemed unrelated. She would talk of rains on a sunny day, she was found shivering as if it was winters on a hot day, she would stand alone in the garden for the entire day till someone forcibly took her to her room. Her friends also found that she had stopped taking care of herself and would not bathe for several days. They reported the matter to the college principal.*

Case Study 4: *Mihir is thirty years old. He works in a reputed law firm. One day he complained about a stomach-ache and went to see a doctor. After all his investigations, the doctors could not figure out any problem. Then he started complaining of a tickling feeling on his back which turned painful when he tried to sleep. Later, he also felt that both his legs were swollen and he had some water retention. Doctors could not diagnose any problem. All his reports were normal but Mihir was convinced that he had some very rare and serious disease.*

The teacher can discuss each case in detail. Learners must underline key symptoms that they identify. Then they can correlate these with the symptoms described in the book. The first case indicates claustrophobia. They teacher can also discuss what could be the underlying reasons for this kind of phobia. The second case indicates generalised anxiety disorder; the third case is indicative of the initial stage of schizophrenia. The final case seems to indicate hypochondriasis.

Synthesis: The case study approach can be useful in introducing disorders and for recapitulating what has already been discussed in the class. It depends on the teacher's discretion, how he/she uses them. The purpose of using fabricated cases is to introduce cases which are simple so that learners can easily identify the disorder. At the next level, learners will have to find more complex cases and discuss them in class.

ACTIVITY 5: CASE PRESENTATION

Route: The teacher may divide the class in groups of two to three learners, each. Each group will be asked to do research on any one of the disorders. They have to present three case studies for each disorder to the class and discuss the symptoms of the disorder. The teacher can send them to the library and give them the names of some reference books. The next day, they can be asked to present their research in front of the class. Some of the significant disorders are as follows:

- Phobia
- Obsessive Compulsive Disorder
- Pain disorders
- Dissociative amnesia, Dissociative identity disorder
- Bipolar Mood disorder
- Schizophrenia
- Attention Deficit Hyperactivity disorder
- Autism
- Anorexia nervosa and Bulimia
- Substance-use disorders

The teacher can use this activity for evaluation too since it represents a project mode. After each presentation, the team will be permitted to ask five questions based on what they presented, to the rest of the class. The team that answers maximum questions will win.

Synthesis: This can be used for recapitulation.

ACTIVITY 6: RESEARCH

Route: The teacher can give another group assignment in which learners will be divided into groups comprising of more than two learners. Each group will be assigned the task of finding out about the disorders that some famous personalities have lived through. The learners must list down the key symptoms of each disorder. They will also have to think of probable reasons that could have led to those disorders. Some of the famous personalities and their disorders are as follows:

- Isaac Newton: Bipolar disorder
- Princess Diana: Bulimia and Borderline Personality Disorder
- John F. Nash: Paranoid Schizophrenia

- Vincent Van Gogh: Depression
- Deepika Padukone: Depression
- Manisha Koirala: Substance abuse (Alcoholic and Nicotine)
- Lady Gaga: Eating disorder and Depression
- Robin Williams: Depression
- Oprah Winfrey: Panic Disorder
- Abraham Lincoln: Anxiety Disorder
- Adolf Hitler: Hypochondria

The teacher will discuss the information that each group presents.

Synthesis: This activity is intended to encourage learners to understand that despite disorders, people move on in life and cope with it and that there are ways of managing disorders. This activity may also help to de-stigmatise psychological disorders and at the same time encourage learners to read more about this unit.

ACTIVITY 7: DISCUSSING MEDIA REPRESENTATION OF PSYCHOLOGICAL DISORDERS

Route: The teacher may show clippings of some movies such as 'A Beautiful Mind', 'Sadma', 'One flew over the Cuckoo's Nest', 'Burfee', 'Kartik calling Kartik', 'U Me Aur Hum', 'Forest Gump', 'It's a wonderful life', 'On the Edge', 'Shutter Island', '50 First Dates', '16 Park Avenue', or some you-tube videos to explain different types of disorders. Alternatively, she/he can suggest that learners can watch some of these movies during their vacation and make notes on what they observed. They can be asked to write a few lines on the following areas:

- Which disorder does the film try to show?
- How did people in the film deal with it?
- What are your thoughts about it?
- Which techniques did the psychologist of the patient in the film use, to help the patient?
- What can we as a society do to help people with psychological disorders?

Synthesis: This activity can be used both as an introductory activity and for summarising the entire unit. Film analysis can give learners a reference to understand and discuss psychological disorder. The teacher must see and prepare notes in advance and then initiate discussion on symptoms, causes and treatment of psychological disorders.

Recent Trends

Much criticism has been raised about the idea of a 'disorder' and the understanding of 'normalcy' underlying it. To make this point clear, learners may be asked to research about the position of American Psychological Association (APA) and Diagnostic and Statistical Manual (DSM) along with International Statistical Classification of Diseases and Related Health Problems (ICD) about homosexuality. This will inform them about the impact of social and cultural factors in labelling anything as a disorder.

Advanced learners may be asked to make a project about DSM and ICD classification for psychological disorders. They may also be asked to present the various critiques that are raised against any such classification and also analyse how such a classification can also act as a political tool. They may be asked to find more about rights of the patients living in the mental health care facilities by making a visit to a nearby mental health care facility. Learners may also plan an awareness campaign about any disorder, to sensitize the neighbourhood about it.

Weblinks and Readings

Brown, T. A., & Barlow, D. H. (2016). *Casebook in Abnormal Psychology*. Australia: Cengage Learning.

CrashCourse. (2014, August 25). *Psychological Disorders: Crash Course Psychology #28-#34*. Retrieved from YouTube: https://www.youtube.com/watch?v=wuhJ-GkRRQc

Freud Museum London. (2015, October 22). *What is Psychoanalysis? Part 1 of 4: Is it Weird?* Retrieved 03 10, 2016, from YouTube: https://www.youtube.com/watch?v=pxaFeP9Ls5c

Kearney, C., & Trull, T. J. (2014). *Abnormal Psychology and Life: A Dimensional Approach*. Stamford : Cengage Learning.

Webb, D. (n.d.). *Top 10 Best Psychological Movies*. Retrieved March 8, 2016, from All About Psychology: http://www.all-about-psychology.com/best-psychological-movies.html

Therapeutic Approaches*

Introduction

The Psychology curriculum, at the beginning level, places a lot of emphasis on understanding 'self' and the 'context' in which a person is located. The endeavour of teaching Psychology at this level, is to enable learners to appreciate the diversity of people around them. There is a tendency to label people who are different from oneself. The attempt, thus, is to bring about an attitude change in the learners and make them more accepting of others. This unit does not promise to make learners counsellors, but, the significance of introducing diverse therapeutic approaches is to familiarise learners with the process of counselling. This will probably help all learners to understand that there is no stigma attached to seeking help from a Psychologist. It will further help them to understand that people in distress, need to seek professional help to restore their sense of wellness without feeling odd or awkward.

The teacher, while teaching this unit, should try to create opportunities where learners learn to listen to others carefully and empathetically. They should discuss the common problems of adolescents and attempt to arrive at some ways of dealing with them. These classes can also help some learners in the class to open up and share their ideas freely. The teacher should encourage participation and ensure that everyone's ideas are expressed and heard.

ACTIVITY 1: THERAPEUTIC RELATIONSHIP

Route: The teacher can show a video of a therapeutic session in the class. Alternatively, the teacher can take a print of the sample case, in which a conversation between a therapist and client is

---

* Vikas Baniwal

presented. Preferably, the teacher can take an excerpt of the conversation from a unit on Person-Centred Counselling, since this will help learners to identify the significant points that form the basis for a therapeutic relationship.

Following this, the teacher can ask the learners to reflect upon and write their responses to the following questions:

- What is the nature of interaction that took place between the therapist and the client?
- What is the role of the therapist in the process?
- What in your view are the desirable characteristics that a therapist should possess?

The teacher can then use the responses given by learners to explain the nature and process of therapy.

Synthesis: The teacher should discuss that a therapist and client share a voluntary relationship. Therapy cannot be forced on a person and one must wait till the person is willing to be a part of the process. Beside this the teacher must emphasise that the purpose of therapy is to help the client to control, change, or modify his/ her own actions, feelings, thinking, and reduce the distress that the client is experiencing. The therapeutic session should also foster the growth of the client. Since, the client confides in the therapist, trust is an important factor.

ACTIVITY 2: MULTIPLE APPROACHES TO THERAPY

Route: To facilitate better theoretical understanding of this unit, the teacher can ask learners to collate different approaches in a tabular format. She/he can either give a worksheet to the learners, or draw the following table on the blackboard and ask learners to complete it. They can complete the worksheet as they proceed in the unit.

Name of therapy, Who pro-posed it?	Aims of the therapy	Cause of the disor-der, accord-ing to the therapy	Techniques of therapy	Nature of relation-ship b/w therapist and the client	Advantages & Disadvantages

Synthesis: This will help learners summarise what they have learnt from the Unit and draw a comparative analysis between various therapies.

ACTIVITY 3: PSYCHODYNAMIC THERAPY

Route: The teacher can divide the learners into four groups and ask them to view four different videos on Psychoanalysis (Freud Museum London, 2015). The focus given to them would be on observing and trying to understand the therapeutic setting and process of therapy. Each group would later be asked to present their observations and share their understanding with the entire class. Based on this, collective understanding can be built.

The teacher can also give learners a sample case from a book on counselling to explain terms such as free association, dream analysis, transference and resistance.

Synthesis: The teacher should remind the learners the main tenets of the psychoanalytic perspective. He/she must emphasise the central role of the unconscious in this framework. The importance of free recall and dream analysis as two key strategies to reach the unconscious also need to be explicitly discussed. The teacher, in addition may also focus on the ethical issues and problems that a therapist faces, during these sessions.

ACTIVITY 4: BEHAVIOUR THERAPY

Route: The teacher may present a case study of a person who is suffering from phobia of closed places or height. The learners will then be guided to take the role of the therapist, using systematic desensitization as the therapeutic method. They will be asked to make a list of all anxiety inducing feelings and situations related to being in a closed place or at a height. Following this, they will then be told to arrange all the identified anxiety inducing stimuli in a hierarchy, from the least anxiety-provoking stimulus to the most anxiety-provoking stimulus. They can then be asked to participate in a role play representation of the problem. Through this, the teacher can then help them understand the finer nuances of the objectives and steps of systematic desensitization. Later, the discussion can move to other techniques used in behaviour therapy.

Synthesis: The teacher must recapitulate the main points of the behavioural approach. He/she must revisit the core concepts such as learning by consequences, reinforcement, generalisation, and discrimination. Then, he/she can discuss various strategies used by a behaviour therapist. Finally, the teacher must discuss systematic desensitisation based on the principle of reciprocal inhibition as an important technique that is utilized to treat people with phobias.

ACTIVITY 5: BEHAVIOUR MODIFICATION THERAPY

Route: Learners can be encouraged to reflect on the techniques that their teachers and parents have used to change their behaviour. They would have come across instances of positive reinforcement such as a verbal praise, medal, or any monetary gift that they received, when they performed well. Likewise, they will be able to recall the different forms of punishment that had to face, such as when they were asked to stand outside the class or repeat the work again if they had not done it as per the teachers' expectations. The teacher can then ask the learners to reflect on the efficacy of these techniques in terms of how their behaviour changed.

Subsequently, the learners can be asked to think about the various ways in which these techniques can be modified and used in a clinical set up. They may be encouraged to list out all the concepts they had read in the Unit on Learning and think of possible ways in which the concepts drawn from there, can be utilized to modify maladaptive behaviour.

The learners should be able to list the following:

- Learning by consequences
- Associative learning
- Positive reinforcement
- Negative reinforcement
- Punishment
- Generalisation
- Discrimination
- Extinction

Using this list, the teacher can discuss the principles and processes of behaviour modification. He/she can also discuss that unlike parents and teachers, therapists use these principles in a more systematic manner. Every client is very closely monitored and their progress is carefully tracked.

Synthesis: This activity can enable learners to think of applications of learning principles postulated by behaviourists. It will also help teachers to build on the existing knowledge base that learners have.

ACTIVITY 6: FACTORS CONTRIBUTING TO HEALING

Route: After the learners have discussed all the therapeutic approaches, they should brainstorm about the various factors that would affect the healing process of a client, in a therapeutic setting. The teacher can ask the following questions to initiate the discussion:

- What do you think will be the outcome of therapy on someone who is not willing to take sessions with a psychologist?
- What should be nature of interaction between a therapist and patient/client?
- What is the first step that can initiate healing?
- What should be the characteristics of the patient-therapist that can help in making the sessions meaningful?

Synthesis: The topic should culminate with discussion about the significance of the patient and therapist relationship, readiness of the patient for therapy, significance of catharsis and the role that personal qualities of both therapist and client play in the process of counselling.

ACTIVITY 7: ALTERNATIVE THERAPIES

Route: The teacher can invite an expert speaker or any teacher from the school who practices Yoga, *Vipassana* or any other meditation technique, to speak about what these are about, how they are practiced, what their underlying premises are, and how they can help in dealing with mental disorders.

Alternatively, the teacher can also give instructions to learners to sit quietly for five minutes with their eyes closed. They should just focus on their thoughts and concentrate on their breath. They should avoid thinking about any particular thing. After five minutes the teacher can encourage the learners to share their experiences and think about whether practicing meditation has benefits in the long run.

Synthesis: The teacher should also discuss that apart from clinical therapies, there are other techniques which many people use to cope with stress and deal with their psychological problems. *Ashtanga* Yoga, *Vipassana, Sudershan kriya,* Transcendental Meditation and Chanting are some techniques that are practiced by people to tide over their problems. Students can be asked to find out more about these alternative therapies. They may be given an enrichment project on the same.

ACTIVITY 8: CASE ANALYSIS FROM MULTIPLE PERSPECTIVES

Route: The teacher can divide the class into four groups. This activity will be in the form of a role play. One group will play the therapist and the other will play the role of a client. Three groups will be assigned the three therapeutic approaches respectively: Existential, Behavioural, and Psychodynamic. Each group will have to read about these approaches from different sources. The fourth group will present four different problem cases. The task assigned to the three groups is to propose strategies to deal with the problems cited in each of the case scenarios.

Case Scenario 1: *A five-year-old boy is very stubborn. He refuses to write anything in class and also does not participate in any activity. He has no friends and stays aloof. He does not like going to school and prefers to stay at home. His parents say that he throws temper tantrums at home too and they have to yield to most of his demands then. He seeks a lot of attention from them.*

Case Scenario 2: *A fifteen-year-old girl is suffering from Anorexia Nervosa. She weighed 80 kgs when she was in class VII and everyone around her seemed to be making fun of her. Most of her friends were thin and they wore nice dresses. One day she decided to lose weight and started dieting without consulting a specialist. She would throw away her tiffin and tell her mother that she ate it. At home, she managed to skip meals. She also started exercising and walking. Slowly she lost weight and the more she lost weight, the more stringent she became about her diet. In the next one year, she became very thin and weak. Despite their best attempts, her parents could not deal with her behaviour, so they decided to consult a psychologist.*

Case Scenario 3: *A ten-year-old boy has stage phobia. He feels very nervous and scared to even step on the stage to read a small prayer. When he was five, he fell on the stage during a performance and his friends made fun of him. Since then, he is very scared of any public speaking and starts stammering when there are people paying attention to what he is saying. His parents took him to a speech therapist and they found out that there is no physiological reason for any of his problem.*

Case Scenario 4: *A seventeen-year-old girl is addicted to internet. She has posted more than 2000 pictures on her Facebook page. She changes her display picture every two hours. She has tried hard to stop herself but feels helpless. She is in class XII now and fears that if she does not* *stop spending time on the internet she will have to face serious repercussions. She feels that she needs help.*

One member from each group will play the role of a therapist and the client will interact with him/her. Then the therapist and client will have to discuss the problem and find out the probable causes. The therapist will then have to propose strategies to help each of the cases. Other group members will help the person who is playing the therapist. Each group will have to create a small section in the classroom that will be appropriate for their therapy. They can use props too. This will be an interactive session and learners will be able to experience the process.

Synthesis: This activity will enable learners to read up about psychotherapies from different sources and references and then apply their understanding of what they have read, in a simulated setting. This can become an opportunity for experiential learning.

ACTIVITY 9: REHABILITATION OF THE MENTALLY ILL

Route: The learners will be asked to design a campaign to create awareness about mental health, different forms of therapy, and rehabilitation. The teacher can talk to the school coordinators and ask for a display board at a strategic location. Learners can make a collage, write slogans, or script a small play that can be performed during the recess time. They should be allowed to think freely and come up with more such ideas.

Synthesis: The purpose of this activity is to engage learners in thinking about mental disorders and work towards de-stigmatising it. It will also encourage learners to read more about this area.

Recent Trends

The various forms of psychotherapy and their methods are rooted in different assumptions of human beings and the context they live in. The therapeutic approaches base on Existentialism and Humanism have found a space for themselves in both the theory and practice of therapy. Behaviour Therapy and Cognitive Behaviour Therapy continue to dominate therapeutic practice with children and adolescents in schools and clinics. Transactional Analysis has also gained considerable visibility. The spiritual dimension of human beings has also found space in therapies like Transpersonal Psychotherapy and Integral Psychology which are informed by the works of Carl Jung (2001), Ken Wilber (2000), Stanislav Grof (2000) and others. In India, a more culturally rooted approach to psychotherapy has emerged, which is popularly known as Indian Psychology. Apart from these, there are many spiritual practices that are followed. Learners may be encouraged to take up projects that explore these practices and traditions.

Web-links and Readings

Brown, T. A., & Barlow, D. H. (2010). *Casebook in Abnormal Psychology*. Australia: Cengage Learning.

Corsini, R. J., & Wedding, D. (2010). *Current Psychotherapies*. Belmont: Cengage Learning.

Freud Museum London. (2015, October 22). *What is Psychoanalysis? Part 1 of 4: Is it Weird?* Retrieved 03 10, 2016, from YouTube: https://www.youtube.com/watch?v=pxaFeP9Ls5c

Grof, S. (2000). *Psychology of the Future: Lessons from Modern Consciousness Research*. Albany: State University of New York.

Jung, C. G. (2001). *Modern Man in Search of a Soul*. Psychology Press.

Wilber, K. (2000). *Integral Psychology: Consciousness, Spirit, Psychology, Therapy*. Boston: Shambhala Publications.

Messer, S. B., & Gurman, A. S. (2011). *Essential Psychotherapies: Theory and Practice* (3rd ed.). New York: Guilford Publications.

Developing Psychological Skills*

Introduction

Sometimes, as teachers, we emphasise a lot on the definitions, theories, and models of the core psychological concepts. We try to leave no stone unturned to ensure that our learners master the key concepts of Psychology and perform well in assessment tests as well. As a result, some topics from the syllabus are emphasised more against others, which do not occupy a significant space in the classrooms and in the minds of learners. This topic on developing psychological skills is especially in danger of such treatment.

However, at this point, it becomes significant to reiterate that both the importance and popularity of the discipline of Psychology come from its applicability. This entails that the theories, research findings, and insights from the studies in Psychology, be utilised to solve real life problems. After all, as asserted by Kurt Lewin (1951), in his opposition to the theory-practice schism, there is nothing as practical as a good theory. Thus, for beginners, developing psychological skills is as essential as the theories of Psychology.

Moreover, the joy of learning Psychology, especially for the beginners, comes from being able to relate the discipline with the world and apply this understanding, to do things differently in daily life. Apart from teaching the concepts and theories, the teacher should try to inspire learners to relate Psychology to their life and see its relevance in understanding their own thought processes, their choices, and their relationships.

This Unit introduces the learners to some psychological skills, which are indispensable for budding psychologists. After studying

* Anshu Chaudhary

this Unit, the learners are also likely to be better prepared to deal with queries and curiosities about human nature, which other people frequently present to them, knowing that they are learners of Psychology.

As far as teaching this Unit in the classroom is concerned, given its nature, activity-based teaching seems to be the most apt method, as it facilitates the acquisition of the skills. Even among varied activities, role-play is likely to be a particularly useful technique as it facilitates learners acting as both the actor and the observer, which not only gives them an opportunity to practice the newly acquired skill as actors, but, they also learn from mistakes of each other as observers. Constructive feedback from peers and teachers also helps in the honing of the skills. In order to demonstrate examples of behaviours and capture the interest of the learners, the teacher can also make use of certain audio-visual clips and relate them to the text book reading.

In this Unit, an attempt is made, to present activities that can be utilized readily by the teacher to teach diverse psychological skills, such as, observation skills, communication skills, counselling skills, and inter-personal skills. This is not to say that all the possible psychological skills have been covered under these categories, but that an attempt has been made to include skills that are most frequently included in the curriculum for beginners. Wherever possible, the activities are short, simple and flexible so that they can be adapted as per the context and the environment of the teacher. An attempt has also been made to direct teachers to the necessary resources and literature, in order to help them devise their own activities, as per their specific requirements.

ACTIVITY 1: OBSERVATION SKILLS: "CHECK IT OUT FOR 30 SECONDS"

Route: The main purpose of this activity is to position learners in a situation to learn to make observations and record them in a limited time frame. For this activity, the teacher should identify 5-6 images with rich details such as photographs/ paintings/ maps, etc. The teacher would label each of the images and project/ display them to the class one by one with the following instructions:

> *"Today you will view a few interesting images, one by one for 30 seconds each. Concentrate on each of the images to the best of your ability, as you will have to recall their details, later. Observe each image very carefully and try to remember as many*

details as possible. After seeing the image, you will have 30 seconds to note down your observations, individually. You are not to discuss or talk to others while recording the observations. You are not allowed to note down the details while the image is on display."

After making sure that the learners have understood the instructions, the teacher should display each image only for 30 seconds and give learners another 30 seconds to record their observations before the next image is shown. After all the images have been displayed, the teacher should quiz the learners on details of each of the images. In order to ensure that the activity goes smoothly, the questions on the details of each of the images (such as number of people/objects of a certain kind present, colors, expressions, words or sentences etc.) should be prepared in advance by the teacher.

After the learners have discussed their observations, the teacher can display the image once more for learners to see the details they might have missed or recorded incorrectly.

Synthesis: After posing the questions associated with each of the images, the teacher should try to direct the discussion towards highlighting the missing details, details captured immediately and accurately, conflicting observations, etc. The learners can also be made to compare their own observations with others. The teachers should also encourage learners to reflect on and identify the techniques/ strategies of observations they could have used in the exercise and relate them to the strategies presented in the textbook for developing/ improving observation skills. Based on the inputs from the classroom discussion, the factors influencing observation can also be discussed.

This exercise is likely to make them understand that making observation and recording those details as data, is not a casual task. It is a task that requires considerable degree of skill/ expertise and thus can be developed with practice and guidance. This is also a very useful activity for demonstrating non-participant observation to the learners.

The teacher can supplement this activity by taking excerpts from "The Adventures of Sherlock Holmes", stories by Arthur Conan Doyle where the protagonist, detective Sherlock Holmes, is known for his extraordinary observation skills and deductive reasoning. Most of his stories are readily available and are full of examples where Holmes draws extraordinary inferences from the ordinary data available. The teacher can also use video clips from numerous television series and film series based on the adventures of Sherlock Holmes to demonstrate the power of observation. Through these and other examples, the learners should also be made to appreciate the scientific nature of observation and the importance of making accurate observations and drawing accurate inferences based on them.

ACTIVITY 2: PARTICIPANT OBSERVATION

Route: The main purpose of this activity is to make learners collect information/ data about behaviour of people in a social space and analyse it, using the participant-observation method. This activity can be given either as a short class activity or as a detailed home assignment with a quick follow-up discussion in the class.

The teacher may divide the class in pairs for this activity. The learners may be permitted to select their own partners, as the activity requires coordination and collaboration. The teacher may instruct the learners as follows:

> *"In this task, you and your partner would be gathering information about behaviour of people in a social space using the participant observation method. Social space is any kind of context where people participate socially and display typical behaviour. For example, you can observe playground, canteen, corridor, assembly etc. (if working in school) or a party, rally, shopping mall, hospital, park, movie theatre etc. (if working outside school). It is advisable that you choose a context that genuinely interests you. After you finalize the context of observation, participate in that context along with your partner for 20-30 minutes and record your observations in as much detail as possible."*

Once the observations are made, the pair should also analyse the data to draw inferences about the patterns of behaviour in the chosen context. They should present their findings in the class.

Synthesis: After learners present their findings to the class, the teacher should facilitate a discussion around the following points:

- Content of observation (i.e. what was observed- conversations, body language, mannerisms, expressions etc.)
- Differences in the roles of learner as 'participant' and learner as 'observer'

- Techniques used for recording the observations (checklists, diaries, recordings etc.)
- Making sense of the recorded data i.e. techniques for drawing the inferences and interpretations
- Challenges encountered during the observation
- Comparison of participant and non-participant observation techniques

The teacher should also help learners understand the difference between the data and its interpretation so that they are able to appreciate that there are multiple interpretations possible, based on the same data. The issues concerning the reliability and validity of observation technique can also be presented briefly here. As closing remarks in this section, 'ethnographic' research may be introduced. This exercise can also be used to teach naturalistic observation to the learners.

ACTIVITY 3: COMMUNICATION SKILLS: THE DRAWING TASK

Route: The purpose of this activity is to demonstrate effective and non-effective communication scenarios to learners. This activity may be used to introduce the basic communication process in the classroom. For this activity, all the learners should be provided with a blank drawing sheet and pencils/sketch pens, scale and compass. The teacher should instruct learners as follows:

> *"All of you have a blank sheet of paper and markers with you. Be ready with them as today, you would be drawing a figure as per my instructions. You should all very carefully listen to me and draw the figure, as instructed. Do not ask any questions in between. You are also not permitted to talk or look at each other's drawings. Are you ready?"*

After making sure that the learners are following, give the following instructions for drawing the figure:

1. Draw a big circle.
2. Draw a triangle inside the circle.
3. Draw a rectangle at the corner.
4. Write your name inside the rectangle.

The teacher should now ask all the learners to hold the drawing up and in their hands for everyone to see. Ask learners to observe each other's drawings. Most drawings are going to look significantly different from each other. After the first part of the activity, the teacher should ask the learners as to why all the drawings are so different from each other, despite everyone receiving the same instructions. They are most likely to respond, saying that there was no time to think through the instructions, or that instructions were vague and non-specific and there was no scope for seeking clarifications.

After taking their responses, repeat the same activity but with different instructions as follows:

> *"So now let us take your feedback into consideration and repeat the activity. You will all be drawing the figure once more at the back of the sheet. Now you can ask me questions if necessary. Are you ready?"*

After learners affirm, instruct them as follows:

1. Draw a circle with two-inch radius at the centre of the page
2. Draw a triangle inside the circle in a fashion that its three corners touch the circumference of the circle
3. Draw a rectangle with three-inch length and one-inch breadth at the upper right corner of the paper
4. Write 'your name' as both first name and surname inside the rectangle

Now the teacher should ask them to hold up their drawing once more for everyone to see. This time the drawings are likely to look remarkably same. The teacher should ask learners as to why they think that this time the drawings were similar.

Synthesis: The aim of the activity is to make learners realize that, different people often understand the same message differently and therefore, communication is a complex process. This should be followed by a discussion on the basic communication model where the problems related to encoding, decoding and medium and channel of communication are discussed in detail. The strategies and tips for effective communication can also be discussed.

ACTIVITY 4: COMMUNICATION SKILLS: CHINESE WHISPER

Route: For this activity, the teacher should divide the class into groups comprising of 10-11 learners each. The learners in a group should get together and stand in a circle. The teacher should assign a number to each learner in the group going in the clockwise direction, and direct them to write it on a piece of paper, which they should keep handy.

Now, the teacher should instruct the learners as follows:

"Most of you might have played the game of 'Chinese Whisper' as kids. Today, we would be playing this game again, but, with a slight variation. I am going to whisper a statement into the first person's ear who is going to whisper the statement into the second person's ear and so on until we reach the last person in the group. A slight improvisation here is that after hearing the message, not during, you can write it down on the piece of paper you are holding and then, you can whisper it to the learner next to you. The last person is going to speak the statement aloud to the group.

The rule is that you can only whisper the statement once, no repetition is permitted. So, whatever you hear, write it down and pass it along to the next person. You would be proceeding in the clockwise direction in the group."

In all probability, by the time last learner reads the message aloud to the group, the original statement will be significantly altered. The group can compare the final statement with the original statement (i.e. the one whispered by the teacher). After the completion of the exercise, one of the learners should collect the slips of paper with written messages from all the learners and organise them in a sequence. From this sequence, the group can discern how the message got altered with each communicator.

For the purpose of this exercise, the teacher can formulate a statement of moderate length and complexity. Some examples are as follows:

- Every weekend, I clean my room, wash my clothes and go out with my friends. Sometimes, I also play soccer and watch movies.
- In the upcoming winter holidays, I am planning to go to the mountains and learn skiing. I also want to join a course on mountaineering next year.
- Mona, her mother and her cousin went shopping to the mall the other day. They bought three pair of shoes, some cosmetics and two dresses.
- Next month, I am going to Kerala with my parents and brother. We are attending a family wedding. My cousin sister is getting married in Cochin.

Synthesis: This activity is an adaptation of the classical game of Chinese Whisper, aimed at making learners appreciate that in inter-personal communication, often, what is said, and what is heard are often quite different. Thus, minimizing these differences by dealing with the different barriers of effective communication is at the core of effective communication.

After the group-activity, the teacher should facilitate a class discussion on the following questions:

- Why do you think the initial statement changed so much? What happened to its meaning? (Relate it to various barriers of communication.)
- Do you think messages get altered like this in our daily life? What are its implications? (Discuss how misunderstandings in relationship, gossip and rumours arise due to miscommunications.)
- How do you think we can minimize these miscommunications? (Discuss the pre-requisites and strategies for effective communication.)
- Can you think of a person who, according to you, is a good communicator? What makes him/her a good communicator? (Highlight the characteristics of effective communicators and impress upon them the importance of refining one's communication skills.)

ACTIVITY 5: COMMUNICATION SKILLS: ACTIVE LISTENING AND PARAPHRASING

Route: Active listening is a skill that, when honed, has the power to improve our communication with people around us. It involves being attentive, receptive, patient and responsive while listening to others. The objective of this exercise is to make learners practice active listening skills through a role play scenario. This exercise should be carried out after the teacher has discussed the importance and techniques of active listening (such as paraphrasing, emotional labelling, mirroring etc.).

After carrying out a detailed discussion on what qualifies and does not qualify as active listening and techniques promoting active listening, the teacher should divide the class into groups comprising of three learners each. These three learners are going to assume roles as the actor, the listener and the observer. The 'actor' would be enacting a pre-decided active listening scenario. The 'listener' would be engaged in active listening to paraphrase and report the conversation after acting. The 'observer' would be observing both the actor and the listener to ensure if they are adequately fulfilling their responsibilities of enacting and active listening. The observer would be required to share his/her observations after each enactment and paraphrasing.

To facilitate this activity, the teacher should keep few active listening scenarios ready for the role play. These could be any situation warranting animated and interesting sharing in the group. Presented below are few examples:

Scenario 1: You are talking to your friend about how you escaped an accident while going back home from school yesterday.

Scenario 2: You are sharing the details of educational trip you have just come back from, with your parents. It was a wonderful learning experience for you where you had great time with your friends.

Scenario 3: You are sharing with your best friend about how upset you are with your girlfriend/boyfriend as s/he has been avoiding you for apparently no reason.

Scenario 4: You are discussing your career plans with your elder cousin and sharing how confused and concerned sometimes you feel about the different career choices.

Scenario 5: You are having an enthusiastic conversation with your sister/brother about the plans of your upcoming birthday party where you are planning to invite all your friends.

Each group would be provided with the active listening scenario sheet from where the actor can select the scenario he/she wishes to enact. Each of the groups should engage in three enactment scenarios and rotate roles so that each group member acts as the actor, listener and observer. After all the groups have completed the activity, the teacher should reconvene the class for the discussion.

Synthesis: After the conclusion of the exercise, the teacher may ask learners to share their experience of playing different roles in the activity. The specific issues they faced while adopting each of the roles can also be probed further. Since, the focus of the activity was active listening, the learners may be asked to highlight problems they encountered in their role as listeners. The learners can also discuss the strategies of active listening that worked well during the exercise. As concluding remarks for this activity, the teacher may encourage learners to think about the various applications of the skill of active listening in their daily life.

At the end of the activity and the follow-up discussion, the learners should be able to appreciate that often, people jump to conclusions and make up their mind without completely following what the other person is saying. This frequently leads to conflict. The learners should also realize that being a good listener is extremely important for being a good communicator.

ACTIVITY 6: COMMUNICATION SKILLS: NON-VERBAL COMMUNICATION AND MIXED MESSAGES

Route: The objective of this simple activity is to introduce the concept of non-verbal communication through a demonstration of 'mixed messages' in the class.

Option 1: 'Liar Liar'

This option involves some acting on the part of a learner volunteer from the class. A day before the class is scheduled, the teacher should select a learner volunteer who would be demonstrating the 'mixed message' in the class through a role-play. The capable volunteer should be carefully selected for this activity and he/she should be given detailed instruction about the role-play scenario by the teacher.

The role play scenario involves a learner coming late to the class and giving verbal excuses which are contradictory with his/her body language. The exercise involves learners observing this contradiction and making use of this observation to understand the significance of non-verbal communication. The teacher should instruct the volunteer to enter the class late by 5-7 minutes. Upon enquiry by the teacher, the learner should say that something terrible happened due to which he/she is late for the class, such as getting caught in a scuffle in the playground, meeting with an accident in the laboratory, visiting the medical room for a terrible headache etc. The teacher should calmly probe the excuse of the learner with some further questions. While giving the excuse and responding to the probes of the teacher, the learner should maintain a mischievous grin and maintain an excited fidgety demeanour. The learner may also look nervous and speak in an under-confident manner. This role-play involving the teacher and learner may go on up to 5 minutes. In order to ensure that everything goes as per the plan, a detailed script of the role-play may be prepared in advance by the teacher and the volunteer. Upon completion of the role-play, the learner may be instructed to take his place in the class.

Learners are likely to observe this episode intently. Without revealing that it was a role play, the teacher should involve learners in a discussion on following questions:

- What do you think just happened?
- Do you believe the reason for the learner getting late for the class? If no, why? If yes, why?
- How did you assess if the learner was telling the truth? Did you believe the verbal message? Or, did you rely more on the body language and facial expressions?

After the initial discussion, the teacher may disclose that the episode was a role-play. The learner volunteer should be appreciated for the initiative and the effort.

Option 2: 'Catch me if you Can'

In case the teacher is not able to identify a learner volunteer in advance to demonstrate mixed messages, the activity may be easily improvised. The teacher may ask any four learners to volunteer for a role-play. The teacher should take three volunteers outside the class and narrate a scenario involving deception. For e.g., they may be told that three of them work at a jewellery store where a theft has taken place the previous night. Two of them are innocent and do not know anything about the incident while one of them is the culprit as he/she has assisted the thieves. The teacher may assign the roles to all three volunteers accordingly. They should also be told that they all are going to be questioned by an investigative officer.

Now, the teacher should get back to the class and narrate the scenario to everyone. The fourth volunteer should now be told to assume the role of investigative officer and identify the culprit through interrogation. The teacher should also tell the rest of the class to observe the investigation carefully so that they can also identify who the real culprit is. The role play may go on for ten minutes after which the investigative officer declares who the culprit is. After the role play, the teacher may also ask the rest of the class to share their observations and speculations.

Synthesis: Learners are likely to observe these episodes intently. Through these exercises, the teacher can introduce the definition and significance of non-verbal communication in our day to day life. The different channels of non-verbal communication such as body language, gestures, facial expressions can also be highlighted. The discussion can be concluded with teacher highlighting the application of mixed messages, incongruence, and inter-channel discrepancy in detection of deception. Certain clips from the American drama series, *'Lie to me'*, can be used as examples here.

ACTIVITY 7: INTERVIEWING SKILLS

Route: The objective of this exercise is to give learners an opportunity to apply the newly acquired interviewing skills. In this exercise, learners would be developing an interview schedule and would be exploring the attitudes and beliefs of their partner on a socially relevant topic. This activity should be introduced after a detailed discussion on interviewing skills has happened in the class.

For this exercise, the teacher should ask learners to select a socially relevant topic that they find interesting. Since, they would be interviewing a person on the chosen topic, they should develop a probe-list and interview schedule in the class as per the guidance of the teacher.

After the learners finalize the interview schedule, the teacher should divide the class in pairs. Each pair should get together and take turns in interviewing each other. While these interviews are taking place, the teacher can observe the interviews and record the common errors. After the interview session, the teacher should reconvene the class to discuss the following:

- The experience of conducting the interview
- The experience of being an interviewee
- The challenges of being the interviewer
- The ways in which the interviews could have been improved
- Key learnings from the exercise

Synthesis: After completion of the exercise, the teacher should share her observations with the class and give learners feedback on their interviewing skills. The common mistakes that learners might be making while interviewing others should be highlighted. The teacher may also encourage learners to observe different interviews on TV and assess the effectiveness of interviewer. Towards the end, the significance of interview as a tool of data collection in psychological research may also be iterated by the teacher as concluding remarks.

ACTIVITY 8: COUNSELLING SKILLS: EMPATHY

Route: The purpose of this activity is to introduce the concept of 'empathy' by making students reflect on certain instances and the feelings associated with them. To begin with the activity, the teacher may distribute blank flashcards to all the students and instruct them as follows:

> *"All of you have a flashcard in front of you. On one side of the card, think and write about something someone did to you good or bad that evoked certain feelings. For example, "I was surprised by my best friend on my birthday" or "My parents scolded me in front of my teacher". On the other side, write about the feeling that incident evoked in you, for example, "I felt wonderful" or "I felt rejected". Do not write your name on the card."*

After the students are done writing on the flash cards, the teacher can divide the class in two groups (group A and B) and collect their cards in separate heaps. Now the teacher may engage the class in a simple competitive game - "Guess my feelings". Ask a member of team A to come forward and read the incident from flashcard to a member from team B who would then be required to guess the feeling associated with the incident as written on the other side of the flashcard. One point should be given to team B if the members guesses correctly. The same should be repeated with team B and likewise the game goes on. The team gathering more points wins the game.

The teacher may want to make sure that the point should only be given if the student guesses the feeling precisely. For example, if the flash card mentions both betrayed and sad, then, point may not be given if the person only mentions sad. Also, if the written feeling on the flashcard is ecstatic or wonderful, then, point may not be given for happy. This is likely to bring about a discussion on how the experience of closely related feelings, when examined, is actually different and thus, empathy requires precise understanding of other person's state of mind.

Synthesis

After the activity culminates, the teacher can facilitate the discussion around the following questions:

- What do you think was the purpose of the activity? (The

definition and meaning of empathy may be introduced here.)

- Why do you think it was significant to come up with the precise feeling written on the flashcard during the game? (Importance of understanding precisely may be highlighted here along with the difference between empathy and sympathy.)
- How do you think this activity is related to counselling? (Significance of empathetic understanding and listening may be emphasized here.)
- What do you think are the ways to enhance empathy? (Strategies for fostering empathy may be discussed here.)

ACTIVITY 9: COUNSELLING SKILLS: ROLE PLAY AND FEEDBACK

Route: The purpose of this exercise is to demonstrate a counselling session to learners and give them some hands-on training in newly acquired counselling skills. This exercise should be carried out after the learners have learned about counselling process, steps, counselling skills and ethics. Teachers may also discuss these skills using some counselling videos.

Role-play is a scenario where participants are assigned specific roles which they act out in an imaginary context. For the purpose of this exercise, the context would be of a counselling scenario, such as a couple seeking help for resolving the marital discord, a learner seeking career counselling, parents discussing the hyperactivity and misbehaviour of their child, an employee looking for better stress management, etc. The participants in the role-play would be assigned the following roles:

- *Counsellor*: The role involves a person acting as an expert in guidance/counselling. This person would be getting an opportunity to demonstrate/practice counselling skills.
- *Client*: The role requires the actor to assume position of a person seeking help for any personal issue and present in detail his/ her concerns.
- *Observer*: The role of the observer is to carefully observe what is happening in the role-play i.e. the counselling skills employed by the counsellor, the coherence of the issues being presented by the client, the content of the discussion, the body-language of the actors etc. The task of the observer is to provide adequate feedback to the actors, particularly, the one acting as the counsellor.

These roles can be assumed either by the learner or by the teacher depending upon the purpose and type the role-play. Some major types of role-plays useful for teaching counselling skills are as follows:

- *Demonstration role-plays*: This role play is helpful to introduce different counselling skills. The teacher can act as counsellor and a learner volunteer can act as a client. The purpose is to present an example of effective counselling so that learners learn from observing the session.
- *Relay role-plays*: This type of role-play gives learners an opportunity to practice counselling skills. Here, the teacher can act as a client and learners take turn in acting as a counsellor. The first learner starts the session as counsellor and when he/she gets stuck anywhere, the next learner takes off as the counsellor from that point. The advantage of this type of role-play is that it engages many learners simultaneously.
- *Triad role-plays*: This involves participants assuming three roles-the counsellor, the client and the observer. It can be either carried out as a demonstration where the learners assume the role of the client and the counsellor while the teacher acts as the observer. Or, it can also be carried out as a class activity where the whole class is divided into triads and learners keep on switching roles after every 10 minutes so that they all get an opportunity to play the client, counsellor and observer.
- *Freeze-frame*: This is a technique used to improve the quality of a demonstration role play where the learners act as the client and the counsellor. Here, as the quality of the role-play deteriorates, the teacher freezes the play to discuss what is happening and what else the counsellor can do in this situation. If necessary, the learner playing the counsellor can also be switched. This technique not only keeps the audience engaged but also gives the teacher an opportunity to give the right direction to the efforts of the role-players

Synthesis: After the role-play, the teacher would ask the role-players to reflect on their experience and assess their performance. Both reflection and self-assessment are essential to learning counselling skills. No role-play exercise is complete without feedback. After the self-assessment, either the appointed observer or the teacher should give feedback to the learners. The purpose of the feedback is to allow the learner what he/she did well and where lies the scope of improvement. Therefore, no role-play exercise is complete without a feedback session. But, for feedback to take effect, it should be constructive, corrective and specific.

ACTIVITY 10: STRESS MANAGEMENT: DEFINING STRESS AND IDENTIFYING ITS CAUSES

Life is not the same for everyone or on every day. It comes with many problems, impediments, and hazards. In a way, every day throws new challenges and each person has to deal with them in his/ her own unique way. This gives rise to stress and, thus, stress is conceptualised as a life challenge. These challenges helps one to become a better person on the one hand and on the other hand, they have the power to shatter and destroy someone's life. One needs to appreciate this dual nature of stress and must equip oneself to transform every negative challenge into a possibility of growth and development.

Learners must have experienced some circumstances where stress would have helped them in meeting deadlines, performing well in exams, and in competing with others; whereas, in other situations, stress might have impeded their usual performance and in an extreme situation, might have even led to debilitating psycho-physiological concerns. This Unit will enable learners to identify the nature, sources, and types of stress. Learners need to be given opportunities to think about their lives and write autobiographical accounts of times when they experienced stress. Teachers can make this unit engaging by adding opportunities for conducting surveys, interviews, or micro studies to understand people's perceptions about stress and stressors and their ways of dealing with these challenges.

Route: The teacher can ask the learners to think of times when they experienced stress. S/he can give the following instructions-

> "Write about two to three most stressful situations that you have experienced in life, till now. Give a detailed description of those events including how you felt and thought at that moment, your physiological responses and how you chose to respond to those situations. Do not write your name on top of the sheet".

The teacher can collect the response sheets and distribute them in the class randomly. Now the teacher would ask the learners to read the response sheet that they have received and answer the following questions:

- Do you think stress resides in the person or the environment?
- How did the person respond in the situation?
- If you were in a similar situation, would you have responded in a similar manner?
- What factors influence responses to a stressful situation?
- Why do people vary in their responses to a stressful situation?'

The teacher should allow learners to come up with ideas and share their views freely. Every learner must have experienced some stressful event in his/her life. This activity is intended to give them an opportunity to put it in a perspective. This session is like a brainstorming session where there are no right or wrong answers.

Synthesis: After the discussion, the teacher may conclude by emphasising the following:

- Stress resides in the process that involves the person interacting with his/her environment. It resides neither in the person nor in the environment alone.
- Every person appraises the situation and the resources available, to cope with the situation. The appraisal of the situation for every person may be different depending on their past experiences. Thus, there is an element of subjectivity in this process.
- Stress refers to a dynamic mental state which is constantly changing. This is because the person is constantly appraising the situation and thinking of possible solutions.
- Stress can also be understood as a disruption in a balanced state. A person strives to return to that state of balance.

ACTIVITY 11: STRESS MANAGEMENT: IDENTIFYING THE STRESSORS

Route: The teacher should ask the learners to make a list of stressors and ask five to seven people to rank them from things that cause maximum stress to those which cause minimum stress:

A suggestive list is as follows:

1. Traffic jams
2. Death of a near and dear one
3. Electricity cut
4. Road rage
5. Accident
6. Fight with a friend
7. Exams
8. Weekly tests
9. Going for a date
10. Peer pressure
11. Completing a project
12. Debate
13. Participating in a competition
14. Public speaking

The teacher would ask learners to work in groups and develop the list further. Learners must collect the data from people outside their classroom. Subsequently, all the lists can be collated and one final list can be made, like the following table:

Stressors	Ranks assigned
9.	Traffic jams
10.	Death of a near and dear one
11.	Electricity cut
12.	Road rage
13.	Accident
14.	Fight with a friend
15.	Exams
16.	Personal illness
17.	Going for a date
18.	Peer pressure
19.	Completing a project
20.	Debate
21.	Participating in a competition
22.	Public speaking

Plot a graph depicting those stressors which received maximum number of 1st and 2nd ranks. They must then compare their results with the results given in different books on General Psychology.

Synthesis: There are a number of situations that can lead to stress. Broadly, they are categorised under three major heads i.e. life events, hassles, and traumatic events.

ACTIVITY 12: STRESS MANAGEMENT: MANAGING STRESS

Route: The teacher can assign the task of analysing case vignettes to the learners. First of all, the teacher would ask the learners to go through techniques of stress management from different books. Then s/he can ask them to read the case vignettes that are given to them and propose individualised strategies for managing the stress of each of those persons. The teacher can give the following instructions- '*Imagine you are a counsellor and the following people come to meet you. How would you counsel them? Prepare a plan for managing their stress.*'

Case 1: *Raman is a Ph.D. scholar. His date of submission is nearing and he is experiencing a block. He is unable to think, work or sleep. He gets extremely restless these days and snaps at everyone around him. He wakes up every night shivering and then he has to take sleeping pills to catch some sleep. He dreads the thought of going to his department and avoids meeting any of his acquaintances from there.*

Case 2: *Mridul is a class XII student. He is preparing for his board exams and IIT entrance exams. He aspired to be an engineer since he was in class VIII and started preparing for it from then. He now studies through the night and does not waste even a minute. He has stopped meeting people and only tries to focus on his aim. Finally, when he wrote the exam, he was unable to clear it. He could not take the set back and attempted suicide.*

Case 3: *Tanya is a very talented musician. However, she is not taken very seriously because she is a girl. Her parents too do not support her cause because they believe that getting her married in due course is very important. She is very passionate about music and feels frustrated that nobody understands her need. She sometimes regrets that she is a girl and feels that had she been a boy, things would have been a bit easier. She wants to prepare for a performance but is feeling very low and despondent. She needs help.*

Case 4: *Ayesha, was a very talented girl. She was a very good artist and her teacher always felt that she should go to one of the best art schools for further studies. One day, she met with an accident in which she lost her vision. Since then, she has lost her zest for life and is unable come to terms with her loss of vision. She weeps through the night and feels that* *everything is over for her. She refuses to meet her friends and relatives. She does not want sympathy. How can she cope?*

This activity may be done in groups of 2-3 learners, as there are many strategies fór stress management which merit discussion. An open discussion on the analysis of situations and recommendations by the various groups would enable learners to view the case-studies from different perspectives.

Synthesis: There are various strategies to manage stress such as relaxation techniques, meditation procedure, biofeedback, cognitive behavioural therapy etc. that are given in different books of psychology. Learners will have to read these on their own and relate them to the concerns of each case. Then they will be able to propose a plan that can be best suited for managing their stress levels.

Web- links and Readings

Field, R. G. (2012, September 26). *Depression treatments - Psychodynamic psychotherapy - Westport CT*. Retrieved March 20, 2016, from YouTube: https://www.youtube.com/watch?v=IC2BYbMuy-k

Hall, T. (2014, May 13). *Eliminate depression - Hypnosis session - By Thomas Hall*. Retrieved March 20, 2016, from YouTube: https://www.youtube.com/watch?v=-MWCzkqcbzY

Johnson, J. (2014, October 23). *Case study clinical example CBT: First session with a client with symptoms of depression (CBT model)*. Retrieved March 20, 2016, from YouTube: https://www.youtube.com/watch?v=7LD8iC4NqXM

Lewin, K., (1951). Field theory in social science: Selected Theoretical papers by D. Cartwrigth (ed.), New York: Harpers.

Valles, B. (2013, August 21). *Mindfulness therapy session on help for anxiety and depression medication reduction*. Retrieved March 20, 2016, from YouTube: https://www.youtube.com/watch?v=0mrgqXoQI80